MYSTERY TRAIN

New Edition,
Revised and Expanded

MYSTERY TRAIN

Images of America
in Rock 'n' Roll Music

GREIL MARCUS

E.P. Dutton, Inc.   New York

A Dutton Paperback

The paperback edition of MYSTERY TRAIN first published 1976 by E. P. Dutton & Co.,
Inc. The Revised edition first published 1982.

Every effort was made to obtain permission to use the lyrics quoted in this book.
Some lyrics appear without acknowledgement because we received no reply from
the proprietors.

Published in the United States by
E. P. Dutton, Inc., 2 Park Avenue, New York, N.Y. 10016

Library of Congress Cataloging in Publication Data
Marcus, Greil.
Mystery train.
Discography: p.
1. Rock music—United States—History and criticism.
2. United States—Popular culture. 3. Rock musicians—
United States—Biography. I. Title.
ML3534.M36 784.5'4'00973 81-12647
AACR2

ISBN: 0-525-47708-X

Published simultaneously in Canada by
Clarke, Irwin & Company Limited, Toronto and Vancouver
10 9 8 7 6 5 4 3 2 1

Designed by The Etheredges

To Emily and Cecily

CONTENTS

AUTHOR'S NOTE

Writing these opening notes reminds me of the prefaces to the American history books that were written during World War II, when the authors, looking back for the meaning of the Revolution or the Civil War or whatever, drew modest but determined parallels between their work and the struggle. They were affirming that their work was part of the struggle; that an attempt to understand America took on a special meaning when America was up for grabs. Those writers were also saying—at least, this is what they now say to me—that to do one's most personal work in a time of public crisis is an honest, legitimate, paradoxically democratic act of common faith; that one keeps faith with one's community by offering whatever it is that one has to say. I mean that those writers were exhilarated, thirty years ago, by something we can only call patriotism, and humbled by it too.

Well, I feel some kinship with those writers. I began this book in the fall of 1972, and finished it late in the summer of 1974. Inevitably, it reflects, and I hope contains, the peculiar moods of those times, when the country came face to face with an obscene perversion of itself that could be neither accepted nor destroyed: moods of rage, excitement, loneliness, fatalism, desire.

Like a lot of people who are about thirty years old, I have been listening and living my life to rock 'n' roll for twenty years, and so behind this book lie twenty years of records and twenty years of talk. Probably it began when a kid pushed a radio at me and demanded that I listen to a song called "Rock Around the Clock," which I disliked at the time and still do. I know the music came together for me in high school, thanks to my cruising friend, Barry Franklin. We spent years on the El Camino, driving from Menlo Park to San Francisco to San Jose and back again, listening to Tom Donahue and Tommy Saunders on KYA, trying to figure out the words to "Runaround Sue" and translating "Little Star" into French. Later, we followed the sixties trail to college, Beatle shows, and Dylan concerts.

About a month before the Beatles hit I met my wife Jenny, who confirmed my enthusiasms and who has always kept them alive; it means more to me to say that this book wouldn't have been written without her than to say that it couldn't have been.

The time I have spent talking rock 'n' roll with my friends Bruce Miroff, Langdon Winner, Ralph Gleason, Ed Ward, Michael Goodwin, and many more, has gone into this book; so has talk with my brothers Steve and Bill, with teachers and students, and with my daughter Emily, who picked "Mystery Train" as her favorite song at the age of two. My daughter Cecily is not as yet so discriminating, but I have hopes. As much as anything, rock 'n' roll has been the best means to friendship I know.

I have been writing about the music since 1966 —professionally, for publication, since 1968. Before I got up the nerve to see my efforts in print I put together a book of pieces by myself and some friends; one of them, Sandy Darlington, taught me a lot about music and a lot more about writing. After the book was finished I took over Sandy's music-space in the San Francisco *Express-Times*, then edited and inspired by Marvin Garson. Until the events of Peoples' Park sent it reeling into mindlessness, the *Express-Times* was the best underground newspaper in America, and I've always been proud to have been part of it. When it changed I moved across town to *Rolling Stone*, where I wrote and edited for a year. In 1970 I left, and ultimately ended up with *Creem*, a magazine that seemed like a place of freedom and was. *Creem* gave me the chance to try out many of the ideas that eventually found their way into this book.

There would be little to those ideas without the study I did in American political thought and American litera-ture with three Berkeley teachers: John Schaar, Michael Rogin, and Norman Jacobson. And there are a few books that mattered a great deal to the ambitions of my own book, and to its content: D. H. Lawrence's *Studies in Clas-sic American Literature*, Leslie Fiedler's *Love and Death in the American Novel*, James Agee's *Let Us Now Praise Famous Men*, Pauline Kael's *I Lost It at the Movies*, Alexis de Toc-queville's *Democracy in America*, and, in a way that is still pretty mysterious to me, Ernest Hemingway's short stories.

Many people helped me in many ways while I was writing: Mary Clemmey, Greg Shaw, Richard Bass, Pat Thomas, Ms. Clawdy, Bill Strachan of Anchor Press, and Wendy Weil. Jenny Marcus, Peter Guralnick, Bruce Miroff, Bob Christgau, and Dave Marsh read every page of the manu-script, and made it far better than it would have been with-out their help.

Bob and Dave deserve special thanks. They have been part of my work from beginning to end; they encouraged it, at times inspired it, always cared about it. No critic could ask for better colleagues, and no one could ask for better friends.

And I owe as much to my editor, Bill Whitehead. Without his commitment to the book, mine would have faded out a long time ago.

What I have to say in *Mystery Train* grows out of records, novels, political writings; the balance shifts, but in my intentions, there isn't any separation. I am no more capable of mulling over Elvis without thinking about Herman Melville than I am of reading Jonathan Edwards (*not*, I've been asked to point out, the crooner mentioned in the Randy Newman chapter, but the Puritan who made his name with "Sinners In the Hands of An Angry God") without putting on Robert Johnson's records as background music. What I bring to this book, at any rate, is no attempt at synthesis, but a recognition of unities in the American imagination that already exist. They are natural unities, I think, but elusive; I learned, in the last two years, that simply because of those unities, the resonance of the best American images is profoundly deep and impossibly broad. I wrote this book in an attempt to find some of those images, but I know now that to put oneself in touch with them is a life's work.

Berkeley, August 9, 1974

INTRODUCTION
TO THE SECOND EDITION

When this book was first published in 1975, I imagined that I was telling part of an ongoing story. "The Band, Sly Stone, Randy Newman, and Elvis Presley are still vital performers," I wrote then; not long after, the careers of all but Newman had effectively come to an end. Through these individual performers I wanted to raise the question of the relationship between rock 'n' roll and American culture as a whole; that, and not a few careers, turned out to be the ongoing story.

Of the two men I chose as "ancestors" of a quartet of "inheritors," black blues singer Robert Johnson had been dead since 1938; Harmonica Frank, a white medicine-show entertainer, though now past seventy, still performs occasionally. Elvis Presley, of course, died in 1977. The previous year, the Band broke up. Sly Stone has attempted numerous halfhearted comebacks since radically challenging popular music with *There's a riot goin' on*, but each has left less of a mark than the one before it. Only Randy Newman's career demanded reconsideration—as everyone's cult hero got himself a hit with the outrageous "Short People," and came face to face with the perils of mass success—and I've tried to provide that in an addendum to his chapter.

For these reasons, I've left the main text of the book substantially as I wrote it: even the long chapter on Elvis Presley remains in the present tense, perhaps because Elvis's story seems big enough to hold that tense even though the man himself is dead. (When asked what he would do now that his meal ticket was in the grave, Col. Tom Parker, Elvis's manager, said, "Why, I'll go right on managing him.") The essays in the "Notes and Discographies" section, though, have been greatly revised and expanded (taking in the discovery of the facts about Robert Johnson's life, the final stages of the Band's career, some new Stagger Lee tales, and the explosion of records, books, and movies that followed Elvis's death), and they are as up to date as publishing deadlines permit.

As for the music *Mystery Train* takes as its subject, it sounds no less remarkable today than it did when it first appeared, five or fifty years ago.

Berkeley, October, 1981

PROLOGUE

OUR STORY BEGINS just after midnight, not so long ago. The Dick Cavett Show is in full swing.

Seated on Cavett's left is John Simon, the New York Critic. On Cavett's right, in order of distance from him, are Little Richard, Rock 'n' Roll Singer and Weirdo; Rita Moreno, Actress; and Erich Segal, Yale Professor of Classics and Author of *Love Story*. Miss Moreno and Mr. Segal adored *Love Story*. Mr. Simon did not. Little Richard has not read it.

Cavett is finishing a commercial. Mr. Simon is mentally rehearsing his opening thrust against Mr. Segal, who is very nervous. Miss Moreno seems to be falling asleep. Little Richard is looking for an opening.

Mr. Simon has attacked Mr. Segal. Mr. Segal attempts a reply but he is too nervous to be coherent. Mr. Simon attacks a second time. Little Richard is about to jump out of his seat and jam his face in front of the camera but Mr. Simon beats him out. He attacks Mr. Segal again.

"NEGATIVE! NEGATIVE NEGATIVE NEGATIVE!" screams Mr. Segal. He and Simon are debating a fine point in the history of Greek tragedy, to which Mr. Simon has compared *Love Story* unfavorably.

" 'Neg-a-tive,' " muses Mr. Simon. "Does that mean 'no'?"

Mr. Segal attempts, unsuccessfully, to ignore Mr. Simon's contempt for his odd patois, and claims that the critics were wrong about Aeschylus. He implies that Simon would have walked out on the *Oresteia*. Backed by the audience, which sounds like a Philadelphia baseball crowd that has somehow mistaken Mr. Simon for Richie Allen, Segal presses his advantage. Little Richard sits back in his chair, momentarily intimidated.

"MILLIONS OF PEOPLE were DEEPLY MOVED by my book," cries Segal, forgetting to sit up straight and slumping in his chair until his body is near parallel with the floor. "AND IF ALL THOSE PEOPLE LIKED IT—" (Segal's voice has now achieved a curious tremolo) *"I MUST BE DOING SOMETHING RIGHT!"*

The effort has exhausted Segal, and as he takes a deep breath Little Richard begins to rise from his seat. Again, Simon is too fast for him. Simon attempts to make Segal understand that he is amazed that anyone, especially Segal, takes this trash to be anything more than, well, trash.

"I have read it and reread it many times," counters Segal with great honesty. "I am always moved."

"Mr. Segal," says Simon, having confused the bull with his cape and now moving in for the kill, "you had the choice of acting the knave or the fool. You have chosen the latter."

Segal is stunned. Cavett is stunned. He calls for a commercial. Little Richard considers the situation.

The battle resumes. Segal has now slumped even lower in his chair, if that is possible, and seems to be arguing with the ceiling. *"You're* only a critic," he says as if to Simon.

"What have *you* ever written? What do you know about art? Never in the history of art . . ."

"WHY, NEVER IN THE HISTORY!"

The time has come. Little Richard makes his move. Leaping from his seat, he takes the floor, arms waving, hair coming undone, eyes wild, mouth working. He advances on Segal, Cavett, and Simon, who cringe as one man. The camera cuts to a close-up of Segal, who looks miserable, then to Simon, who is attempting to compose the sort of bemused expression he would have if, say, someone were to defecate on the floor. Little Richard is audible off-camera, and then his face quickly fills the screen.

"WHY, YES, IN THE WHOLE HISTORY OF AAAART! THAT'S RIGHT! SHUT UP! SHUT UP! WHAT DO YOU KNOW, MR. CRITIC? WHY, WHEN THE CREEDENCE CLEARWATER PUT OUT WITH THEIR 'TRAVELN' BAND' EVERYBODY SAY WHEEE-OOO BUT I KNOW IT CUZ THEY ONLY DOING 'LONG TALL SALLY' JUST LIKE THE BEATLES ANDTHESTONESANDTOMJONESANDELVIS—I AM ALL OF IT, LITTLE RICHARD HIMSELF, VERY TRULY THE GREATEST, THE HANDSOMEST, AND NOW TO YOU (to Segal, who now appears to be *on* the floor) AND TO YOU (to Simon, who looks to Cavett as if to say, really old man, this *has* been fun, but this, ah, *fellow* is becoming a bit much, perhaps a commercial is in order?), I HAVE WRITTEN A BOOK, MYSELF, I AM A WRITER, I HAVE WRITTEN A BOOK AND IT'S CALLED—

"HE GOT WHAT HE WANTED BUT HE LOST WHAT HE HAD! THAT'S IT! SHUT UP! SHUT UP! SHUT UP! HE GOT WHAT HE WANTED BUT HE LOST WHAT HE HAD! THE STORY OF MY LIFE. CAN YOU DIG IT? THAT'S MY BOY LITTLE RICHARD, SURE IS. OO MAH SOUL!"

Little Richard flies back to his chair and slams down into it. "WHEEEEE-OO! OOO MAH SOUL! OO mah soul . . ."

Little Richard sits with the arbiters of taste, oblivious to their bitter stares, savoring his moment. He is Little Richard. Who are they? Who will remember Erich Segal, John Simon, Dick Cavett? Who will care? Ah, but Little Richard, Little Richard *Himself!* There is a man who matters. He knows how to rock.

A phrase that Little Richard snatched off Erich Segal stays in my mind: "Never in the history—*in the whole history of art*. . . ." And that was it. Little Richard was the only artist on the set that night, the only man who disrupted an era, the only man with a claim to immortality. The one who broke rules, created a form; the one who gave shape to a vitality that wailed silently in each of us until he found a voice for it.

He is the rock, the jive bomber, the savant. "Tutti Frutti" was his first hit, breaking off the radio in 1955 to shuffle the bland expectations of white youth; fifteen years later the Weirdo on the Cavett Show reached back for whatever he had left and busted up an argument about the meaning of art with a spirit that recalled the absurd promise of his glory days. "I HAVE WRITTEN A BOOK, MYSELF, AND IT'S CALLED . . ."

Listening now to Little Richard, to Elvis, to Jerry Lee Lewis, the Monotones, the Drifters, Chuck Berry, and dozens of others, I feel a sense of awe at how fine their music was. I can only marvel at their arrogance, their humor, their delight. They were so sure of themselves. They sang as if they knew they were destined to survive not only a few weeks on the charts but to make history; to displace the dreary events of the fifties in the memories of those who heard their records; and to anchor a music that twenty years later would be struggling to keep the promises they made. Naturally, they sound as if they could care less, so long as their little black 45's hit number one and made them rich and famous. But they delivered a new version of America with their music, and more people than anyone can count are still trying to figure out how to live in it.

Well, then, this is a book about rock 'n' roll—some of it—and America. It is not a history, nor a purely musical analysis, nor a set of personality profiles. It is an attempt to broaden the context in which the music is heard; to deal with rock 'n' roll not as youth culture, or counter culture, but simply as American culture.

The performers that I have written about appeal to me partly because they are more ambitious and because they take more risks than most. They risk artistic disaster (in rock terms, pretentiousness), or the alienation of an audience that can be soothed far more easily than it can be provoked; their ambitions have a good deal to do with Robbie Robertson's statement of his ambitions for the Band: "Music should never be harmless."

What attracts me even more to the Band, Sly Stone, Randy Newman, and Elvis, is that I think these men tend to see themselves as symbolic Americans; I think their music is an attempt to live up to that role. Their records—the Band's *Big Pink*, Sly's *There's a riot goin' on*, a few of Randy Newman's tunes, Elvis Presley's very first Tennessee singles—dramatize a sense of what it is to be an American; what it means, what it's worth, what the stakes of life in America might be. This book, then, is an exploration of a few artists, all of whom seem to me to have found their own voices; it is rooted in the idea that these artists can illuminate those American questions and that the questions can add resonance to their work.

The two men whose tales begin the book—white country hokum singer Harmonica Frank and black Mississippi blues singer Robert Johnson—came and went before the words "rock 'n' roll" had any cultural meaning at all. Both men represent traditions crucial to rock 'n' roll, and both are unique. They worked at the frontiers of the music, and they can give us an idea of what the country has to give the music to work with—a sense of how far the music can go. Harmonica Frank sang with a simple joy and a fool's pride; he caught a spirit the earliest rock 'n' roll mastered effortlessly, a mood the music is always losing and trying to win back. Robert Johnson was very different. He was a brooding man who did his work on the darker side of American life; his songs deal with terrors and fears that few American artists have ever expressed so directly. In this book, Frank and Johnson figure as metaphors more than musical influences. Their chapters are meant to form a backdrop against which the later chapters can take shape, a framework for the images the other artists have made.

The Band, Sly Stone, Randy Newman, and Elvis Presley share unique musical and public personalities, enough ambition to make even their failures interesting, and a lack of critical commentary extensive or committed enough to do their work justice. In their music and in their careers, they share a range and a depth that seem to crystalize naturally in visions and versions of America: its possibilities, limits, openings, traps. Their stories are hardly the whole story, but they can tell us how much the story matters. That is what this book is about.

> . . . to be an American (unlike being English or French or whatever) is precisely to *imagine* a destiny rather than to inherit one; since we have always been, insofar as we are Americans at all, inhabitants of myth rather than history. . . .
>
> LESLIE FIEDLER, "Cross
> the Border, Close the Gap"

It's easy to forget how young this country is; how little distance really separates us from the beginnings of the myths, like that of Lincoln, that still haunt the national imagination. It's easy to forget how much remains to be settled. Since roots are sought out and seized as well as simply accepted, cultural history is never a straight line; along with the artists we care about we fill in the gaps ourselves. When we do, we reclaim, rework, or invent America, or a piece of it, all over again. We make choices (or are caught by the choices others have made) about what is worth keeping and what isn't, trying to create a world where we feel alive, risky, ambitious, and free (or merely safe), dispensing with the rest of the American reality if we can. We make the oldest stories new when we succeed, and we are trapped by the old stories when we fail.

That is as close as I can come to a simple description of what I think the performers in this book have done—but of course what they have done is more complex than that.

In the work of each performer there is an attempt to create oneself, to make a new man out of what is inherited and what is imagined; each individual attempt implies an ideal community, never easy to define, where that new man would be at home, where his work could communicate easily and deeply, where the members of that ideal community would speak as clearly to the artist as he does to them.

The audiences that gather around rock 'n' rollers are as close to that ideal community as anyone gets. The real drama of a performer's career comes when the ideal that one can hear in the music and the audience that the artist really attracts begin to affect each other. No artist can predict, let alone control, what an audience will make of his images; yet no rock 'n' roller can exist without a relationship with an audience, whether it is the imaginary audience one begins with, or the all-too-real confusion of the audience one wins.

The best popular artists create immediate links between people who might have nothing in common but a response to their work, but the best popular artists never stop trying to understand the impact of their work on their audiences. That means their ideal images must change as their understanding grows. One may find horror where one expected only pleasure; one may find that the truth one told has become a lie. If the audience demands only more of what it has already accepted, the artist has a choice. He can move on, and perhaps cut himself off from his audience; if he does, his work will lose all the vitality and strength it had when he knew it mattered to other people. Or the artist can accept the audience's image of himself, pretend that his audience is his shadowy ideal, and lose himself in his audience. Then he will only be able to confirm; he will never be able to create.

The most interesting rock 'n' rollers sometimes go to these extremes; most don't, because these are contradictions they struggle with more than resolve. The tension between community and self-reliance; between distance from one's audience and affection for it; between the shared experience of popular culture and the special talents of artists who both draw on that shared experience and change it—these things are what make rock 'n' roll at its best a democratic art, at least in the American meaning of the word democracy. I think that is true because our democracy is nothing if not a contradiction: the creed of every man and woman for themselves, and thus the loneliness of separation, and thus the yearning for harmony, and for community. The performers in this book, in their different ways, all trace that line.

If they are in touch with their audiences and with the images of community their songs hint at, rock 'n' rollers get to see their myths and parables in action, and ultimately they may even find out what they are worth. When the story is a long one—a career—they find the story coming back to them in pieces, which of course is how it was received.

Here is where a critic might count. Putting the pieces together, trying to understand what is novel and adventurous, what is enervated and complacent, can give us an idea of how much room there is in this musical culture, and in American culture—an idea of what a singer and a band can do with a set of songs mixed into the uncertainty that is the pop audience. Looking back into the corners, we might discover whose America we are living in at any moment, and where it came from. With luck, we might even touch that spirit of place Americans have always sought, and in the seeking have created.

ANCESTORS

HARMONICA FRANK
1951

In 1951 Sam Phillips was the owner of a shoestring operation that cut records by young black blues singers in Memphis, Tennessee. A few years later he would shape the careers of such founding rockers as Elvis Presley, Carl Perkins, Roy Orbison, and Jerry Lee Lewis; today, he counts his money. But at least one writer has stepped forward to call him "America's Real Uncle Sam," a title he might like.

Phillips was raised on a plantation in Alabama; when he was a little boy an old black man named Uncle Silas Payne would take him aside and sing him the blues, playing Jim to Sam's Huck. In the fifties, bored by the music business and itching for something new, it would be quite natural for Phillips to look for someone to complete a role that was sketched out in his own past. "If I could find a white man who had the Negro sound and the Negro feel," he was saying in those days (as Huck Finn met the Riverboat Gambler),

11

"I could make a billion dollars." Harmonica Frank Floyd, a white man in his early forties, who held a harmonica in one side of his mouth and sang out of the other, was Sam Phillips's first try.

Harmonica Frank was never famous. Born in 1908 in Toccopola, Mississippi, a short ways from Elvis Presley's birthplace in Tupelo, he was a drifter, who left home at the age of fourteen and bummed his way around the country for the next forty years, a man who came up with his own idea of the country's music, black and white.

In 1973, an old man, Frank wrote: "Just one thang I would love to say the first time I played a rock and roll tune on my oath I had never heard no one else do that type therefore I am almost sure I am the originator of rock and roll regardless of what you may have heard at the time I could not read or write music but now I can I am truly a hillbilly from the state of miss but have traveled all over played in old time vaudeville shows medicine shows on the streets barber shops court house lawns auctions sales woodman halls radios television you name it I've played it comedy fire eaters with carnivals tricks or magic so at least I'm an old showman picked cotton picked fruit dug mussel shells in Ark pan some gold in calif one time on KELW in Hollywood with Bustie steel and log cabin wranglers. . . .

". . . You see I played rock and roll before I ever heard of elvis presley I saw him in memphis before he ever made a record with sam phillips on north main in memphis tennessee. . . ." *

Frank cut many sides in 1951 for Phillips, who leased a few to Chess, the Chicago blues label. They didn't sell. Phillips put out two remaining tracks as a single on his own Sun label in 1954, just before Elvis Presley's first record was released, but the disc went nowhere.

Harmonica Frank's music was a joke, mostly, because there was a little more money for a street-singer who could make people laugh. Yet there was an edge to Frank's music, a

* From a letter Frank wrote to Greg Shaw.

fool's resistance to the only role he knew; and that, along with the vitality and invention of the sounds Frank made, was a key to the inarticulate desires shared by Sam Phillips and the impatient new audience whose presence he sensed. "Old Sam Phillips only had one thing to tell me," Harmonica Frank says today. "Said it over and over. 'Gimme something different. Gimme something unique.' "

In his own way Harmonica Frank was as much a maniac as Little Richard. He sounded like a drunken clown who's seen it all, remembers about half of that, and makes the rest up. He put together a style of country rock that did not really find an audience until years later, when Bob Dylan caught the same spirit and much of the sound with "Mixed-Up Confusion," his first single, a lot of the *Freewheelin'* album, and his "I Shall Be Free" songs. In a broader sense Frank can be heard every time a rocker's secret smile breaks open: when Randy Newman sings from the bottom of a bottle, or when Levon Helm gurgles "Hee, hee!" in the middle of "Up on Cripple Creek," the Band's sexiest song.

Harmonica Frank was perhaps the first of the rock 'n' roll vocal contortionists—like Buddy Holly, Clarence "Frogman" Henry, and Bob Dylan—whose mission in life seemed to be the willful destruction of the mainstream tradition of popular singing and the smooth and self-assured way of life it was made to represent. Frank screeched, he bellowed, croaked, cackled, and moaned, carrying his songs and never mind about the tune. He was a noisemaker.

What matters about Frank is the sense of freedom he brought to his music: a good-natured contempt for conventional patterns of life combined with a genius for transforming all that was smug and polite into absurdity. The result was a music of staggering weirdness, dimly anchored by the fatalism of the blues and powered by the pure delight of what was soon to be called rock 'n' roll. Frank wasn't sexy, like the rockabilly singers who were to make Sam Phillips' fortune; he was more like a dirty old man. He was ribald, and he had flair. "I am," he growled in one of his numbers, "a howling tomcat."

His only Sun single was his best—"The Great Medical Menagerist," a wonderful talking blues, backed by "Rockin' Chair Daddy," a first-rate piece of nonsense that really does set the stage for rock 'n' roll. Here he reaches for falsettos, talks to himself, corrects himself, roaring into town

> *Rock to Memphis, dance on Main*
> *Up stepped a lady and asked my name*
> *Rockin' chair daddy dont have to work*
> *I told her my name was on the tail of my shirt!*

and pounding away to the finish: "Never been to college, never been to school, if you want some rockin' I'm a rockin' fool!"

"The Great Medical Menagerist" is simply a triumph. Probably a miniature autobiography, it is a catalogue of all the prim and decent people Frank made asses of, and of the jobs his fun cost him. The first lines have the perfection of myth:

> *Ladies and gentlemens, cough white dodgers and*
> *little rabbit twisters, step right around closely,*
> *tell ya all about a wonderful medicine show I*
> *useta work with. . . .*

"We have Doctor Donicker here with us," he drawls, too sly to believe, "The Great Medical Menagerist . . . *of the World.*" That little pause charges the performance with wit and even menace; Frank sings with a squeak. Frank barely lets on that the menagerie is none other than Doctor Donicker's audience, which is to say, his.

His most compelling record was "Goin' Away Walkin'," one of the sides on Chess. It is a classic country blues, and a kind of final statement. If the form is blues, though, the spirit and the sound come from the high, lonely whine of the white mountain music that goes back to the Revolution. The notes seem to hang in the air like ghosts; the song is bitter, unrepentant, and free. "I ain't gonna get married," Frank

Floyd sings. "I ain't gonna settle down. I'm gonna walk this highway, till my whiskers drags the ground."

That was his promise, and he kept it. Of all the characters who populate this book, only Harmonica Frank did more than keep the legend of Huckleberry Finn alive—he lived it out. He showed up, made his records, and lit out for the territory, banging his guitar and blowing his harp, dodging Greyhounds and working the fields, setting himself free from an oppression he never bothered to define.

His humor, his cutting edge, came like Twain's from that part of the American imagination that has always sneered at the limits imposed by manners; the strain that produced both obscenity and the tall tale, two forms of a secret revolt against the Puritans who founded the country and against the authority of their ghosts. It is a revolt against the hopeful morality of Twain's aunts and the tiresomeness of Ben Franklin doing good and being right; a revolt against pomposity, and arrogance.

And this revolt is powerful stuff, after all. How long would Ahab have lasted if he'd been up against howling weirdo like Harmonica Frank instead of a dumb Christian like Starbuck?

A DIGRESSION THAT MAY PROVE WORTHWHILE TO THOSE READERS WHO DO NOT SKIP IT

Our latest Ahab almost had it both ways, because there was a lot of Harmonica Frank in Lyndon B. Johnson, once President of All the People; one of America's secrets is that the dreams of Huck and Ahab are not always very far apart. Both of them embody an impulse to freedom, an escape from restraints and authority that sometimes seems like the only really American story there is. That one figure is passive and benign, the other aggressive and in the end malignant; the one full of humor and regret, and the other cold and determined never to look back; the one as unsure of his own authority as he is of anyone else's, the other fleeing authority only to replace it with his own—all this hides the common bond between the two characters, and suggests how strong would be a figure who could put the two together. For all that is different about Ahab and Huck Finn, they are two American heroes who say, yes, they will go to hell if they have to.

The obsessiveness and the wish for peace of mind that most easily set Ahab and Huck off from each other—on the surface, anyway—are cornerstones of how rock 'n' roll works and what it is for, but we will find the two spirits together more often than not.

LBJ had his year on the road, quitting college and hoboing his way out to California, digging ditches and washing dishes, finally coming home after having gone far enough to say, years later, that any member of his generation that hadn't been a communist or a dropout wasn't worth a damn. Deeply contemptuous of Eastern gentility (and attracted by it too), Johnson coupled a devastating talent for obscenity that no Easterner could match with an image of himself as a latter-day Pecos Bill; the American, Johnson might have been telling us, is alive only as long as he is uncivilized. Thus Johnson carefully received his guests on the toilet, because it threw them off guard. Bob Dylan was pouting that even the President of the Yew-Nited States had to stand naked, but LBJ was way ahead of him: he forced heads of state to strip for a swim and got the upper hand. He showed his scar and the *New York Review of Books* never forgave him. He told them his name was on the tail of his shirt.

But Johnson's best defense was his verbal obscenity, that side of Huck that Twain left out of the book and kept for himself.

Norman Mailer was the only one of Johnson's adversaries who understood this side of the man, and so he took LBJ on with *Why Are We in Vietnam?* It was the most gloriously obscene book Mailer could write, a book whose hero was in fact a Texas Huck on his way to becoming a Texas Ahab, changing fast from a reckless kid into a killer.

The job, Mailer knew, was to find the sources of Johnson's power—not merely his political power, but his personal strength. That meant Mailer had to understand the language LBJ really spoke, and then beat him at his own game. And so the obscenity of Mailer's book, at first so funny, so full of honest rebellion, becomes more and more cruel, until finally it is part and parcel with brutality, and murder.

But Mailer didn't win the fight with Lyndon Johnson. The richest, riskiest passages of his book cannot compare with the off-hand remark Johnson made when he was asked why he had not told the people more about Vietnam: "If you have a mother-in-law with only one eye, and that eye is in the middle of her forehead, you don't keep her in the living room."[*]

If anything could redeem the arrogant obsessions of the man who introduced us to the obscenity of the burnt baby, it was a style of personal obscenity. This allowed Johnson to transcend, for a time, the self-righteousness (and righteousness pure and simple) of those who vilified him with every obscenity at *their* command. After all, compared to the crowds who hounded him with their mechanical chants, Lyndon Johnson was a poet.

Perhaps, if the political language of America was as free as its secret language, LBJ could have made King Shit a title to be reckoned with. Perhaps, in the presidential election of our dreams, he could have beaten even Lenny Bruce.

And maybe he would have kept Harmonica Frank on retainer, down there on the LBJ ranch.

Harmonica Frank's music, like LBJ's language, has a spirit that occasionally emerges to redeem those impulses in American life that are cold, bitter, and corrupt—just as that book about a river and a raft was meant to displace Mark Twain's dread of what, hard into the Gilded Age, the country seemed eager to believe it was all about. The idea

[*] Cited in David Halberstam, *The Best and the Brightest*, (New York: Random House, 1972).

that the two Americas are separable, I suppose, is the heart of our romanticism.

A good part of the impact of rock 'n' roll had to do with its anachronistic essence, the way it seemed to come out of nowhere—the big surprise that trivialized the events that governed daily life. Rock 'n' roll gave the kids who had seen no alternative but to submit to those events a little room to move. Any musicologist, neatly tracing the development of the music, can tell us that rock 'n' roll did not come out of nowhere. But it sounded as if it did. It was one of those great twists of history that no one anticipated—no one, that is, except a few men like Sam Phillips, who were looking for it, looking for something to break the boredom they felt when they turned on the radio.

Harmonica Frank was part of Phillips' quest for the weird, and weird it had to be if it was to crack the ice that was seeping into Memphis in 1951. When Phillips looked at his town he must have seen the thousands of good country people, the people who worked hard and prayed harder, who had migrated to Memphis after World War II. They wanted a home that was safe, orderly, and respectable, and as far as the old wide-open riverboat town was concerned, they were perfectly satisfied to visit it in a museum. There was a sense that life was set in a pattern; winding down.

"It seemed to me that Negroes were the only ones that had any freshness left in their music," Phillips has said of those days when he was looking for a white man. Maybe it was a white man who sounded like a cross between a barn-yard and a minstrel show—Harmonica Frank, say; maybe a cocky kid, child of those new Memphians, who sang a new kind of blues. Certainly it had to be someone who toyed with race, the deepest source of limits in the South.

The alternative for Phillips, as a record producer, was the white country music of the Carter Family, Jimmie Rodgers, Hank Williams, Patsy Cline. But leaving aside the fact that Phillips was not likely to make a billion dollars on it, there was a problem with that music. It so perfectly expressed the acceptance and fatalism of its audience of poor and striving whites, blending in with their way of life and endlessly reinforcing it, that the music brought all it had to say to the surface, told no secrets, and had no use for novelty. It was conservative in an almost tragic sense, because it carried no hope of change, only respite. By the early fifties this music was all limits. Country music was entertainment that made people feel better, as all true American folk music is before it is anything else, but at its deepest country music was a way of holding on to the values that were jeopardized by a changing postwar America. Country music lacked the confidence to break things open because it was not even sure it could find space to breathe. Hank Williams was eloquent, but his eloquence could not set him free from the life he sang about; he died proving it, overdosing in the back of a car, on his way to one more show.

Phillips had not even worked out the sound he wanted; it was music toward which he was only groping, and most important, ready to accept. Frank Floyd, a white man with some life in him, whose music wasn't exactly blues but was too strange to peddle as anything else, couldn't have sounded less like Hank Williams (though he might have picked up some of his twinkle from Jimmie Rodgers, whom he met on the road years before). Maybe Frank's music was something that would make people take notice if they heard him on the radio, which they rarely did; whatever it was, it was music to turn things around a bit—a clue to what Phillips was looking for, to what made rock 'n' roll happen and to what keeps it alive.

What Phillips was looking for was something that didn't fit, that didn't make sense out of or reflect American life as everyone seemed to understand it, but which made it beside the point, confused things, and affirmed something else. What? The fact that there *was* something else.

What finally arrived was a music of racial confusion, Huck and Jim giving America's aunt the slip, no dead-end "white Negroes" but something new, men like Harmonica

Frank and Elvis Presley, whose styles revealed possibilities of American life that were hardly visible anywhere else with an intensity and delight that had no parallel at all.

The music unleashed by Elvis, Little Richard, and the rest of the early rockers was a thrill, and it was also unnerving. I recall hearing Little Richard's "Rip It Up" for the first time, loving the sound but catching the line, "Fool about mah money dont try to save," and thinking, well, that *is* foolish. Had Harmonica Frank's "Rockin' Chair Daddy" been on my radio, I would have been appalled that anyone could skip college *and be proud of it*.

I know that when Elvis was drafted I felt a great relief, because he made demands on me. It was close to what I felt when the politics of the sixties faded—an ambivalent feeling of cowardice and safety. I loved his records—"Hound Dog" was the first I ever owned; "All Shook Up" the first I bought; and "(You're So Square) Baby I Don't Care" (the title may sum up this dilemma) my first private treasure, a record I loved that no one else seemed to like.

But I didn't like—that is, didn't understand—what the Big E did to the girls I went to school with or the way he looked on the cover of his first album, demented, tongue hanging down his chest, lost in some ecstasy completely foreign to me. What was this? Harmonica Frank wasn't the source of this confused delight, not in terms of musicology anyway, because almost no one ever heard him. But he was in on it: he helped Sam Phillips open the doors the King walked through. More than that, he was a harbinger of a certain American spirit that never disappears no matter how smooth things get.

ROBERT JOHNSON
1938

When the train
Left the station
It had two lights on behind
When the train left the station
It had two lights on behind
Well, the blue light was my blues
And the red light was my mind.
All my love's
In vain.

ROBERT JOHNSON, "Love in Vain"

You know how it feels—you understand
What it is to be a stranger, in this unfriendly land.

BOBBY BLUE BLAND, "Lead Me On" *

* Lyrics as used in the composition, "Lead Me On," by D. Malone. Copyright © 1960 by Lion Publishing Co., Inc., 8255 Beverley Boulevard, Los Angeles, California, 90048. Used by permission only. All rights reserved.

It may be that the most interesting American struggle is the struggle to set oneself free from the limits one is born to, and then to learn something of the value of those limits. But on the surface, America takes its energy from the pursuit of happiness; from "a love of physical gratification, the notion of bettering one's condition, the excitement of competition, the charm of anticipated success" (Tocqueville's words); from a memory of open spaces and a belief in open possibilities; from the conviction that you *can* always get what you want, and that even if you can't, you deserve it anyway.

Most of the big shore places were closed now and there were hardly any lights except the shadowy, moving glow of a ferryboat across the Sound. And as the moon rose higher the inessential houses began to melt away until gradually I became aware of the old island here that had flowered once for Dutch sailors' eyes—a fresh, green breast of the new world. Its vanished trees, the trees that had made way for Gatsby's house, had once pandered to the last and greatest of human dreams; for a transitory enchanted moment man must have held his breath in the presence of this continent, compelled into an aesthetic contemplation he neither understood nor desired, face to face for the last time in history with something commensurate to his capacity for wonder.

No one ever captured the promise of American life more beautifully than Fitzgerald did in that passage. That sense of America is expressed so completely—by billboards, by our movies, by Chuck Berry's refusal to put the slightest irony into "Back in the U.S.A.," by the way we try to live our lives—that we hardly know how to talk about the resentment and fear that lie beneath the promise. To be an American is to feel the promise as a birthright, and to feel alone and haunted when the promise fails. No failure in America, whether of love or money, is ever simple; it is always a kind of betrayal, of a mass of shadowy, shared hopes.

Within that failure is a very different America; it is an America of desolation, desolate because it is felt to be out of place, and it is here that Robert Johnson looked for his images and found them.

Robert Johnson was a Mississippi country blues singer and guitarist, born in 1911; he was murdered, by a jealous husband, in 1938. He died in a haze: if some remember that he was stabbed, others say he was poisoned; that he died on his hands and knees, barking like a dog; that his death "had something to do with the black arts."

Nearly forty years after his death, Johnson remains the most emotionally committed of all blues singers; for all the distance of his time and place, Johnson's music draws a natural response from many who outwardly could not be more different from him. He sang about the price he had to pay for promises he tried, and failed, to keep; I think the power of his music comes in part from Johnson's ability to shape the loneliness and chaos of his betrayal, or ours. Listening to Johnson's songs, one almost feels at home in that desolate America; one feels able to take some strength from it, right along with the promises we could not give up if we wanted to.

Like Charley Patton, Tommy Johnson, Son House, or Skip James—the men who worked out the country blues form in the late teens and twenties—Robert Johnson sang an intense, dramatic music, accompanied only by his guitar. He put down twenty-nine of his songs for the old Vocalion label in 1936 and 1937; his songs lasted, in the work of other bluesmen, long after Johnson was dead, and in the early sixties Johnson's original versions began to appear on albums. Today Johnson's presence can be felt behind many of the best modern guitar players; in a more subtle and vital way, his presence can be felt behind many of our best singers. And a good musical case can be made for Johnson as the first rock 'n' roller of all. His music had a vibrancy and a rhythmic excitement that was new to the country blues. On some tunes—"Walking Blues," "Crossroads Blues," "If I Had Possession Over Judgment Day"—Johnson sounds like a complete rock 'n' roll band, as full as Elvis's first combo or the group Bob Dylan put together for the *John Wesley Harding* sessions, and tougher than either. Johnson's way of looking at things, though, is just beginning to emerge.

I have no stylistic arguments to make about Johnson's "influence" on the other performers in this book, but I do have a symbolic argument. It seems to me that just as they all have a bit of Harmonica Frank in their souls, the artistic ambitions of the Band, Sly Stone, and Randy Newman can at times be seen as attempts to go part of the way into the America Robert Johnson made his own; that since his journey into that America knew few limits, his music can help us understand the limits of other artists and the risks they take when they try to break through them.

And as for Elvis Presley—well, his first music might be seen as a proud attempt to escape Johnson's America altogether.

Johnson's vision was of a world without salvation, redemption, or rest; it was a vision he resisted, laughed at, to which he gave himself over, but most of all it was a vision he pursued. He walked his road like a failed, orphaned Puritan, looking for women and a good night, but never convinced, whether he found such things or not, that they were really what he wanted, and so framing his tales with old echoes of sin and damnation. There were demons in his songs—blues that walked like a man, the devil, or the two in league with each other—and Johnson was often on good terms with them; his greatest fear seems to have been that his desires were so extreme that he could satisfy them only by becoming a kind of demon himself. When he sings, so slowly, in "Me and the Devil Blues,"

> *Early this morning*
> *When you knocked upon my door*
> *Early this morning*
> *When you knocked upon my door*
> *I said, Hello, Satan*
> *I believe it's time, to go*

the only memory in American art that speaks with the same eerie resignation is that moment when Ahab goes over to the devil-worshiping Parsees he kept stowed away in the hold of the *Pequod*. That is a remarkable image, but Johnson's images were simply part of daily life.

> *Me and the devil, was walking side by side*
> *Oooo, me and the devil, was walking side by side*
> *I'm going to beat my woman, until I get satisfied*

It may seem strange that in the black country South of the twenties and thirties, where the leap to grace of gospel music was at the heart of the community, the blues singers, in a twisted way, were the real Puritans. These men, who had to renounce the blues to be sanctified, who often sneered at the preachers in their songs, were the ones who really believed in the devil; they feared the devil most because they knew him best. They understood, far better than the preachers, why sex was man's original sin, and they sang about little else.

This side of the blues did not come from Africa, but from the Puritan revival of the Great Awakening, the revival that spread across the American colonies more than two hundred years ago. It was an explosion of dread and piety that Southern whites passed onto their slaves and that blacks ultimately refashioned into their own religion. The blues singers accepted the dread but refused the piety; they sang as if their understanding of the devil was strong enough to force a belief in God out of their lives. They lived man's fear of life, and they became artists of the fear.

Or perhaps that is not the truth; perhaps Robert Johnson was very different from other blues singers. For all his clear stylistic ties to Son House, Skip James, and others, there are ways in which he stands apart. Part of this is musical—it has to do with the quality of his imagery, his impulse to drama, the immediacy of his singing and guitar playing—but mostly it is Johnson's determination to go farther into the blues than anyone else, and his ability, as an artist, to get there. Anyone from Muddy Waters to Mick Jagger to Michael Jackson could put across the inspired pornography of Johnson's "Terraplane [a good, rough car of the thirties] Blues"—

I'm gonna get deep down in this connection
Keep on tangling with your wires
I'm gonna get deep down in this connection
Keep on tangling with your wires
And when I mash down on your little starter—
Then your spark gonna give me fire

—but as for "Stones in My Passway," which was the other side of sex, no one has been fool enough to try.

Few men could brag like Robert Johnson: "Stuff I got'll bust your brains out, baby," he sang in "Stop Breaking Down Blues," "It'll make you lose your mind." Women crowded around him at the back country juke joints to find out if it was true, and no doubt it often was. But such tunes gave way to songs like "Phonograph Blues," where Johnson sings, with far too much emotion it seems, about his broken record player. "What evil have I done . . . what evil has the poor girl heard." That one line shows us how far he is trying to go.

The poor girl is the phonograph, softly personified; she refuses to play Johnson's wicked records and breaks down. With a blazing insistence, Johnson intensifies his personification, unveils his metaphors. At once, you see him struggling with his machine, and in bed with his girl. The records are his sins; the phonograph his penis. The song ends as a confession that the sins his records embody have made him impotent.

What Johnson found on his road was mostly this: ". . . the sense that life is essentially a cheat and its conditions are those of defeat, and that the redeeming satisfactions are not 'happiness and pleasure' but the deeper satisfactions that come out of struggle." So wrote Fitzgerald to his daughter, about what he had found in Lincoln and Shakespeare and "all great careers." His words make good company for Stanley Booth's: "The dedication [the blues] demands lies beyond technique; it makes being a blues player something like being a priest. Virtuosity in playing blues licks is like virtuosity in celebrating the Mass, it is empty, it means nothing. Skill is a necessity, but a true blues player's virtue lies in his acceptance of his life, a life for which he is only partly responsible. When Bukka White sings a song he wrote during his years on Parchman Prison Farm, 'I wonder how long, till I can change my clothes,' he is celebrating, honestly and humbly, his life."

When acceptance and celebration mean the same thing, or when the two words must fill the same space in the mind at once, we can begin to grasp the tension and the passion of Robert Johnson's music—because when one accepts one's life by celebrating it, one also asks for something more. In Johnson's blues the singer's acceptance is profound, because he knows, and makes us see, that his celebration is also a revolt, and that the revolt will fail, because his images cannot deny the struggles they are meant to master.

It is obvious that man dwells in a splendid universe, a magnificent expanse of earth and sky and heavens, which manifestly is built upon a majestic structure, maintains some mighty design, though man himself cannot grasp it. Yet for him it is not a pleasant or satisfying world. In his few moments of respite from labor or from his enemies, he dreams that this very universe might indeed be perfect, its laws operating just as now they seem to do, and yet he and it somehow be in full accord. The very ease with which he can frame this image to himself makes the reality all the more mocking. . . . It is only too clear that man is not at home in this universe, and yet he is not good enough to deserve a better.

PERRY MILLER, on the Puritan view of the world *

When Robert Johnson traveled through the Deep South, over to Texas and back to Memphis, into the Midwest and up to Chicago, across the border to Canada and back to Detroit to sing spirituals on the radio, to New York City (the sight of this primitive blues singer gazing up at the lights of

* From *The New England Mind: The Seventeenth Century* (Boston: Beacon Press, 1968).

Times Square is not only banal, it is bizarre), to the South again, he was tracing not only the miles on the road but the strength of its image. It was the ultimate American image of flight from homelessness, and he always looked back: the women he left, or who left him, chased him through the gloomy reveries of his songs, just as one of them eventually caught up. Like a good American, Johnson lived for the moment and died for the past.

Sometimes the road was just the best place to be, free and friendly, a good way to put in the time. In "Four Until Late" there is even a girl waiting at the other end.

> *When I leave this town,*
> *I'm gonna bid you fair, farewell*
> *When I leave this town,*
> *I'm gonna bid you fair, farewell*
> *And when I return again,*
> *You'll have a great long story to tell.*

There is the grace and bitterness of "Rambling on My Mind" (which Johnson played with his walking bass figure that was to define Chicago blues, making the song sound just like a man pushing himself down the highway, half against his will); the slow sexual menace of "Traveling Riverside Blues"; the nightmare of "Crossroads," where Johnson is sure to be caught by whites after dark and does not know which way to run; there is always one more "strange man's town," one more girl, one more drink; there is the last word of "Hellhound on My Trail."

> *I got to keep moving, I got to keep moving*
> *Blues falling down like hail, blues falling*
> *down like hail*
> *Blues falling down like hail, blues falling down*
> *like hail*
> *And the days keep on 'minding me*
> *There's a hellhound on my trail*
> *Hellhound on my trail, hellhound on my trail*

It wasn't the open road, to say the least; more like Ish-
mael falling in behind funeral processions, because they
made him feel more alive, and on good terms with death.
You could imagine what the two travelers would have to say to
each other: *This is no way for a young man to act!*

That spirit gives us what might be Johnson's most American image, these lines from "Me and the Devil Blues"—
most American because, as a good, defiant laugh at fate, they
are vital not only beneath the surface of American life, but
on it. They are often called in as proof of Johnson's despair,
and they are part of it, but also his most satisfied lines, a
proud epitaph:

> *You may bury my body, down by the highway side*
> *Babe, I don't care where you bury my body when*
> *I'm dead and gone*
> *You may bury my body, ooooo, down by the*
> *highway side*
> *So my old evil spirit*
> *Can get a Greyhound bus, and ride.*

Robert Johnson had a beautiful high voice, a tragic voice
when he meant it to be. In "Walking Blues" he wakes up to
find that his woman has left him without even his shoes. He
is plainly in awe of this woman ("Well!" he sings to himself,
"she's got Elgin movements, from her head down to her toes
. . . From her head down to her toes!"); when he says the
worried blues are the worst he ever had, he's still too full of
admiration for that woman to make you believe him.

So he will sing, with a distracted, comic determination:

> *Lord I—feel like blowin' my, old lonesome home*
> *Got up this morning, my little bunny ears was gone*
> *Now, up this light, ooooo, my lonesome home*

and then with utter grace his voice rises, almost fades away,
and there is a soft moan that could echo in your heart for a
long time, a melancholy too strong to step around:

Well, I got up this morning . . . all I had, was gone.

Johnson was in his mid-twenties when he sang these songs (Don Law, the great recording engineer who handled the sessions, thought of him as a teenager). Johnson didn't have the worldly dignity of Son House or Skip James. Neither House nor James ever sounds confused; they sing as men who live deeply, but within limits. In Johnson's voice, there is sometimes an element of shock—less a matter of lost innocence than of innocence willfully given up and remembered anyway.

Johnson seemed to take more pure pleasure out of making music than any other Delta singer; there is rock 'n' roll fun in his guitar playing you can hear anytime you like. He was, I think, working out a whole new aesthetic that rock 'n' roll eventually completed: a loud, piercing music driven by massive rhythms and a beat so strong that involvement was effortless and automatic. Yet Johnson also had more to say than other singers. His music was half seduction, half assault, meant to drive his words home with enormous force. His technique was not only more advanced, it was deeper, because it had to be.

Only his weakest songs move on an even keel; the greatest shudder and break and explode, or twist slowly around quietly shaking strings into a kind of suspension, until Johnson has created a mood so delicate and bleak one feels he cannot possibly get out of his song alive. Johnson's most distinctive performances have the tension that comes when almost everything is implied, when the worst secrets are hiding in plain talk. With "Come on in My Kitchen" Johnson plays out the sound of a cold wind on his guitar, and his voice rides it; there is a stillness in the music. The loneliness is overpowering and the feeling of desolation is absolute. The most prosaic lines take on the shape of pure terror.

When a woman gets in trouble
Everybody throws her down
Looking for her good friend

None can be found.
You better come on, in my kitchen
There's going to be rain in our door.

It was songs like this one—the combination of voice, guitar, words, and the mythical authority that comes when an artist confirms his work with his life—that made Eric Clapton see Johnson's ghost, and his own, in Jimi Hendrix's death. "Eric wanted to do a Robert Johnson," one of Clapton's friends said when Hendrix died. "A few good years, and go."

Johnson's music is so strong that in certain moods it can make you feel that he is giving you more than you could have bargained for—that there is a place for you in these lines of his: "She's got a mortgage on my body, a lien on my soul." It is no exaggeration to say that Johnson changed the lives of people as distant from each other as Muddy Waters, who began his career as a devoted imitator; Dion, who made his way through the terrors of his heroin habit with Johnson's songs for company; and myself. After hearing Johnson's music for the first time—listening to that blasted and somehow friendly voice, the shivery guitar, hearing a score of lines that fit as easily and memorably into each day as Dylan's had—I could listen to nothing else for months. Johnson's music changed the way the world looked to me. Over the years, what had been a fascination with a bundle of ideas and dreams from old American novels and texts—a fascination with the foreboding and gentleness that is linked in the most interesting Americans—seemed to find a voice in Johnson's songs. It was the intensity of his music that changed fascination into commitment and a bundle of ideas into what must serve as a point of view.

But commitment is a tricky, Faustian word. When he first appeared Robert couldn't play guitar to save his life, Son House told Pete Welding; Johnson hung out with the older bluesmen, pestering them for a chance to try his hand, and after a time he went away. It was months later, on a Saturday night, when they saw him again, still looking to be heard. They tried to put him off, but he persisted; finally, they let him play for a lull and left him alone with the tables and chairs.

Outside, taking the air, House and the others heard a loud, devastating music of a brilliance and purity beyond anything in the memory of the Mississippi Delta. Johnson had nothing more to learn from *them*.

"He sold his soul to the devil to get to play like that," House told Welding.

Well, they tell a lot of stories about Robert Johnson. You could call that one superstition, or you could call it sour grapes. Thinking of voodoo and gypsy women in the back country, or of the black man who used to walk the streets of Harlem with a briefcase full of contracts and a wallet full of cash, buying up souls at $100 a throw, you could even take it literally.

If there were nothing else, the magic of Johnson's guitar would be enough to make that last crazy interpretation credible. But in a way that cannot be denied, selling his soul and trying to win it back are what Johnson's bravest songs are all about, and anyone who wants to come to grips with his music probably ought to entertain Son House's possibility. I have the feeling, at times, that the reason Johnson has remained so elusive is that no one has been willing to take him at his word.

Let us say that Johnson sought out one of the Mississippi Delta devil-men, or one of the devil-women, and tried to sell his soul in exchange for the music he heard but could not make. Let us say he did this because he wanted to attract women; because he wanted to be treated with the kind of awe that is in Son House's voice when he speaks of Robert Johnson and the devil; because music brought him a fierce joy, made him feel alive like nothing else in the world. Or let us say that the idea of the devil gave Johnson a way of understanding the fears that overshadowed him; that even if no deal was made, no promises passing from one to another, Johnson believed that his desires and his crimes were simple proof of a consummation quite beyond his power to control; that the image of the devil appealed to Johnson when he recognized (singing, "I mistreated my baby, but I can't see no reason why") that his soul was not his own, and, looking at the disasters of his life and the evil of the world, drew the one conclusion as to whom it did belong.

Blues grew out of the need to live in the brutal world that stood ready in ambush the moment one walked out of the church. Unlike gospel, blues was not a music of transcendence; its equivalent to God's Grace was sex and love. Blues made the terrors of the world easier to endure, but blues also made those terrors more real. For a man like Johnson, the promises of the church faded; they could be remembered—as one sang church songs; perhaps even when one prayed, when one was too scared not to—but those promises could not be lived. Once past some unmarked border, one could not go back. The weight of Johnson's blues was strong enough to make salvation a joke; the best he could do was cry for its beautiful lie. "You run without moving from a terror in which you cannot believe," William Faulkner wrote in one of his books about the landscape he shared with Robert Johnson, just about the time Johnson was making his first records, "toward a safety in which you have no faith."

We comfort ourselves that we do not believe in the devil, but we run anyway; we run from and straight into the satanic images that press against the surface of American life. I think of Robert Mitchum, the mad preacher in *Night of the Hunter*, with LOVE tatooed between the knuckles of his right hand, HATE tatooed between the knuckles of his left—and he seems, again, like the legacy of the men who began the American experience as a struggle between God and the devil, the legacy of a Puritan weirdness, something that those who came after have been left to live out.

The dreams and fears of the Puritans, those gloomy old men, are at the source of our attempts to make sense out of the contradictions between the American idea of paradise and the doomed facts of our history; they emerge when "solving problems" is not good enough nor even the point, when the hardest task is not to denounce evil, but to see it.

Unlike Fitzgerald's Dutch sailors, the Puritans did not take their dreams from the land; they brought them along. They meant to build a community of piety and harmony, what their leader, John Winthrop, called "a city on a hill"— an idea, in its many forms, that we have never gotten over, nothing less than America as the light of the world. They had a driving need to go to extremes, as if they could master God and the devil if only they could think hard enough; that, and a profound inability to make peace with the world as they found it. They failed their dreams, and their community shattered. "This land," Winthrop wrote before he died, "grows weary of her inhabitants."

The Puritans came here with a utopian vision they could not maintain; their idea was to do God's work, and they knew that if they failed, it would mean that their work had been the devil's. As they panicked at their failures, the devil was all they saw. Their witch trials were a decadent version of their America—schlock, as it were, but their biggest hit.

Their initial attempts to shape America, and their failures, set the devil loose in the land—as a symbol of uncontrollable malevolence, of betrayal, of disaster, of punishment. Just as the Puritans' failures and compromises anticipated our own, there is something in us that responds, not always quite consciously, to the original image of American failure—to the terror that image can speak for.

If the presence of that image has been felt from the Puritans' day to ours, it is, perhaps, because that image is a way of getting to the idea of an American curse. The image of the devil is a way of comprehending the distance between Fitzgerald's shining image of American possibility and his verdict on its result; it is a way of touching the sense (there in Fitzgerald's beautiful image of America as "an aesthetic contemplation [man] neither understood nor desired") that America is a trap: that its promises and dreams, all mixed up as love and politics and landscape, are too much to live up to and too much to escape. It is as if to be an American means to ask for too much—not even knowing one is asking for too much—and to trade away one's life to get it, whatever it is; as if this is what makes America special, vital, murderous, and noble.

The Puritan devil endures as a face on the betrayal of the promises we mean to keep; the Puritan commitment to extremes, the willingness to live in a world where the claims of God and the devil are truly at odds, has lasted as a means to comprehend the depths of the promise and the failure alike.

This world may have survived most completely in the tension between the blues and the black church. Robert Johnson inherited this world, and, as a black blues singer, he made a new kind of music out of it. The image of the devil was played out within the matrix of Johnson's struggle with women, and with himself. It was a drama of sex, shot through with acts of violence and tenderness; with desires that no one could satisfy; with crimes that could not be explained; with punishments that could not be escaped.

The most acute Americans, in the steps of the old Puritans, have been suspicious, probing people, looking for signs of evil and grace, of salvation and damnation, behind every natural fact. Robert Johnson lived with this kind of intensity, and he asked old questions: What is man's place in the world? Why is he cursed with the power to want more than he can have? What separates men and women from each other? Why must they suffer guilt not only for their sins, but for the failure of their best hopes?

This is a state of mind that gives no rest at all. Even if you have sold your soul to the devil, you cannot rest with him; you have to keep looking, because there is never any end to the price you have to pay, nor any certainty as to the form that price will take. Every event thus becomes charged with meaning, but the meaning is never complete. The moments of perfect pleasure in Johnson's songs, and the beauty of those songs, reminds one that it is not the simple presence of evil that is unbearable; what is unbearable is the impossibility of reconciling the facts of evil with the beauty of the world.

This shadow America comes to a verge with "Stones in My Passway." It is the most terrifying of Johnson's songs, perhaps because his desolation can no longer be contained in the old, inherited image of the devil—those lines from "Me and the Devil Blues" seem suddenly almost safe, comfortable, the claims of a man who thinks he knows where he stands. In "Stones in My Passway" terror is too ubiquitous to have a face: it is formless, elusive, overpowering.

A few months before he recorded "Stones in My Passway," Johnson sang these astonishing lines:

> *If I had possession, over Judgement Day*
> *If I had possession, over Judgement Day*
> *Then the woman I'm lovin', wouldn't have no right to pray*

No right to pray—that is a staggering demand to make on life; it is to ask for the same power the devil has over one who has sold his soul. "Stones in My Passway" is the song of a man who once asked for power over other souls, but who now testifies that he has lost power over his own body, and who might well see that disaster as a fitting symbol of the loss of *his* soul. There is no way to "know"; there are no Gothic images in this song. The idea simply takes shape as the song draws in all the echoes of hellhounds, devils, the weirdness of blues walking like a man, draws in those images and goes past them. If those images were a means to expression, they are no longer necessary—they are no longer good enough.

Because not even his body is his own, Johnson cannot satisfy his woman. Because that matters more than anything else in his life, that fact, as a symbol, expands to create more facts, more symbols. Finally, with stones in every passway and no way clear, there is a way in which the singer's life is resolved: he has seen all around his life, for as long as he can hold onto the image. Because the stakes of the song are so high, every word and every note is fashioned to carry the weight of what Johnson wants to say. The four knife-stroke notes that open the song are like a warning; the song is stark.

It communicates so directly any distance between the singer and the listener is smashed.

> *I got stones in my passway*
> *And my road seems dark as night*
> *I got stones in my passway*
> *And my road seems dark as night*
> *I got pains in my heart—*
> *They have taken my appetite.*

The tune darts forward on a high, almost martial rhythm; one shattering note freezes the music and the image just before the last line of each verse. "Shock technique," a friend called it.

> *My enemies have betrayed me*
> *Have overtaken poor Bob at last*
> *My enemies have betrayed me*
> *Have overtaken poor Bob at last*
> *And there's one thing certain—*
> *They have stones all in my passway.*

If the passway is in his body, immediately it must stand for every invisible trap on the road; if the stones are at first the most direct, physical description of the sexual collapse that has made Johnson afraid to look his lover in the face, those stones must be made to stand for the men who will soon block the way to his lover's door.

> *I'm crying please*—please, *let us be friends*
> *And when you hear me howlin' in my passway, rider*
> PLEASE *open your door and let me in.*

The song is enormous. I cannot put it any other way. The image of the words is subsumed into Johnson's singing, his guitar, into the eerie, inevitable loudness of the song. The music has its claims to make: no matter how low you set the volume, the music creeps up louder, demanding, and the only way to quiet this music is to shut it off.

I got three legs to truck on
Boys, please don't block my road
I got three legs to truck on
Boys, please don't block my road
But I been 'shamed by my rider—
I'm booked and I got to go.

"Stones in My Passway," like a few others of Johnson's songs—"Love in Vain," "Come on in My Kitchen," "Me and the Devil Blues"—is a two-minute image of doom that has the power to make doom a fact. One hardly knows if it is the clarity of the world Johnson revealed in his music, or Johnson's resilience as he made his way through that world that is most exhilarating; but that so many people—people who have never left the American mainstream that Johnson was never part of—respond to his music is perhaps not such a mystery. Because of our faith in promises, the true terror of doom is in the American's natural inability to believe doom is real, even when he knows it has taken over his life. When there is no way to speak of terror and no one to listen if there were, Johnson's songs matter.

What Robert Johnson had to do with other bluesmen of his time is interesting to me, but not nearly so interesting as what Johnson has to do with those discovering him now, without warning and on their own. The original context of Johnson's story is important, and it is where his story is usually placed; but a critic's job is not only to define the context of an artist's work but to expand that context, and it seems more important to me that Johnson's music is vital enough to enter other contexts and create all over again. Off in the Netherlands to teach college, my friend Langdon Winner wrote back:

. . . the truth of the matter is that in my first months here I found out a lot more about America than I did about Holland. Hundreds of things which are second nature to us just do not play a part here. Dissatisfaction, for example. Dutch musicians know the techniques pioneered by America's black masters. But they are not interested in extremes of rage, ecstasy, dissipation, or religious enlightenment. And this sums up the place: While jazz has long been popular in the Netherlands, *the blues has never arrived.* How can you understand Aeschuylus, Augustine, Shakespeare, and Nietzsche if you can't listen to Robert Johnson in your own time?

Which is to say that if Robert Johnson is an ancestor, or even a ghost, he is really a contemporary.

It is the inescapable pull of Johnson's music that gives us Mick Jagger singing "Love in Vain" in the middle of a rock 'n' roll show—and a rock 'n' roll show is a celebration that is rooted in Little Richard's kind of revolt, or in Harmonica Frank's, far more than it is in Robert Johnson's. Robert Johnson is a presence these days, as rock 'n' roll fans find the world less of a home than it used to be, and yet accept more and more their inability to do anything about their displacement; Johnson is a sort of invisible pop star. He has caught up with us.

The music that is animated by Robert Johnson today is not really found in new rock 'n' roll versions of his songs; Johnson's spirit is not so easy to capture. All of Eric Clapton's love for Johnson's music came to bear not when Clapton sang Johnson's songs, but when, once Johnson's music became part of who Clapton was, Clapton came closest to himself: in the passion of "Layla" and "Any Day." Finally, after years of practice and imitation, Johnson's sound was Clapton's sound: there was no way to separate the two men, nor any need to. And perhaps to keep the story straight, there is, in "Layla," one lost echo buried under Clapton's screams and who knows how many guitars: "Please don't say/You'll never find a way/And tell me, all my love's in vain."

This music sounds like real Delta blues to me, forty years after: Duane Allman's solos on Boz Scagg's "Loan Me a Dime"; Sly Stone's "Thank You for talkin' to me Africa"; Randy Newman's "God's Song"; much of the Rolling Stones' music from *Let It Bleed* on down; Bob Dylan's "All Along the Watchtower"; Eric Clapton's "Layla." If someone were to ask me where Johnson's spirit had found a home, I would play these songs.

All the beauty of the world and all the terror of losing it is there in Eric Clapton's rock 'n' roll; Robert Johnson's music is proof that beauty can be wrung from the terror itself. When Johnson sang his darkest songs, terror was a fact, beauty only a glimmer; but that glimmer, and its dying away, lie beneath everything else, beneath all the images that hit home and make a home. Our culture finds its tension and its life within the borders of the glimmer and the dying away, in attempts to come to terms with the betrayal without giving up on the promise. And so at the borders of Elvis Presley's delight, of his fine young hold on freedom, there is, in his "Peace in the Valley," a touch of fear, of that old weirdness:

> *And I'll be changed*
> *Changed from this creature*
> *That I am* *

And at another frontier there is Robert Johnson, pausing for a moment in "Hellhound on My Trail," frightened, running down his road, but glancing over his shoulder with a smile:

> *If today was Christmas Eve, if today was Christmas Eve*
> *And tomorrow was Christmas Day*
> *If today was Christmas Eve*
> *And tomorrow was Christmas Day*
> *Aw, wouldn't we have a time, baby?*

* Copyright 1939 by Hill and Range Songs, Inc. Copyright renewed 1966 and assigned to Hill and Range Songs, Inc. Used by permission.

INHERITORS

THE BAND
Pilgrims' Progress

The Band—four Canadian rockers held together by an Arkansas drummer—staked their claim to an American story from the beginning. The story had its veils, but the fact of the story was plain. "This is *it*," my editor Marvin Garson said in the spring of 1969, as he sent me off to cover the Band's national debut in San Francisco. "This is when we find out if there are still open spaces out there."

Marvin was a New Yorker; living in California sometimes made him talk like Natty Bumppo, but his words were accurate. By out there he meant right here, and he was talking about the Band because it was obvious they were committed to the very idea of America: complicated, dangerous, and alive.

Their music gave us a sure sense that the country was richer than we had guessed; that it had possibilities we were only beginning to perceive. In the unique blend of instruments and good rhythms, in the shared and yet completely individual vocals, in the half-lost phrases and buried lyrics, there was an ambiguity that opened up the world with real force. The songs captured the yearning for home and the fact of displacement that ruled our lives; we thought that the Band's music was the most natural parallel to our hopes, ambitions, and doubts, and we were right to think so. Flowing through their music were spirits of acceptance and desire, rebellion and awe, raw excitement, good sex, open humor, a magic feel for history—a determination to find plurality and drama in an America we had met too often as a monolith.

The Band's music made us feel part of their adventure; we knew that we would win if they succeeded and lose if they failed. That was what Marvin Garson meant. It was a good feeling.

CROSSING THE BORDER

When the Band surfaced in 1968 with *Music from Big Pink*, they had been playing rock 'n' roll music for more than half as long as there had been such a thing. What mattered most, though, was that they had put in their years together, as a group. A rock 'n' roll group is a banding together of individuals for the purpose of achieving something that none of them can get on their own: money, fame, the right sound, something less easy to put into words. But what begins as a marriage of convenience sometimes takes on its own value. An identity comes into being that transcends individual personalities, but does not obscure them—in fact, it is the group, sometimes only the group, that makes individuals visible. The Beatles, after all, were the most satisfying and complex testament to the limits of self-reliance most of us have ever known; they were also proof of the limits of a common bond. Groups are images of community. That the Band had created itself through the years, and had come to our attention bent on demonstrating just what their years together had been worth, was perhaps the most potent image of all.

Like John Lennon and Paul McCartney, Booker T. & the MG's, Bob Dylan, and a few thousand others, drummer Levon Helm, guitarist Robbie Robertson, piano man Richard Manuel, bass Rick Danko, and organist Garth Hudson started out in the high school bands that appeared overnight in the flash of the first great rock explosion.* Still in their teens in the early sixties, they came together in Toronto as the Hawks, back-up band for Ronnie Hawkins, a small-time Arkansas rockabilly singer who had brought Levon north with him around 1958.

Hawkins, though he brushed the charts twice in 1959—with a Chuck Berry remake and his own "Mary Lou"—was too little and too late to pass for the next Elvis Presley; his task was to keep himself alive. In the U.S.A. he was one of too many; in Canada, where authentic American rockers were a solid commercial rarity, Hawkins could bill himself "The King of Rockabilly" and get away with it. Sometimes he liked to call himself "Mr. Dynamo." It was, as so many have testified, better than working.

Ronnie Hawkins was a windjammer in the grand style. He claimed to have picked cotton right alongside Bo Diddley; to have made the first rock 'n' roll record of all, back in 1952 (no one, so far as I know, has ever found it, but Hawkins, keeping his story straight, says it was the first version of "Bo Diddley"); to have passed up a chance for stardom when he graciously offered the sure-hit "It's Only Make Believe" to his old pal Conway Twitty; to know more back roads, back rooms, and backsides than any man from Newark to Mexicali. His singing was only fair, though in one sense it was quite distinctive: Hawkins is the only man I have ever heard who can make a nice sexy song like "My Gal Is Red Hot" sound sordid. "None of us rock 'n' rollers could understand all that fuss about Jerry Lee Lewis marrying a

---

* The names of those bands are too good to leave out: the Robots, the Consuls, Thumper and the Trombones (Robbie); Paul London and the Capters—what are "Capters"? Shouldn't it be "Copters"? "Captors"? (Hudson); the Rockin' Revols (Manuel); and the Jungle Bush Beaters. The last was Levon's original Marvel, Arkansas, outfit—and as the soubriquet of a bunch of Southern white boys chasing the blues across the tracks, it's rock 'n' roll poetry if anything is.

thirteen-year-old girl," he is reputed to have said. "All us Southern cats knew she was only twelve."

Hawkins was no fool; he needed a band to carry him, and when the razorbacks he had imported began to scatter, he and Levon recruited the Canadian kids one by one. As characters in the classic bildungsroman that tells of the wise old philosopher who initiates innocent young boys into the mysteries of life, Hawkins and his Hawks played their way through the collected works of Gene Vincent, Chuck Berry, Larry Williams, Fats Domino, and the rest, filling out their shows with tunes about the whores they met.

Robbie wrote his first song, "Hey Boba Lu," which Hawkins recorded; on stage, Manuel and Levon handled most of the singing. "When Ronnie sang," Robbie remembers fondly, "we had to count out the beat for him. It was, 'Oh, Carol—one, two, three, *four*—Don't let him steal. . . .' "

The Hawks were looking for their music. When Robbie was fifteen Levon took him into the South, with hopes of putting the Bush Beaters back together. That came to nothing, but the trip changed something in Robertson; just what it was is elusive even to him, but listening to the man retrace his steps, one gets the sense that an enormous creative ambition was set free when he discovered that the place that had put magic into his life was real. There had been the music, of course—rock 'n' roll from Memphis, rock 'n' roll from New Orleans—and Robbie already had the beginnings of his idea that the land makes the music. But there were also the family histories and local legends Levon had told him; the inexplicably exciting foreign names, suddenly right there on billboards and coming over the drifting Southern radio dial in between the fiddles and sermons, names like "Dr. Pepper" and "Ko-Ko bars"; there was the fact of seeing people, black and white, living out the sounds he had heard on his records. The reality only made the magic that much more fierce. Here was a different world, with more on its surface than Canada had in its abyss; you could chase that world, listen to it, learn from it. Perhaps you could even join it.

Before too long, Howlin' Wolf, Junior Parker, Bobby Bland, and other bluesmen were climbing the Hawks' charts, and Hawkins' repertoire no longer seemed so romantic. Robbie had tried to get Kenny Paulsen, Hawkins' original guitarist, to teach him how to play—Paulsen, with a good eye for the competition, told the kid to get lost—but now Robbie was in a position to feel the competition himself. For a white boy, that meant James Burton, star of "Suzie Q" and hero of Ricky Nelson's hits; Roy Buchanan, the lonesome master of the blues; Lonnie Mack, who sang from the church and played straight from the alley. To live up to all that Levon had shown him, and to satisfy his own brash self, Robbie had to be better than any of them.

He was listening hard to Wolf's guitarists: Willie Johnson on "How Many More Years" and Hubert Sumlin on "Wang Dang Doodle." Johnson and Sumlin had created a guitar style so chaotic and fast it demanded a rhythm section as quick as it was hard just to keep a performance from flying to pieces. There was none of the polite formality of a band setting up a solo, taking turns; there was no showcasing. Wolf's best records came on like three-minute race riots. The drums, bass, piano, and harp converged on the beat, hammering, shoving; for a moment they let the beat take the song, let you think you had the sides sorted out and the picture clear, and then the guitarist leaped in, heaved himself through the crowd like a tornado, and the crowd paid no attention and went right on fighting. This was the sound the Hawks were after, and on an unbelievably demonic recording of Bo Diddley's "Who Do You Love," they got it. Hawkins' vocal (his only real claim to greatness, but it will do) was one ghastly scream; Robbie fought back with a crazed, jagged solo that to this day has never been matched. It is still possibly the most menacing piece of rock 'n' roll ever made.

The Hawks, however, did not need their front man—fooling around in the studio after the dry sessions for Hawkins' *Mojo Man* LP, Levon took over the mike for Bobby Bland's hard-rocking "Further on Up the Road" and Muddy Waters' slow and sexy "She's 19," and the group left

behind the most exciting white blues recordings since the
early days of Elvis Presley. "White blues" doesn't really describe the music—though they were white, and the songs
were blues—Levon's singing and Robbie's guitar playing fell
into no genre. This wasn't like the early Paul Butterfield
Band, or John Hammond, Jr., to be judged on how precisely
the white music matched the sound of the black idols. The
Hawks were a long way past questions of technique; the
problem was to find out what they could do with that technique.

Unfortunately, they were making music in a vacuum; in
America, those great sides were never released, not that they
would have fit the commercial demands of the radio anyway.
Like most of the best bands forming at the time, the Hawks
were a walking jukebox that played only other people's hits,
and the jukebox was a few years out of date to boot. Over in
Hamburg, the Beatles too were jamming out five sets a night,
as John Lennon shouted "Dizzy Miss Lizzy" with a toilet
seat around his neck; Van Morrison and the Monarchs were
peddling their Ray Charles imitations to homesick GIs in
Germany; the Rolling Stones were up all night trying to figure out how Sonny Boy made his harp sound like that; Elvis
was having fun in Acapulco; and Creedence Clearwater, calling themselves the Blue Velvets, were scuffling up and down
the road from Sacramento to San Jose, fighting a battle of the
bands with Peter Wheat and the Breadmen, while John
Fogerty scribbled the bayou fantasies that would lift him out
of a world he hated. In the early sixties, rock 'n' roll was a
waiting game.

After a year or two apprenticed to Hawkins, Levon led
the Band out on their own as Levon and the Hawks, sometimes as the Crackers, sometimes as the Canadian Squires.
They traveled Hawkins' circuit of honky-tonks and dives—a
tough, loud band that played, as Garth Hudson once put it,
"for pimps, whores, rounders, and flakeouts." "We had one
thing on our minds," Robbie says. "Stomp."

They cut occasional 45's, whenever they found someone

to let them into a studio: "Go Go Liza Jane," the old folk song; a good hard punch-out of a record called "Leave Me Alone"; an odd, churchy paean to "this righteous land" with the even odder title of "The Stones I Throw (Will Free All Men)"—crude stuff, but hopeful. "Down in L.A., you know they got everything," Levon sang on "Uh-Uh-Uh." "Think I'll move out there, become the new Southern King."

This was not earthshaking. By 1965 the Beatles and the Stones were running the scene, and from their name to their nightclubs, the Hawks were an anachronism. Still, they built up a vague word-of-mouth reputation on the East Coast; eager to take on the world with a new sound and perhaps feeling a bit anachronistic himself, Bob Dylan got in touch. The combination clicked: suddenly Dylan was singing like a demon, and the Hawks—never introduced, always anonymous—twisted around him with a noise that not even they could have been prepared for. The Hawks backed Dylan through the rough, mean tours of 1965 and 1966, and the Stones sat in the audience. The Hawks left the stage as the best band in the world.

Levon, a pro when Bob Dylan was still hard at work scaring his high school principal, did not go along; the Hawks, after all, had been *his* band. But when the Canadians followed Dylan to Woodstock once the tours were over, Levon joined up again, and the Band made a second founding.

Out of all this they fashioned a music that sounded not at all like what had preceded it; they seemed to draw less on their old music than on the friendship they had discovered making it. Calling themselves "The Band" was proof of their arrogance, but there was a depth of experience in their music that could not be denied, and the fans they won had no wish to deny it. It was, in fact, precisely what a lot of people were looking for.

In 1968 rock 'n' roll was coming out of its San Francisco period—psychedelic music, rebel energy, Father-Yes-Son-I-Want-To-Kill-You, drum solos, drug visions, bright and happy dancing crowds—a fabulous euphoria in the middle of a war, innocence and optimism running straight into the election of Richard Nixon. It had been a fine time, with many chances taken and many chances blown, but it was over, it was soft underneath the flash and it had exhausted itself. There was a peculiar emptiness in the air, and in the music; *Sgt. Pepper*, generally enshrined a year earlier as the greatest achievement in the history of popular music—by some, in the history of Art—now seemed very hollow, a triumph of effects. The Yippies showed up to take over the politics of the decade, and defrauded them. There were heroes and heroines of the era just past who had only a year or two to live; some of the political heroes had already been murdered. We had gone too far, really, without getting anywhere.

With Bob Dylan, the Band had seen much of this world from the inside, seen it as it was born, even helped bring it into being; but they came through on the other side, in a place very much of their own making. They stepped out, very consciously, as an alternative.

The pictures inside *Big Pink*—of the Band, their friends and relatives, and their ugly but much-loved big pink house—caught some of what they had to say. Against a cult of youth they felt for a continuity of generations; against the instant America of the sixties they looked for the traditions that made new things not only possible, but valuable; against a flight from roots they set a sense of place. Against the pop scene, all flux and novelty, they set themselves: a band with years behind it, and meant to last.

Many young Americans had spent the best part of the decade teaching themselves to feel like exiles in their own country; the Band, particularly songwriters Robbie Robertson and Richard Manuel, understood this, and were sure it was a mistake. They had come here by choice, after all. They had fallen in love with the music, first as they sought it out on the radio and on records, later as they learned to play it, and, wonder of wonders, define it. Coming out of Canada into the land that had kicked up the blues, jazz, church music, country and western, and a score of authentic rock 'n' roll heroes, playing their way up and down the spine of the continent, they fell in love with the place itself.

They felt more alive in America. They came to be on good terms with its violence and its warmth; they were attracted by the neon grab for pleasure on the face of the American night, and by the inscrutable spookiness behind that face. American contradictions demanded a fine energy, because no one could miss them; the stakes were higher, but the rewards seemed limitless. The Band's first songs were a subtle, seductive attempt to get this sense of life across. Their music was fashioned as a way back into America, and it worked.

STRANGER BLUES

With *Music from Big Pink*, the Band presented a rough moral drama. It had none of the mythic clarity of, say, John Ford's movies; it came through a modern haze, something like Robert Altman's *McCabe and Mrs. Miller*, obscure in its plots, dialogue hard to catch, communicating with a blind humor and a cryptic intensity nothing in rock 'n' roll has ever remotely touched.

They began with "Tears of Rage," an eerie invocation of Independence Day, dragging the organ and their secretive horns across a funeral beat, changing the Fourth of July into an image of betrayal, and of loneliness: America betrayed by those who would no longer be part of it. The Band made a claim to an identity others no longer wanted, and the album opened up from there. In its stories, its feel for place and language, its music, and most of all in its quest, this was an American mystery.

The liveliest songs (half Robertson's, half Manuel's, and all of a piece) shared an oddly familiar actor: the voice of "Lonesome Suzie," "Caledonia Mission," "To Kingdom Come," "We Can Talk About It Now," "Chest Fever," "The

Weight," and "Long Black Veil."* His part is taken by Levon (gutty, carnal, bewildered, always hanging onto the end of his rope), Rick Danko (quivering, melancholy, hesitant), Manuel (the Band's great sentimentalist, devastated and bursting with joy by turns), Robbie (anxious, yelping), or the four of them at once; but as I hear them now, years after I thought I knew this record, the vocals, like the writing, complete a single story.

The hero of this story (such as I find him, and I ought to note that I am setting the story down—or, if you like, making it up—simply. as I hear it, without much regard for song sequence, cross-checked lyrics, or other formalities) has *Big Pink* pretty much to himself. He almost disappears on the next album, *The Band*, returns with *Stage Fright*, loses his voice on *Cahoots*, and perhaps hits the end of his road with Richard Manuel's singing on a handful of the rock 'n' roll classics that make up *Moondog Matinee*. To follow his trail is to leave out a good bit of what the Band has done—wonderful tunes like "Get Up Jake" and "Strawberry Wine," and their work with Bob Dylan. But there is a storyteller in their music, and in one form or another, his tale is the one I'm after, because it seems to be the one the Band tells best: the story of the worried man.

"Delivered Under the Similitude of a Dream, Wherein Is Discovered the Manner of His Setting Out, His Dangerous Journey, and Safe Arrival at the Desired Country," as John Bunyan put it. That, really, is only the beginning of his adventure.

He first appears on *Big Pink* as a wanderer, a quester,

---

*This last, a modern country tune in the guise of an old Kentucky murder ballad, was not the Band's song, but it fits in perfectly with the rest. "This Wheel's on Fire" and "I Shall Be Released" (the former by Dylan and Danko and the latter by Dylan) don't fit in, not because the lyrics are out of place but because as performances the songs are not emotionally convincing, and the quality of emotion is what makes *Big Pink* a great album, not merely an interesting one. The music and the singing sound strained, contrived, probably because the Band felt obligated to replace the original arrangements they had worked out with Dylan when the songs were first put down on the famous Basement Tape. "Tears of Rage" is another Basement composition, but it works, perhaps because it was so necessary to what the Band was after; but the other two sound like filler on a record that needs nothing of the sort.

hoping to brazen his way through a strange land and learn something. He lives by his wits, moving across the territory explored by Robert Johnson and Harmonica Frank, taking his spirit from the best of both men.

To use a dark old word the worried man would recognize, these two men are his familiars. Like Johnson, he is obsessed by choices he never asked for, because he sees too clearly to avoid the guilt and fear that worm out of the Bible he carries in his carpetbag; like Harmonica Frank, he is saved by his sense of humor, and he refuses to take his fears too seriously.

The combination gives us a resurrection shuffle: prophecy, cut with jive. "Been sittin' in here for so darn long, waitin' for the end to come along," he complains in "To Kingdom Come"—Judgment Day is supposed to deliver the answers he wants, but unlike some people he will meet in *Big Pink*, he can't hang around forever. He moves on, but before he is even out of the song a stranger appears to suggest that it might be wiser for him to turn back. " 'Tarred and feathered, thistles and thorns—One or the other,' he kindly warned." Well, that's not much of a choice—what else can you show me? The seeker knows the stakes are high, but he can't believe the game is fixed. He keeps looking, scared to death and full of optimism—careful to watch out for himself, once he's fallen into a trap. The devil might be anywhere—though, thanks to the touch of Harmonica Frank in the story, the devil comes on like the Headless Horseman—so the quester only wants to do the right thing; given the clutch of all-too-human doomsters that fly through the album, he'd better. "Time will tell you well," he offers hopefully, "if you truly, truly fell."

And so he dives headlong into a Gothic world of tricksters, fortunetellers, mummers, lunatics, witch doctors, cops, and lovers, struggling to find a home at the heart of that world. The music, like the character it shapes, is full of chance, uncertainty, and humor; the sound of *Big Pink* is one version of the quester's struggle, and of the world that makes his struggle interesting.

That sound is an uncanny blend of ancient folk songs,

New Orleans jazz, postwar blues, white gospel groups, the Monotones, and Motown; and these sources are only a few of the obvious, picked almost at random. Al Kooper, reviewing *Big Pink* in 1968, heard the Beach Boys, the Association, the Swan Silvertones (*black* gospel), Hank Williams, the Beatles, Bob Dylan, and the Coasters. He's right, of course: *Big Pink* music is as dense as it is elusive. All those people are in it, and anyone's listening will turn up dozens more. The richness of *Big Pink* is in the Band's ability to contain endless combinations of American popular music without imitating any of them; the Band don't refer to their sources any more than we refer to George Washington when we vote, but the connection is there. The Band's music on *Big Pink* is personal, their own invention, but not merely personal; it is an unpredictable resolution of a common inheritance, something we shared in pieces. This was a new sound, but you could recognize yourself in that sound. *That* connection is what gives this music its natural authority, and makes it so exhilarating.

There are times when Richard Manuel sounds like the ghost of Johnny Ace (that sweet-voiced fifties R&B singer who died in a game of Russian roulette)—Johnny Ace condemned to haunt a gloomy radio, from which "Pledging My Love," the first posthumous rock 'n' roll hit, issues every time you spin the dial. There are times when the tone is desperate, close to the panicky feeling Marvin Gaye got on "I Heard It Through the Grapevine." But more often than not, the music is simply ominous.

This has to do, I think, with Robbie's hide-and-seek guitar, Garth Hudson's slithery organ, and the Band's collective sense of timing—which is really a sense of freedom. In most blues or rock bands, each musician has to give something up in order to make a performance work; the men in the Band played and sang with second sight, and they made no concessions at all. The beat is tough, but open; fast little riffs shoot out from behind vocals without warning; vocals twist around seemingly random chords. The parts combine to pull the listener into a labyrinth, with no idea of what might be lurking around the next turn.

When the music is most exciting—when the guitar is fighting for space in the clatter while voices yelp and wail as one man finishes another's line or spins it off in a new direction—the lyrics are blind baggage, and they emerge only in snatches. This is the finest rock 'n' roll tradition ("I learned the words to Little Richard's songs the best I could and what I couldn't figure out didn't matter," Robbie said once), but on *Big Pink* such a style also seems to link up with an older tradition: the instinct of the American artist to put his story in disguise, to tell his tale from the shadows, probably because that is where he usually finds it. Those who mean to seduce do not announce their intentions through megaphones.

On the other hand, those who are too subtle wind up plying their seductions in the mirror. If *Big Pink* wasn't good to hear from a distance, no one, certainly myself included, would ever bother to get close to it. The first virtue of the album is that the danger, promise, and craziness of the quester's adventure come across directly in the music; not only can't you understand the words, you don't have to. Garth Hudson's satanic organ playing (straight out of *Sunset Boulevard*, with Erich von Stroheim at the pipes) is the key to "Chest Fever"—the words couldn't be, no one has ever deciphered them anyway. You don't need to analyze the lyrics of "The Weight" to understand the burden Miss Fanny has dropped on the man who sings the song; as Jon Carroll has written, Levon Helm is the only drummer who can make you cry, and drums are all he needs to get across the weary, fated sense of a situation that simply cannot be escaped. We never find out who Miss Fanny is, let alone what the singer is supposed to do for her; but the music, not to mention the singing, is so full of emotion and complexity it makes "the weight"—some combination of love, debt, fear, and guilt—a perfect image of anyone's entanglement.

So the story is revealed, and concealed, in flashes, dreams, pieces of unresolved incident, rumbles of doubt exiting through a joke. Yet if the music is part of the story, it is also the landscape against which the story takes place.

Blurred at the edges and unsure of its center, this America is still a wilderness—the moral, social wilderness that is left even when the natural wilderness is gone. Excited and intrigued by the place for just that reason, the worried man has to get on without maps.

He has, however, brought along a lot of time-honored, prudent advice; unfortunately, it's never equal to the imprudent dilemmas life persists in forcing upon him. "Be careful what you do, it all comes back on you," he says, poking his head out of the mad confusion of "To Kingdom Come" (recalling, perhaps, a Sunday School lesson); but a few songs later, stuck in "The Weight" and surrounded by the suddenly comic riddles first set out in Robert Johnson's "Me and the Devil Blues," this is not quite good enough. Miss Fanny has given him his job, packed him off "with her regards for everyone," and since that phrase is as mysterious to him as it is to us, all he can do is stick out his hand and hope that whoever grabs it will eventually let go.

> *I picked up my bag, I went looking for a place to hide*
> *Then I saw Carmen and the devil, walking side by side*
> *I said, Hey, Carmen, come on, let's go downtown*
> *She said, I gotta go, but my friend can stick around.**

The sound of the quester's voice tells us that his first desire is simply to be left alone—left alone by friends, enemies, neighbors, women, relatives, dogs, good and evil—but he was born with his eyes and ears wide open, and he misses nothing. He can't stop asking questions (which is not to say that there aren't times when he wouldn't mind stopping—the golden calf that chases him through "To Kingdom Come" is not his idea of a good time); with nothing but the best intentions, he stumbles into everything in his way. And because he is fascinated by everything the rest of us take for granted, he finds himself caught up with his fellow men and women, and inevitably, their troubles become his own.

Looking for salvation, he ends up trying to save others: the woman of "Caledonia Mission" (she lives hidden behind a wall, and the city has a lock on her gate), "Chest Fever" ("She drinks from the bitter cup," he declares; "I'm trying' to get her to give it up"), the daughter in "Tears of Rage," and many more. Whether he succeeds is never made clear, but what is clear is that his salvation is tied to theirs.

There is Lonesome Suzie, for one; an outcast, or maybe an aging spinster, in the timeless and mythical American town in which *Big Pink* seems to be set. She dearly needs a friend, and though the quester isn't willing, he thinks, in Manuel's wonderful phrase, that maybe he can loan her one. But that, he knows, only makes him one of the confidence men his search has bound him to unmask, and so he gives in: "I guess just watching you/Has made me lonesome too."

The whole of *Big Pink*, and perhaps the best of what the Band has had to say over the years, seems to dovetail into those modest lines. The man who lives them feels like part of the crowd, and he is only too happy to fade into it; but he recognizes himself in everyone he meets, and so he is drawn out of himself and into the world. He takes his vitality from that paradox. To survive it, he can't afford to be anyone's fool; to make it worth his considerable trouble, he needs a talent for friendship that is as deep as it is broad. "Save your neck, or save your brother," he shouts a couple of years later in "The Shape I'm In," just out of jail and searching for his woman, "Look's like it's one or the other." But it's one more false choice, one more denial of the fraternity he feels in spite of himself, and he can't rest with it. Maybe that's why he sounds so desperate; even running for his life, his mind is on the people he leaves behind.

Now, taken all at once, this is a remarkable figure: the Band's recreation of an American original, the democratic man—trapped, against his better judgment, in a hilarious and scarified recreation of a very old American idea: this is a joint-stock world. A joint-stock world is open to devils and angels alike; all barriers are betrayals, and the man who sees only himself sees nothing at all.

This is the possibility the Band pursue through the tangles of the country itself. The extraordinary diversity of the place, and the claim of every man and woman to do just as they please, make a joint-stock America both necessary and hard to find; the man who looks for it has a right to be worried.

America has a lot of mottoes—common slogans, because they sum up how individuals act among themselves. "We Must All Hang Together, Or We Shall All Hang Separately" is a sentimental favorite, but the edge goes to "Don't Tread On Me"—which is to say that the man who wants to hang together had best take care not to give the good people he meets an excuse to string him up. America, as the quester finds it in his songs, is not a very friendly place. It is suspicious of itself. Most people no longer even know that they have brothers to save, and if they do, "brother" means men, but not women; the young, but not the old; blues singers, but not country singers; Northerners, but not Southerners; whites, but not blacks; or a general vice versa. The man who tells this story becomes who he is, the one who reaches out, because he responds so deeply to the yearning for unity and affection that these facts hide. Perhaps because he comes from outside, he can see the country whole, just as those who have always lived there see it only in pieces. His job, as in "The Weight," no longer a matter of isolated predicament but of vocation, is to drag that affection out into the open, even if it comes hard, as his did.

The song for that is "We Can Talk About It Now," a wonderful Richard Manuel tune that sounds like the best merry-go-round in the world. Full of exultation, exhortation, smiles, and complaints, it is the song of a man who has gone far enough to have become a part of what he sings about. "It's safe now," he says, "to take a backward glance."

It seems to me, we've been holding something
Underneath our tongues

I'm afraid if you ever got a pat on the back
It would likely burst your lungs
Whoa—stop me, if I should sound
Kinda down in the mouth
But I'd rather be burned in Canada
*Than to freeze here in the south! *

If his quest has taught him anything, it is that if he wants to find a home in this country he will have to make it himself, and that means breaking through to the warmth others hide, just as Lonesome Suzie broke through to him. The pure joy of the music unveils the depth of emotion that's his to win; and that must have been the treasure he was after from the beginning, whether he knew it or not. He had to learn, in John Barth's line, that the key to the treasure is the treasure—that to be free is not to get what you want or to settle for what you've got, but to begin to know what you want and to feel strong enough to go after it. So now, out of the claustrophobia of *Big Pink*, he has a glimpse of what he wants. For a moment, to say yes is to say everything.

We can talk about it now
It's the same old riddle, always starts from the middle
I'd fix it but I don't know how
Well, we could try to reason
But you might think it's treason
One voice for all
Echoing around the hall, ECHOING, *echoing around the hall! *

The song is loose and rangy, and the song has plenty of room in it: room for doubt, and room for doubt to turn into love without any explanation at all; room for arguments interrupted by a bottle, room for friends and strangers, room for escape and room for homecoming. For its moment, the song—a free and friendly conversation between the men in the Band and anyone who might care to listen—is that one voice.

* Copyright © 1968 & © 1970 by Dwarf Music. Used by permission of Dwarf Music.

The song creates, out of words and music, a big, open, undeniable image of what the country could sound like at its best, of what it could feel like. One good burst of rock 'n' roll blows the trail clean, and the people our man has seen and the places he has been look brand-new.

"Dontcha see," he shouts, in an extraordinary flash of vision, that seems to reveal the secret America holds, even as it hints at deeper secrets, "There's no need to slave."

"The whip," he sings, "is in the grave."

THIS RIGHTEOUS LAND

Those lines, I think, deserve a pause—there is no bottom to them. Nothing I know captures with such mystery and clarity the circle traced by American optimism, and by the dread that optimism leaves behind and inevitably meets again. You couldn't ask for a more perfect statement of the conviction that America is blessed, nor of the lingering suspicion that it is cursed. When the two ideas come together—in a story, a voice, or a group—all things seem possible. The lines touch both sides of the country's soul at once; the tension they create can push out the limits of what an artist can accomplish, for just so long as the spirit of the lines can support their contradictions. By contradictions I mean that a paradise is made out of a line that turns on the image of a whip; by spirit I mean the joy one feels when Richard Manuel shoots the line across Levon's drums—and the way Levon sounds like a man calling a town meeting to order with a gavel in each hand.

When the spirit fades, those lines will contract, and trap the man who sings them. But until then, what they bring is freedom, and the space to use it. The result is *The Band*.

That second album—arriving in 1969, soon after the group went out on the road on their own for the first time since Levon and the Hawks broke up—is the map *Big Pink*'s quester was missing. The new songs roll right over the surface of American life, proof of how magnificent that surface can be.

Turn the sound up, and the music rocks like "Blue Suede Shoes"; keep it quiet, and it sounds as folksy as an old Charlie Poole 78. The good eye of the last record is still working, but instead of probing the dark for phantoms, there is a loving feel for detail, for nuance. With its warm, happy vocals, and an irresistible snapping rhythm square in the middle of almost every tune, *The Band* is the testament of a man who has come up from a netherworld for a breath of air, a man who can now afford to have himself a good, long look around.

The worried man is a settler now, here to stay, complete with wife and kids, and the album opens with his wife holding a gun on him. As he pleads and jokes with her, trying to explain himself (No matter what you think, honey, I didn't do it), he is drawn back to the days when all he wanted was a place to come home to. He remembers his hard times, his fears, how close he came to giving up the ghost; he thinks he just may have to hit the road again if she doesn't put that gun away. By the time his reverie is finished the fight is over—still, he wouldn't mind knowing where she hid the pistol. . . .

The song is called "Across the Great Divide," an appropriate beginning for an album Robbie once said the Band could have called *America*—might as well kick it off right there where the water runs both ways. But there is more to it than that.

The Band give author's credit to the land because while we usually read our own meanings into the landscape—when we don't miss it altogether—they know that at our best we live and speak according to the metaphors of the land. The land—the image of a place like "The Great Divide," the simple fact that there is such a phenomenon—attracts the Band. The symbol seems full of meaning—the Great Divide is where the two sides of the country separate, but it is also where the two sides meet. If we look into this double metaphor, we can understand the ambitions of *The Band* clearly. That first song and those that follow are meant to cross the great divide between men and women; between the past and the present; between the country and the city; between the North and the South; between the Band and their new audience. The worried man steps back, once he has shown up to play the theme song: he wants to celebrate the country he has discovered, and he celebrates by letting the country speak for itself, in as many voices as can be crammed onto a twelve-inch disc. At home here now, the man from *Big Pink* can sit back and listen with the rest of us.

The songs, all but one by Robbie, are classics now; "Up on Cripple Creek," "Rag Mama Rag," "The Night They Drove Old Dixie Down," "King Harvest (Has Surely Come)" made up the heart of the Band's stage show for years. What they say was clear the moment they were released, and I have nothing to add to that. Their power, though, is too great to take for granted.

The songs were made to bring to life the fragments of experience, legend, and artifact every American has inherited as the legacy of a mythical past. The songs have little to do with chronology; most describe events that could be taking place right now, but most of those events had taken on their color before any of us was born. There is a conviction here that every way of life practiced in America from the time of the Revolution on down still matters—not as nostalgia, but as the necessity of someone's daily life—and the music, though it never bends to any era, never tries for any quaint support of a theme, seems as if it would sound as right to a gang of beaver trappers as it does to us. There is no feeling of being dragged back into the past for a history lesson; if anything, the past catches up with us. Robbie put his stories on the surface, but they hit home because they draw the traces of that legacy out of each of us, bringing them to the surface of our own lives.

"The Night They Drove Old Dixie Down," for one—written for Levon, who sings it—is not so much a song about the Civil War as it is about the way each American carries a version of that event within himself. In this case it is a man named Virgil Kane, who makes no claim to speak for anyone else; but something in his tone demands that everyone listen.

In a few short verses, we learn a lot about him. He is a poor white farmer from the Confederate side of Tennessee, probably not more than twenty years old, a survivor of the attacks made by General Stoneman's cavalry on the Danville train he defended. With the war over, a glimpse of Robert E. Lee is worth as much to him as the memory of his brother, who died fighting for the sense of place Virgil Kane's war was all about. He wants us to understand that the war has cost him almost everything he has.

It is hard for me to comprehend how any Northerner, raised on a very different war than Virgil Kane's, could listen to this song without finding himself changed. You can't get out from under the singer's truth—not the whole truth, simply *his* truth—and the little autobiography closes the gap between us. The performance leaves behind a feeling that for all our oppositions, every American still shares this old event; because to this day none of us has escaped its impact, what we share is an ability to respond to a story like this one.

The scope of the album, words and music, is astonishing. In "King Harvest," probably Robbie's greatest song, we meet a man who might be Virgil Kane's grandson—or our contemporary, you can't tell. He works that same farm, but it fails and sends him into the bitter mills of the New South; when times are slow the mills shut down, and he runs into the arms of a union, hoping for one last chance. Yet wherever he is driven, he carries his roots with him like a conscience. He cannot escape the feel of the land any more than we can escape its myth.

"King Harvest" is the last number on the album; like "Dixie" or the desolate "Whispering Pines" (Richard Manuel's sole contribution), the song is optimistic only because it is so full of desire. It goes against the usual playful, rocking grain of *The Band*, giving the music the tension it must have if it is to work as a version of our own roots, of our own conscience.

The distance between those songs of struggle is marked by a set of easy, honest affirmations that can be summed up in a dozen lines, but perhaps best by this one: "Life has been so good to us all." Jawbone, the Band's unregenerate thief, would say yes to that; certainly the trucker and his semipro girlfriend down in Lake Charles would, along with the little boy and his grandfather in "When You Awake" and the tired sailors of "Rockin' Chair." Even the people scrambling into the storm cellar in "Look Out Cleveland" and the lover stuck with a woman who only wants to dance would show up to sign that pledge. The man who sings "King Harvest" is alone, and he probably could not agree.

With that last reservation ahead of us we ride down the Mississippi, out to California, through the Midwest to Virginia, back again to Canada. We listen to fiddles, what sounds like an amplified jew's-harp, a rock 'n' roll band, laughing horns, good guitar, yodels, sniggers, snorts, and moans; along with the people we meet we take satisfaction in whiskey, in the grinning joys of miscegenation, in Garth Hudson's mad piano, trickling through the fast steps of "Rag Mama Rag." From song to song paradise means good times— and good times are where you find them.

> *Up on Cripple Creek she sends me*
> *If I spring a leak, she mends me*
> *I don't have to speak, she defends me*
> *A drunkard's dream if I ever did see one!* *

Again and again, the music creates that moment of shared recognition first confirmed in "Dixie"—the songs catch it in sex, in work, in failure, in the weather, in the choice of an instrument, in names lifted from half-forgotten Westerns, in the emotion of a vocal, in a memory of family life. The shifts between the songs finally let us understand that the man who sings "King Harvest" wants nothing more from his life than to sing a song like "Rag Mama Rag"; we understand that the voice of "Rag Mama Rag" is real because it has been shaped by the terrors of "King Harvest," and knows a chance to dance them away for what it's worth.

The album tells no lies. It touches the size and the age of the country, takes in its fabulous multiplicity, but that repeated moment links us to each part of the story even as it knits the songs into one.

For as long as that moment lasts, the story seems complete. Every character, every place, every event in the music looms up at once. Crossing the great divide, the Band left community in their wake.

EVEN STRANGER BLUES

The problem with community, as the Band was to discover when they finally followed their records into the country, is that you have to live in it. They had, in fact, made those first two albums from a distance—isolated in the musicians' haven of Bearsville/Woodstock and walled off from the crowd by their manager, Albert Grossman. *Big Pink* had been out for almost a year and *The Band* was in the can when the group arrived in San Francisco to meet their audience for the first time—people had gathered from all over the West to celebrate *them*.

No matter how many rave record reviews the Band might have read, until they stepped onto a stage there was no way they could have understood how fierce and intense the expectations of their audience would be. Their music had cut even more deeply than they could have hoped—to many, *Big Pink* was one of the memorable events of their lives, and the stakes of that first night were as high as they could be.

After hours of delays, excuses, promises, and interminable tuning up, the Band came on with Robbie dazed and sick, dragging along a hypnotist to cure him. The hypnotist stood on the stage conjuring up spells while the Band fell apart before the crowd's very eyes. They struggled through a handful of weak, ragged tunes, and then they turned and ran. The crowd's hopeful energy had been suspended be-

tween disappointment and desire, and it collapsed into fury.
The Band's first concert ended with an outpouring of anger
and rage unlike anything I have ever seen at a rock 'n' roll
show.

Perhaps the crowd's reaction was vicious, but it was certainly real—a good measure of how much the Band had to
live up to. They had it all the next night, playing on and on
with a wild, raucous delight that finally climaxed with Little
Richard's "Slippin' and Slidin'," a number that the five had
likely been playing—in afterschool pick-up bands, as the
Hawks, up in Woodstock—since it came out in 1956. But we
had loved the song as long as the Band had, and as Richard
Manuel tossed off the unmistakable first notes of the tune the
crowd began to dance and cheer. This was a common celebration now: as we made the old song new, what seemed
most remarkable was the recognition that our links to the
Band had been forged so long ago, and that our time together
was just beginning.

Still, I think something of that initial disaster stayed
with the Band. They made a number of cross-country tours
after that, but if they never played as badly as they did that
first night, they never played with the freedom of the show
that followed either. Performing involved all the psychic
risks they had faced and dodged in the adventures of *Big
Pink*; performing also demanded new links, no matter how
tenuous, to the America their audience lived in, which was
very different from their own—a scary place, violent with
blocked hopes and bad dreams, a place where roots were not
enough, where a good concert by the Band was like shelter in
the storm, a means to strength and pleasure. And they had
aimed for more than that.

Sometimes, though, there was less. The Band began to
hedge their bets. They called their next album *Stage Fright*,
and both the new songs and the concerts of the time proved
they meant it. *Stage Fright* was an album of doubt, guilt,
disenchantment, and false optimism. The past no longer
served them—the songs seemed trapped in the present, a

jumble of desperation that was at once personal and social. The music at its best was still special, but in every sense, the kind of unity that had given force to those first two albums, and to the idea of the Band itself, was missing. Now, instead of hearing music that could not really be broken down, one picked at parts for satisfaction—Robbie's guitar and Garth's organ on "The Shape I'm In," Rick Danko's bass and fiddle on "Daniel and the Sacred Harp." Robbie had completely taken over the songwriting; the surprises of three voices wrestling for a lyric were abandoned for solo vocals. There was an edge of separation in the music: the worried man was back, drawing the shade on his window as the police wailed by in one tune, picked up for vagrancy himself in another, spinning a hilarious but ultimately unsettling tale of sin and damnation in a third. He still reaches out to others—*he* needs shelter now—but no one is there.

Facing an audience, the Band hid in their arrangements. The arrangements were tight, disciplined, precise; the open spirit of their music contracted. They were known to spend more time on testing the sound system than they did playing, but often they didn't play loud enough to come across. They presented perfect replicas of their records—to the point where Rick Danko would back off from the mike at the end of "When You Awake," imitating the studio fade—the surest way to please an audience without really moving it.

From the days when they had first paid out their money to hear Howlin' Wolf, there had been a side to the Band that was anarchic, risky, virtually out of control, and when they caught that spirit, they could take it farther than anyone else. Sometimes Robbie made his guitar sound like a musical equivalent of Jim Brown's big scene in *The Dirty Dozen*—that moment when he takes off on a broken-field run around a Nazi chateau, dropping a hand grenade down an air shaft every ten yards and grinning madly as explosions leap up behind him in sequence—but to bring such qualities into your music you have to touch such emotions in yourself. The Band saw chaos in the crowd, in the country, in the commercial pressures that were driving the five of them apart, driving at least one of them into dope and alcohol, and they stepped back.

Almost always, the numbers they had never re-corded—Rick Danko's lovely country version of the Four Tops' "Loving You Is Sweeter Than Ever," or their hard rock assault on Marvin Gaye's "Baby Don't You Do It (Don't Break My Heart)"—were most vital, because you could hear them reaching for the songs and grabbing hold. But most of all they were looking for safety—they rarely cut loose, tried hard not to take chances. Their shows began to lose excite-ment, their music began to lose its drama, and the Band began to lose their audience.

Cahoots came out in 1971, but only the earlier songs gave any weight to the title—and the title was the best thing on the album. The songs were stiff and the music was con-stricted; all the humor and drive had gone. On *The Band* Robbie had breathed life into his characters in a line, and the singers made you care about them; here there were only ab-stractions and stereotypes, and the singers sounded as if they had no real connection to the words they were given.

The music no longer had any life of its own; it took its cues from the lyrics, and when the result wasn't flat, it was cute. "When I Paint My Masterpiece" was about an expatri-ate artist in Europe, so the tune featured a little Michel Le-grand accordion; the utterly pointless "Shootout in China-town" came complete with Fu Manchu guitar, a touch so tasteless it verged on racism. The Band's ability to create a sense of place was reduced to a humorless presentation of fixed images. The failure of language made even the good ideas of the lyrics unsatisfying—made the truth sound false.

That sense of struggle and reward that bled through *Big Pink*, *The Band*, and *Stage Fright*, the balance always chang-ing, had collapsed into a nostalgic pastoralism in which few who had felt the strength of their best songs could believe. The last cut on *Cahoots*, a tribute to the white gospel commu-nities of the South, was as sentimental in its performance as it was honest in its intent; hearing it after the strained failures of the rest of the album, I couldn't help but think of the studio happy ending that was tacked onto Fritz Lang's *You Only Live Once*, wherein Henry Fonda, having died tragically in the last shot, suddenly ascends to heaven with a bewildered smile on his face. *Cahoots* was a commercial disaster; the Band retreated even further, playing only an occasional concert, making no tours at all.

In the last week of 1971 they arranged a special set of shows in New York, and with a horn section unlike anything ever heard in rock 'n' roll to force their music past itself, the Band broke through and said their piece once more. Out of those nights came a magnificent live album, *Rock of Ages*—a claim that their music was meant to last, and certainly the best of it will. But as I listened to the live records when they were released in 1972—so full of playfulness and bite, blazing with soul and love—I was struck by how long it had been since the Band had put out a single new song that mattered.

The Band's vision of the country had darkened as they moved farther apart. If they were to keep the group they had made, they could not ask too much of it. The music seemed to say that they had lost their trust in the country, in themselves, and in each other—that they had to fight harder than they were able to touch the spirit that had made their work worth doing in the first place. Like most good American artists, and like their worried man, they had been romantics, but not fools; when the romance began to go, their talent for asking the right questions went with it. They still looked for community, but like many who cannot find it, they fell back into an even deeper privacy than they started out with. Because their dreams were too real and too beautiful to give up, they felt a sense of guilt; their withdrawal—a separation from the country, from their audience, and from each other—was a betrayal of those dreams.

They had closed out *Stage Fright* with a queer song that had all the warmth of "The Man Who Corrupted Hadleyburg," which it resembles: "The Rumor." The old quester who sings it is afraid now, and his voice is muted—no one else speaks at all. He sings to a crowd he has long since joined, but the bonds between them—of loyalty, affection, fascination—have faded away. When the singer first came to the country, he found it poisoned by suspicion and shame; he meant to change it, but instead, the country changed him.

Someone in the crowd has been harmed: "His name abused, his privacy refused." Why he has been harmed is not spelled out, probably no one really knows, and the mystery deepens the malevolence of the scene. "Feel the good," the seeker calls out, "hang down your heads/Until the fog rolls away—Let it roll away." He means it, but the words no longer mean what they might have, because the community can never be what it was. "He can forgive—and you can regret—but he can never, never forget." Not even the victim is known—the victim might be anyone, as might be the villain.

When the worried man looks into the crowd, as he must, for he has nowhere else to go, the people he sees will seem different to him, as he will to them. The whip will hang over them all.

Perhaps. The last song on *Rock of Ages* was the old Chuck Willis/Jerry Lee Lewis hit, "(I Don't Want To) Hang Up My Rock and Roll Shoes," and it capped a New Year's Eve night when the Band and their fans had put themselves back in touch with each other. But as the Band left the stage, Robbie says, they felt a common sense of depression—no, they didn't wanna, and they weren't gonna, but the song, like so many, was complex in its context. The Band knew that when Chuck Willis's version was on the radio, he was in the grave; that while Jerry Lee kept his rock 'n' roll shoes, he lost his rock 'n' roll audience. The song was not a curse, but it wasn't the simple affirmation they had bargained for either. It simply raised questions they could not answer, about the cheers that had ridden them off the stage; reaching for the past had forced them to think about what they had left to do.

Many months later, in the fall of 1973, an article appeared in *Playboy*, measuring Richard Manuel for a straight-jacket; at the same time, the Band released *Moondog Matinee*, a collection of some favorite oldies. Manuel had been in bad shape for a long time; he had not finished a song of his own for years, but this was his album.

He sang about giving up the bottle in "Saved," deepened his hopes with "A Change Is Gonna Come," and slowly pulled down his mask with "The Great Pretender." If that last had been more than a little overblown when the Platters first sang it in 1955, one would have thought that after nearly twenty years there would be nothing left of the song but nostalgia. Manuel transformed it into the truest kind of soul music; his singing made the Band's more predictable rockers sound tame by comparison.

The best of the album took the Band's tale back to its beginnings, and eased their special voice into its parts. "Third Man Theme," their little instrumental, had a quiet affection in its modesty and humor—the music asked for good times, perhaps for less than before, perhaps not. The finest cut of all, Manuel's gentle, utterly despairing version of Bobby Bland's "Share Your Love," was as lonesome a song as any can be. As he sang, surrounded again by the old simpatico of the Band, it seemed like the last word of that worried man. Share your love with me, share your love with me—what had he ever said but that, what else had anyone ever said to him?

THE WEIGHT

"It was a rowdy life," Robbie once recalled, thinking back over the years before *Big Pink*. "The places we played had tough audiences. They would throw things at you; they were rednecks. Fighting plays a big part in their life, you know—fighting and woman-stealing. And you fall in, you just do what the custom is. If they take off their shoes, you take off your shoes.

"We were all so young—we were sixteen, seventeen years old at the time. We played in joints. That's what they were. Some of it was great and some of it was scary and some of it was horrible, and some of it was very valuable to us, to this day.

"You see—instead of throwing a knapsack over your back and getting out on the highway, to learn about life, we were able to do it together. We were protected by one another. We were secured by one another."

Those are fine words. They tell us that the Band sought in America what they found among themselves: that their music and their stories were not only a version of America, but a reflection of their own unity. All those years on the road had given them their values; in a sense, community was only a projection of comradeship.

The group was its own joint-stock world, but it could not survive the honest demands of the greater joint-stock world that was the country itself. Every song on the first two albums had been written before the Band had played a single show in public; once they began to tour, the group, as men who contributed what was special about themselves to something bigger than any of them, began to fall apart. Richard Manuel never wrote another song; the singers stopped calling out to one another across the verses; the uncanny sense of timing that had made the Band's early music move disappeared altogether. As the Band stepped back from their audience, you could feel the friendship go out of their sound.

In order to save the group, Robbie took it over. He took it over as lyricist, manager, strategist, savant, visionary, and spokesman. No one else in the Band ever gave an interview; after a time, the rock press began to celebrate Robbie as a genius and the Band as his foil, and the other members were not asked to talk. And yet, because the group was no longer truly whole, Robbie could not really draw on it; since his links to the country and to his audience were no longer strong, he could no longer see the country or his audience clearly. *Moondog Matinee*, for all of its satisfactions, had the melancholy tinge of a reunion—a feeling that became all the more unsettling when one realized the five men saw each other all the time.

Friendship, in the end, is not community, though it was the Band's sense of friendship that let them embody community—in their stories, in their music, in their ambitions. Friendship can be the means to community. But if one does not live in the world, then one will feed off the small world of friendship until there is nothing left.

When I went up to Woodstock to talk to Robbie late in 1972, he was ready to leave. The Band had been hiding out there for years, their houses squirreled off in the Catskills; I had never seen that part of the country before, and I understood how one could read its signs as a promise of peace of mind. Woodstock itself looked like the usual American idea of community—quaint, tasteful, small, homogeneous—but in fact it was more like a private club, inhabited by musicians, dope dealers, artists, hangers-on. The town made me nervous; it seemed like a closed, smug, selfish place.

I asked Robbie about his favorite cities. Montreal and New Orleans, he said, and he began to talk about the cultural confusion that he thought gave those cities their spirit—the mix of languages, customs, religions, music, food, architecture, politics. You could spend your whole life in one of those cities and be surprised every day. He had a house in Montreal—that was his wife Dominique's hometown—and they were going back. What that would mean for the future of the Band I didn't ask; the pastoral traps of Woodstock had already taken too much of the soul out of the group. That they had protected each other years ago was only half of their best music—the other half came from what they had protected themselves against: those rowdy audiences, scattered all over the country in dance halls and bars. "They take off their shoes, you take off your shoes"—in those days, the Band could not afford to keep their distance. They learned to lean on each other and to listen to the crowd; that, in a queer way, brought their commitment to friendship and their feel for community together.

Before I left Woodstock I sat and talked for a long time with Dominique Robertson. She told me about the struggles of the Quebec Separatist movement and what that fight meant to her, that she had tried to find someone to talk to when Trudeau imposed a terror on the people after Separatists kidnapped a government official, that no one in Woodstock had any idea there really was a world different from their own. There's nothing here but dope, music, and beauty, she said; if you're a woman, and you don't use dope and you don't make music, there's nothing here at all.

The Band did leave; they moved to Los Angeles, and early in 1974 they set out on a grand tour with Bob Dylan. With Dylan, they were once again the best rock 'n' roll band in the world; their own sets had all the old limits, and not a song was less than four years old. Still, there was a joy in their faces as they played that I had not seen since that great night in San Francisco.

America is a dangerous place, and to find community demands as much as any of us can give. But if America is dangerous, its little utopias, asking nothing, promising safety, are usually worse. "Look at all this," Dominique said, taking in her house, the trees, the mountains. "It's beautiful. It's everything people ought to want, and I hate it." Then she grinned. " 'This country life is killin' me,' " she sang, turning a song we had both heard too many times on its head. "I gotta find my way back to the city, and get some corruption in my lungs."

SLY STONE
The Myth of Staggerlee

I named my son Malik Nkrumah Staggerlee Seale. Right on, huh? Beautiful name, right? He's named after his brother on the block, like all his brothers and sisters off the block. Stagger*lee*.

Staggerlee is Malcolm X before he became politically conscious. *Livin' in the hoodlum world.*

You'll find out. Huey had a lot of Staggerlee qualities. I guess I lived a little bit of Staggerlee's life too, here and there. That's where it's at. You move yourself up from a lower level to a higher level. And at one time brother Eldridge was on the block. He was Staggerlee.

"Staggerlee shot Billy . . ." Billy the *Lion*. "Staggerlee had a sawed-off shotgun and a Model A Ford and he owed money on that as well; his woman kicked him out in the cold 'cause she said his love was growin' old. Staggerlee took a walk down *Ramparts Street*, down where all them baaad son-of-a-guns meet. By the Bucket o' *Bluuuuuud*." You know, the main drag? That's from

Louisiana, Ramparts Street? Yeah, this is where Staggerlee's history is. Staggerlee is all the shootouts that went on between gam-
blers, and cats fightin' over women—the black community.

Staggerlee shot Billy, you know? "Shot that poor boy dead."
Two black brothers fightin' each other. Billy the Lion was bad too.
"Staggerlee walked into a bar and ordered . . . just to get a bite to
eat. And he wound up with a glass of muddy water and a piece of
rotten meat. He asked the bartender, did he know who he was?
And the bartender says, 'I heard o' you across the way,' he says,
'but I serve *bad* son-of-a-guns *three* times a day.' " *Everybody's* bad,
you see?

Something else, huh? That's *life*. And all the little Staggerlees,
a *lot of 'em*! Millions of 'em, know what I mean?

And so I named that brother, my little boy, Staggerlee, because . . . that's what his *name* is.

BOBBY SEALE, from a jailhouse
interview with Francisco Newman, 1970.

STAGGERLEE

Somewhere, sometime, a murder took place: a man called
Stack-a-lee—or Stacker Lee, Stagolee, or Staggerlee—shot
a man called Billy Lyons—or Billy the Lion, or Billy
the Liar. It is a story that black America has never tired of
hearing and never stopped living out, like whites with
their Westerns. Locked in the images of a thousand versions of the tale is an archetype that speaks to fantasies of
casual violence and violent sex, lust and hatred, ease and
mastery, a fantasy of style and steppin' high. At a deeper
level it is a fantasy of no-limits for a people who live
within a labyrinth of limits every day of their lives, and
who can transgress them only among themselves. It is
both a portrait of that tough and vital character that
everyone would like to be, and just another pointless,
tawdry dance of death.

Billy died for a five-dollar Stetson hat; because he beat
Staggerlee in a card game, or a crap game; because Stack was
cheating and Billy was fool enough to call him on it. It happened in Memphis around the turn of the century, in New
Orleans in the twenties, in St. Louis in the 1880s. The

style of the killing matters, though: Staggerlee shot Billy, in the words of a Johnny Cash song, just to watch him die.

Sometimes it was a cautionary tale, as in Mississippi John Hurt's version, recorded in 1929.

> *Po-lice officer, how can it be*
> *You can 'rest everybody, but cru-el Stagolee*
> *That bad man, Oh, cru-el Stagolee*
>
> *Billy the Lion tol' Stagolee*
> *Please don't take my life*
> *I got two little babes, and a darlin' lovely wife*
> *That bad man, Oh, cruel Stagolee*
>
> *What I care about your two little babes*
> *Your darlin' lovely wife*
> *You done stole my Stetson hat*
> *I'm bound to take your life*
> *That bad man, Oh, cruel Stagolee*
>
> *Boom-boom, boom-boom, went a .44*
> *Well, when I spied ol' Billy the Lion*
> *He was lyin' on the floor*
> *That bad man, Oh, cruel Stagolee*
>
> *Gentlemens of the jury, what you think of that*
> *Stagolee shot Billy the Lion 'bout a five-dollar Stetson hat*
> *That bad man, Oh, cruel Stagolee*

If that was something like the original idea of the story, it didn't hold up very long. Usually, no white sheriff had the nerve to take Stack on, and he got away. When he didn't— when he was caught and hung—it was only for a chance to beat the devil. The song carried Staggerlee down to hell, where he took over the place and made it into a black man's paradise.

Innocent Billy was no longer seen as a helpless victim, but as a hapless mark. Staggerlee's secret admirers came out of the woodwork; the women (all dressed in red) flocked to his funeral (it was the best money could buy). Stagolee was a winner. "GO!" shouted Lloyd Price, caught up in the legend, "GO! GO! Stagger Lee!"

Nobody's fool, nobody's man, tougher than the devil and out of God's reach—to those who followed his story and thus became a part of it, Stack-o-Lee was ultimately a stone-tough image of a free man.

In the blues, Stack changed names, but little else. He was the Crawling Kingsnake; Tommy Johnson pouring Sterno down his throat, singing, "Canned heat, canned heat is killing me"; Muddy Waters' cool and elemental Rollin' Stone; Chuck Berry's Brown-Eyed Handsome Man; Bo Diddley with a tombstone hand and a graveyard mind; Wilson Pickett's Midnight Mover; Mick Jagger's Midnight Rambler.

Stack rode free as the Back Door Man in the deadly electric blues of Howlin' Wolf (" 'Cuse me for murder/ First degree/ Judge's wife cried, Let the man go free!/ *I am* . . ."), and gave up the ghost, proud never to rest easy, in "Going Down Slow." Stagolee was a secret, buried deep in the heart as well as ruling the streets: in Bobby Marchan's "There Is Something on Your Mind," Stackerlee crawled out of a man who only wanted love and pulled the trigger that turned love into death. When the civil rights movement got tough, he took over. And Staggerlee would come roaring back on the screen in the seventies, as Slaughter, Sweet Sweetback, Superfly.

"Stagger Lee shot Billy. . . ." The line echoes from Lloyd Price's rock 'n' roll hit through fifty years of black culture, passing, on its way back to its hidden source, thousands and thousands of Staggerlees and Billys. There is an echo for Jimi Hendrix, a star at twenty-four and dead at twenty-seven; for Sly Stone, "not," as was said of Bob Dylan once, "burning his candle at both ends, but using a blow torch on the middle"; for young men dead in alleys or cold in the city morgue; for a million busted liquor stores and a million angry rapes. Stack and Billy merge into a figure innocent on one level and guilty on another: into Robert Johnson, living from town to town and woman to woman, driven and searching for sin and peace of mind; into junkies twisted from their last OD's; into a young George Jackson, drunk and out for easy money, or his brother Jonathan, rising years later with a gun in his hand. Look and you will see King Curtis, stretched out dead in front of his house; Muhammad Ali; Rap Brown, so bad that Congress passed a law against him. Farther on are pimps like Big Red Little, Jack Johnson in a car full of white women, Sportin' Life steppin' out. It is an echo all the way back to the bullet that went through Billy and broke the bartender's glass, a timeless image of style and death.

SLY STONE

Born Sylvester Stewart in 1944, in Dallas, Sly Stone grew up in Vallejo, California, a tough and grimy polyglot town on the north end of San Francisco Bay. He picked up guitar and drums as a kid, led his own gang into the streets, and played his part in the high school race riots that were endemic in the town. He made it into a few semipro bands in the early sixties; by the time he was nineteen, in 1964, he was producing small hits by local white club bands for Autumn Records, the label owned by the baron of San Francisco Top 40, Big Daddy Tom Donahue. This put Sly right in the mainstream of Bay Area rock 'n' roll; up until 1965, the local music scene pretty much came down to Donahue's kind of radio and the big package shows he and his partner, Bobby Mitchell, booked into the Cow Palace.

There was no big money; in fact, a lot of what there was never seemed to find its way from the distributors back to the company. The music that was going to put San Francisco on the rock 'n' roll map was taking shape; it would wipe out the tight, commercial sounds Donahue and Sly were after— that is, it would make them uncool.

Sly went to radio school and got a job on KSOL, the number two black station in the area. Fast on the air, he was a hit. A brilliant, kinetic DJ, he found the straight soul format a fraud on his taste, and salted it with Bob Dylan and the Beatles. At the same time, he was pulling a band together. There were whites as well as blacks, women—who played real instruments—as well as men: "The Family."

By early 1967 the hippie bands of the Haight had the ear of the nation, and San Francisco geared up for the crunch of the Summer of Love. The first hip FM rock station, led by Larry Miller and a reformed Tom Donahue ("Should I change my name?" he once asked his new listeners. "Send in your suggestions."), was breaking the Top 40 monopoly. *Sgt. Pepper* was on the way, as was the Monterey Pop Festival. It was a genuinely exciting time.

And it was a very white scene. If the Jefferson Airplane had little to say to blacks, the fact that they and bands like them brought a white audience into the Fillmore ghetto every weekend seemed unimportant, even if racial tensions were beginning to emerge in the Haight. No one knew what to say about that, so no one said anything, except that they sure dug spades.

Black music, led by Aretha Franklin, Wilson Pickett, and Sam and Dave, had hit a commercial peak and was approaching an artistic impasse, as inspiration turned into formula. Otis Redding became the white hope of the new rock 'n' roll fans, and at Monterey they would cover him with glory because he said they were all right. But six months later he was dead. A musical vacuum was opening up, and the racial contradictions of the counterculture were coming to the surface. There was no music to work out the contradictions, and no music to fill the vacuum.

It was at this point that Sly and the Family Stone emerged from the unhip white bars of Hayward and Redwood City—middle-class suburb towns—with a music they brashly called "a whole new thing," leaving behind (and picking up again on the radio) an audience of small-time boosters, bikers, college students, and the sons and daughters of transplanted Okies.

Sly had mastered the recording studio and a dozen instruments. He was tough and wily, already burned in the record business and determined never to let it happen again;

a man out to build something worth the trouble it would take. He was bursting with ambition and ideas, the wildest dresser rock 'n' roll had ever seen—which is saying something—an outrageous showman whose style was a combination of Fillmore district pimp gone stone crazy and Fillmore Auditorium optimism with a point to it. A cultural politician of the first order, Sly was less interested in crossing racial and musical lines than in tearing them up.

In the manner of the very greatest rock 'n' roll, Sly and the Family Stone made music no one had ever heard before.

In moments you could catch echoes of Sam Cooke, the Beatles, a lot of jazz, and even a little surf music. Not just the singers but the whole band seemed to find much of their inspiration in a few classic rock 'n' roll songs, building off the furious vocal lines of the Silhouettes' "Get a Job," the mad desire of Maurice Williams' "Stay," and the chaos of Stevie Wonder's preteen apocalypse, "Fingertips." The band dismissed the simple, direct sound of the black music of the day, from Stax to James Brown, but took advantage of its rhythmic inventions; the Family Stone had much of the exhilaration of the white San Francisco sound, along with the open spirit that sound was already beginning to lose. And there was a keen ear for the hook lines and commercial punch crucial to the charts of any rock era.

The whole was something other than its parts, perhaps because what came across was not simply a new musical style, though there was that, but a shared attitude, a point of view: not just a brand-new talk, but the brand-new walk of young men and women on the move.

There was an enormous freedom to the band's sound. It was complex, because freedom is complex; wild and anarchic, like the wish for freedom; sympathetic, affectionate, and coherent, like the reality of freedom. And it was all celebration, all affirmation, a music of endless humor and delight, like a fantasy of freedom.

They had hits: "Dance to the Music," "Stand!," "Everyday People," "Hot Fun in the Summertime," "Thank You

falettinme be mice elf agin." A smash with black kids and
white, these records had all the good feeling of the March on
Washington, and the street cachet that march never had.

Sly's real triumph was that he had it both ways. Every
nuance of his style, from the razzle-dazzle of his threads to
the originality of his music to the explosiveness of his live
performance, made it clear he was his own man. If the essence of his music was freedom, no one was more aggres-
sively, creatively free than he. Yet there was room for everyone in the America of a band made up of blacks and whites,
men and women, who sang out "different strokes for different folks" and were there on stage to show an audience
just what such an idea of independence meant. Vocals were
demystified: everybody sang (even Cynthia Robinson, who
screeched). When the band growled out "Don't Call Me
Nigger, Whitey (Don't Call Me Whitey, Nigger)," they gave
pleasure by using the insults for all they were worth, and at
the same time showed how deeply those insults cut.

Sly was a winner. It seemed he had not only won the
race, he had made up his own rules. Driving the finest cars,
sporting the most sensational clothes, making the biggest
deals and the best music, he was shaping the style and ambition of black teenagers all over the country—expanding the
old Staggerlee role of the biggest, baddest man on the block.
Sly was Staggerlee, and the power of the role was his, but he
didn't have to kill anyone to get it.

RIOT

Motown raced to absorb Sly's new music, to catch up.
They tightened his aesthetic and roared back up the charts
with a revamped version of the Temptations and the new
Jackson 5. Sly kept up the pace, breaking the color line at
Woodstock and emerging as the festival's biggest hit. In early
1970 the band cut a new single, called "Everybody Is a
Star," and it was their best—a lovely, awesomely moving
statement of what the band was about and what it was for. A

new album was on the way, Sly told an interviewer, "the most optimistic of all."

But something went wrong. Sly began to show up late for concerts, or not at all. That caused riots, including a very bad one in Chicago. Performances, when they came off, were often erratic, angry, or uncommitted. There was no new album; there was trouble with promoters; lawsuits; rumors of the band breaking up; rumors of bad dope, gangsters, extortion, death threats. Sly's manager said his client had a split personality.

Finally, in late 1971, the new record hit the stores. There was an American flag on the cover (flowers instead of stars) and happy pictures all over the rest of it (with odd, somber shots of Lincoln and the Gettysburg Address here and there). The album was called *There's a riot goin' on*, and the title cut was blank.

The record was no fun. It was slow, hard to hear, and it didn't celebrate anything. It was not groovy. In fact, it was distinctly unpleasant, unnerving. Many people didn't like it, wrote it off as a junkie bummer. If Robert Johnson were alive today there would be someone around to yell "Boogie!" at him.

There's a riot goin' on was an exploration of and a pronouncement on the state of the nation, Sly's career, his audience, black music, black politics, and a white world. Emerging out of a pervasive sense, at once public and personal, that the good ideas of the sixties had gone to their limits, turned back upon themselves, and produced evil where only good was expected, the album began where "Everybody Is a Star" left off, and it asked: So what?

The album contained, in a matrix of parody and vicious self-criticism, virtually all the images and slogans Sly had given to his audience. The new music called all the old music and the reasons for claiming it into question. Like *Bonnie and Clyde*, which angered critics in much the same way, *Riot* was, and is, a rough, disturbing work that can be ignored, dismissed, but never smoothed over.

Riot joined other pop reversals that confused and divided audiences and created new ones, pop acts that risked the destruction of the artist's audience. It was Sly's equivalent of Van Morrison's *Blowin' Your Mind*, his first solo album, where Van reached for the grotesque because it seemed the only rational description of everyday life; of Dylan's *John Wesley Harding*, in that Sly was escaping his own pop past and denying its value; of John Lennon's screaming break with the Beatles, though Sly worked with much greater sophistication and intelligence. Instead of merely orchestrating his confessions, Sly transformed them into a devastating work of art that deeply challenged anyone who ever claimed to be a part of his audience, a piece of music that challenges most of the assumptions of rock 'n' roll itself.

In an age when politics succeeds by confusing and obscuring matters of life and death, the strongest artists must claim those things as their own and act them out. Not many will ever have the nerve or the vision to do it, but at least for as long as it took to make *Riot*, Sly did.

Riot begins with a slow, stuttering beat, a chanting parody of "Stand!" As Sly comes in, wailing and groaning, half-satisfied, half-desperate, the question that comes through is whether it is worth standing up at all, or possible even if it is worth it. In another world, the man who sings this song did not merely "control the decisions that affected his life," to use a phrase from the decade this album left behind, he *made* them; now the words "control" and "decision" have lost their meaning. Tense, nervous, creepy, the song careens to an end, and it sets the tone. What follows is an expertly crafted and brilliantly performed review of folly, failure, betrayal, and disintegration—the confession of a man, speaking for more than himself, who has been trapped by limits whose existence he once would not even admit to, let alone respect: trapped by dope; by the weakness behind a world based on style; by the repression that sent black men and women into hiding, into exile, into the morgue; by the flimsiness of the rewards a white society has offered him. A testament to oppression, the music is, on first listening, itself oppressive.

The songs seem to wander, to show up and disappear, ghostly, with no highs or lows. At their kindest, they are simply ironic. Some, like "Africa Talks to You (The Asphault Jungle)," are morbid: chased into hiding by the band, Sly shouts back, "Timmmmmberrr!" and the guitar mocks him into silence. "Brave and Strong" pleads for survival, but hints that only dope will get it.

Two tracks were released as singles—"Family Affair" and "Runnin' Away"—both were hits, and both had a deceptively easy movement. But the first was about finding your way back to mother and a marriage falling to pieces, and the second used a saucy female chorus to drive nails into a fool.

The album found its end with "Thank you for talkin' to me Africa," a reversal of "Thank you fallentinme be mice elf Agin." There is no vocal music in rock 'n' roll to match it; the voices creep in and out of the instruments, cutting out in the middle of a line, messages from limbo, golem-talk. "I'm a-dyin, I'm a-dyin," you can hear Sly wailing, and the only way to disbelieve is to stop listening. The song gathers up all the devastation of the rest of the album and slowly drives it home, grinds it in, and fades out.

This music defines the world of the Staggerlee who does not get away, and who finds hell as advertised. There is an enormous reality to the music: a slow, level sense of getting by. It is Muzak with its finger on the trigger; the essence of the rhythms James Brown has explored without the compensations of Brown's showmanship or his badass lyrics. It is a reality of day-to-day sameness and an absence of variety— like prison—that requires, if one is to endure it, either a deadening of all the senses, or a preternatural sharpening of them, so that the smallest change of mood or event can be seized on as representing something novel or meaningful.

In this sense, and only at the farthest margin, the music is part of the way out of the disaster it affirms. If you listen, you get sharper, and you begin to hear what the band is hearing; every bass line or vocal nuance eventually takes on great force. The disaster gains an emotional complexity, and you enter it. Finally, *Riot* bears the same relationship to most music as George Jackson's *Soledad Brother* does to *Confidential*. The second is easier to get into, but nothing is there.

Stand!, the brilliant album that preceded *Riot* (and literally turned black music inside out with its flash and innovation), had all the drive and machinery of a big semi-truck; listening to it put you in the driver's seat, made you feel like you owned the road. *Riot* is about getting off the truck. The mood is one of standing still; of performing every act with the care of one who is not sure his mind and his body will quite connect; of falling apart; of running, looking back, realizing you can be caught.

> *Lookin' at the devil,*
> *Grinnin' at his gun.*
> *Fingers start shakin',*
> *I begin to run.*
>
> *Bullets start chasin',*
> *I begin to stop.*
> *We begin to wrestle,*
> *I was on the top.*

"Thank You for talkin' to me Africa"

When the song was released a year earlier as "Thank You fallentinme be mice elf agin," it had a snappy rhythm. It was a winner's song, and neither the music nor the vocals left any doubt as to who was going to stay on top. On *Riot* the song comes slowly, emphasizing the thud of the bass guitar. The words are buried in a slurred half-chant; when Sly sings, "Thank You falletinme be mice elf Agin," the contempt in his voice is inescapable.

Notice how the song reads. The words Sly wrote for *Riot* are some of the most imaginative and forceful in all of rock 'n' roll. The images are perfectly developed; the songs achieve a tense and eerie balance, as each element of the music seems to pull more than its own weight. Not one image, not one note, is wasted. Nothing is gratuitous.

One song, "Poet," was called pretentious, because it said such things as, "I'm a songwriter, oh yeh a poet." The number is intentionally crude, but in the end such a song is pretentious only if it is false. And although for rock 'n' roll the terms themselves are probably false, the words of the songs on this album are better "poetry" than anything the "rock poets" have written. The rock poets are all of them white, of course, because the rock 'n' roll audience—and rock critics—often think in neat racial categories, and "black" does not fit into the "poetry" category. When Bob Dylan quipped that Smokey Robinson was America's greatest poet, most people thought that was some kind of joke.

Of all the nonsense that has been written about the poetry of Neil Young, Paul Simon, or even Bob Dylan, no one has ever said anything about Jimi Hendrix's "Little Wing." The poetry question, especially when we are dealing with a song, has to do with how a writer uses language—and his music will be part of his language—to make words do things they ordinarily do not do, with how he tests the limits of language and alters and extends the conventional impact of images, or rescues resources of language that we have lost or destroyed. The music on *Riot* mostly flattens out what Sly wrote, hiding it, telling the truth, but not quite out loud. The words peek out, and only occasionally do they hit you in the face.

> *Lookin' at the devil,*
> *Grinnin' at his gun.*
> *Fingers start shakin',*
> *I begin to run.*
>
> *Bullets start chasin',*
> *I begin to stop.*

The poetry of those lines is the use of the words "start" and "begin," which slow the usual pace of the violent images Sly is presenting. The eye is working here, taking in the scene from the edge of action; the description is minimal, and the economy is absolute. The eye turns and the listener, or the reader, is given only a vague sense of physical motion, a whole body aware of itself with the precision of the eye in the first three lines. You feel the slowing down, the endless, instantaneous decisions and hesitations involved in turning to face the gun again. It all moves in pieces, and you are in the song, in the riot, breathing its risk.

Sly saw a band as the means by which each member finds his or her own voice; while he is the source of vision, the emotion of every singer, his included, has been authentic because that vision is shared. I think this is so because Sly's vision, whether one of affirmation, as it was in the sixties, or negation, as it is on *Riot*, is always an attempt at liberation.

It is Sly's musical authority that gives his singers freedom, that builds a home where freedom seems worth acting out. The singing on the Family's records—complex, personal, and unpredictable—really was something new. As opposed to the Temptations or the Jackson 5, whose records were not inspired by Sly's sound so much as they formalized it (just as earlier Motown imposed order on the risky spontaneity of gospel music), what you hear in Sly's music are a number of individuals who have banded together because that is the way they can best express themselves *as* individuals. It's the freedom of the street, not the church.

This was made explicit in "Everybody Is a Star." That meant not that everyone lives in the spotlight, but that every man and woman finds moments of visibility appropriate to what he or she has to give. On *Riot* Sly took this aesthetic— of the group that sings like a band plays—away from the context of celebration, which had seemed not only appropriate but necessary, and made it the means to a dramatization of events and moods that are bitter, mocking, and scary. Voices stretch words until they are drained of their ordinary meanings, just as the guitars, drums, bass, horns, and organ reduce the sensational clichés of the earlier music to bone. The superstar clothes are removed, piece by piece, and what is left, in a weird and modern way, is the blues.

The equality is still there: no one is a star.

With "Family Affair," so direct in its musical impact and so elusive in its meanings, Sly comes close to a conventional lead vocal, but here he needs the isolation of the spotlight because he is singing about the need to lean on other people.

> *Both kids are good to mom*
> *You see, it's in the blood*
> *Blood's thicker than the mud*

He sings from a distance, preaching, trying to explain something that matters. Some people give up on you; some don't, no matter what you do. Sometimes it's important to find out who's who. Sly presented this to the Top 40 audience like a philosophy lesson, holding out knowledge he had paid for.

> *You*
> *It's a family affair don't*
> *know*
> *who*
> *turned*
> *you*
> *in.*

With *Riot* Sly gave his audience—particularly his white audience—exactly what it didn't want. What it wanted was an upper, not a portrait of what lay behind the big freaky black superstar grin that decorated the cover of the album. One gets the feeling, listening, that the disastrous concerts that preceded and followed this record were not so much a matter of Sly insulting his audience as they were of Sly attacking that audience because of what the demands of the audience had forced him to produce. The concerts were an attack on himself as well, for having gone along with those demands and for having believed in them. All through *Riot* Sly turned on himself: "Must be a rush for me/ To see a lazy/ A brain he meant to be/ Cop out?" He removed the question mark in the next verse, and ultimately covered the question with poison: "Dyin' young is hard to take/ Sellin' out is harder."

Those last words were shoved under the graveyard chorus, "Thank you, falettinme be mice elf Agin," and it is not hard to see why this record was so hard to listen to, which is to say, hard to take.

The bonds of a peculiar aesthetic democracy held, one last time, to reveal a world of terror and falsehood, that moment when Staggerlee runs into the limits his role was meant to smash, the same limits that turned Selma into Attica and "Satisfaction" into "You Can't Always Get What You Want." The endless fantasies piled onto the Staggerlee myth over the years were simple proof of the force of those limits, of the need to transcend them, but the fantasy, remade again and again, had its own force: it created new Staggerlees.

Staggerlee is a free man, because he takes chances and scoffs at the consequences. Others, especially whites, gather to fawn over him, until he shatters in a grimy celebration of needles, juice, and noise. Finally he is alone in a slow bacchanal, where his buddies, in a parody of friendship, devote themselves to a study of the precise moment of betrayal. Out of this disaster the man who lives it sometimes emerges whole: Malcolm did. Sometimes he dies young; sometimes he cops out.

On the way to this silent riot Sly shouldered the racial and sexual fantasies of a huge audience and staggered under them, as if he were Staggerlee himself back from the dead to live up to his myth. The images of mastery, style, and triumph set forth earlier in Sly's career reversed themselves; his old politics had turned into death, his exuberance into dope, and his old music into a soundtrack for a world that didn't exist. As an artist, Sly used those facts to reverse the great myth itself.

The role is all too real. It was forced on Chuck Berry, who never wanted it, and he paid for it in prison; Hendrix resisted, but in the public mind, the role enclosed him anyway. *Riot* is the secret contained in the whole blazing tradition. Something more than a definition of the risks involved in getting your hands on Staggerlee's kind of freedom, more than an illustration of the neat duality of any cultural archetype, *Riot* claims the story.

When new roles break down and there is nothing with which to replace them, old roles, ghosts, come rushing in to fill up the vacuum. Whether or not he thought in these terms, Sly lived out one side of Staggerlee's life until the other side caught up, and took over. Once the first role broke down in the face of social and personal limits it could not countenance and still survive, the rage of Staggerlee intensified as his mastery was defrauded. Instead of breaking the bartender's glass Stack found himself aiming at the mirror behind the bar, and thus discovered that his target was himself.

SLY VERSUS SUPERFLY

The best pop music does not reflect events so much as it absorbs them. If the spirit of Sly's early music combined the promises of Martin Luther King's speeches and the fire of a big city riot, *Riot* represented the end of those events and the attempt to create a new music appropriate to new realities. It was music that had as much to do with the Marin shootout and the death of George Jackson as the earlier sound had to do with the pride of the riot the title track of this album said was no longer going on.

"Frightened faces to the wall," Sly moans. "Can't you hear your mama call? The Brave and Strong—Survive! Survive!"

I think those faces up against the wall belonged to Black Panthers, forced to strip naked on the night streets of Philadelphia so Frank Rizzo and his cops could gawk and laugh and make jokes about big limp cocks while Panther women, lined up with the men, were psychologically raped.

A picture was widely published. Many have forgotten it; Sly probably had not. This again is why *Riot* was hard to take. If its spirit is that of the death of George Jackson it is not a celebration of Jackson, but music that traps what you feel when you are shoved back into the corners of loneliness where you really have to think about dead flesh and cannot play around with the satisfactions of myth.

The pessimism of *Riot* is not the romantic sort we usually get in rock 'n' roll. Optimistic almost by definition, pop culture is always pointing toward the next thing and sure it is worth going after; rock 'n' roll is linked to a youthful sense of time and a youthful disbelief in death. Pop culture pessimism is almost always self-indulgent; not without the power to move an audience, but always leaving the audience (and the artist) a way out. In retrospect, records made in this spirit often seem like reverse images of narcissism. *Riot* is the real thing: scary and immobile. It wears down other records, turning them into unintentional self-parodies. The negative of *Riot* is tough enough to make solutions seem trivial and alternatives false, in personal life, politics, or music.

Rock 'n' roll may matter because it is fun, unpredictable, anarchic, a neatly packaged and amazingly intense plurality of good times and good ideas, but none save the very youngest musicians and fans can still take their innocence for granted. Most have simply seen and done too much; as the Rolling Stones have been proving for ten years, you have to *work* for innocence. You have to win it, or you end up with nothing more than a strained naïveté.

Because this is so pop needs an anchor, a reality principle, especially when the old ideas—the joy of the Beatles, the simple toughness of the Stones—have run their course and the music has begun to repeat its messages without repeating their impact. Rock 'n' roll may escape conventional reality on a day-to-day level (or remake it, minute-to-minute), but it has to have an intuitive sense of the reality it means to escape; the audience and the artists have to be up against the wall before they can climb over it. When the Stones made "Gimmie Shelter," they had power because their toughness had taken on complexity: they admitted they had doubts about finding even something as simple as shelter, and fought for it anyway. But because the band connected with its audi-

ence when they got that across, and because the music that
did it was the best they ever made, the song brought more
than shelter; it brought life, provided a metaphor that allowed the Stones to thrive when Altamont proved toughness
was not the point, and gave them the freedom to go on to
sing about other things—soul survivors, suffocation, a trip
down a moonlight mile.

Riot matters because it doesn't just define the wall; it
makes the wall real. Its sensibility is hard enough to frame
the mass of pop music, shuffle its impact, jar the listener,
and put an edge on the easy way out that has not really been
won. It is not casual music and its demands are not casual; it
tended to force black musicians to reject it or live up to it.
Some months after *Riot* was released—from the middle of
1972 through early 1973—the impulses of its music emerged
on other records, and they took over the radio.

I don't know if I will be able to convey the impact of
punching buttons day after day and night after night to be
met by records as clear and strong as Curtis Mayfield's "Superfly" and "Freddie's Dead," the Staple Singers' "Respect
Yourself" and the utopian "I'll Take You There," the O'Jays'
"Back Stabbers," War's astonishing "Slipping into Darkness"
and "The World Is a Ghetto," the Temptations' "Papa Was
a Rolling Stone," Johnny Nash's "I Can See Clearly Now,"
Stevie Wonder's "Superstition," for that matter the Stones'
Exile on Main Street (the white *Riot*)—records that were surrounded, in memory and still on the air as recent hits, by
Marvin Gaye's deadly "Inner City Blues," by the Undisputed Truth's "Smiling Faces Sometimes (Tell Lies)," by
the Chi-Lites' falsetto melancholy, by *Riot* itself. Only a year
before such discs would have been curiosities; now, they
were all of a piece: one enormous answer record. Each song
added something to the others, and as in a pop explosion, the
country found itself listening to a new voice.

To me, the Temptations took the prize. Imagine—or
simply remember—the chill of driving easily through the
night, and then hearing, casually at first, then with interest,
and then with compulsion, the three bass patterns, repeated

endlessly, somewhere between the sound of the heart and a judge's gavel, that open "Papa Was a Rolling Stone." The toughest blues guitar you have heard in years cracks through the building music like a curse; the singer starts in.

More than one person I knew pulled off the road and sat waiting, shivering, as the song crept out of the box and filled up the night.

Four children have gathered around their mother to ask for the truth about their father, who has been buried that very day. They don't know him; he was just another street-corner Stagolee. So they ask. Was he one of those two-faced preachers, mama—"Stealing in the name of the Lord?" * A drunk? A hustler? A pimp? With another wife, more kids? They slam the questions into their mother, and all she can give them is one of the most withering epitaphs ever written, for them, as well as for him: "When he died, all he left us was alone."

Some thought "Back Stabbers" hit even harder. It moved with a new urgency, heading into its chorus with an unforgettable thump; it was like hearing the Drifters again, but the Drifters robbed of pop optimism that let them find romance even in the hard luck of "On Broadway." The O'Jays sounded scared when they climaxed the song with an image that was even stronger than the music: "I wish some-body'd take/ Some a' these *knives* outta my back!"

Stevie Wonder reached number one with "Superstition"—his first time on top in ten years. It was the most ominous hard rock in a long while, a warning against a belief in myths that no one understood; Wonder made the old chicka-chicka-boom beat so potent it sounded like a syncopated version of Judgment Day.

All these records were nervous, trusting little if anything, taking *Riot*'s spirit of black self-criticism as a new aesthetic, driven (unlike *Riot*) by great physical energy, determined to get across the idea of a world—downtown or

---

* A reference to Paul Kelly's single of the same name, which, along with Jerry Butler's "Only the Strong Survive," had opened up the new territory the Tempts were exploring.

uptown, it didn't matter—where nothing was as it seemed. These black musicians and singers were cutting loose from the white man's world to attend to their own business—and to do that, they had to tell the truth. And so they made music of worry and confinement that, in their very different way, the Chi-Lites took to even greater extremes.

The Chi-Lites—like all the artists discussed here—had been around for many years, but they broke into the Top 40 in the seventies, with a dark chant called "(For God's Sake) Give More Power to the People." Stylistically, this was an old kind of record, but it was a new kind of politics; instead of a demand, or an affirmation, it was a plea, and a desperate one at that. The Chi-Lites' persona was open and vulnerable, the antithesis of machismo (something they explicitly dismissed with the great "Oh, Girl"). Other hits—"A Lonely Man," "Have You Seen Her," and "The Coldest Day of My Life"—undercut the high-stepping burst of mastery on which Wilson Pickett and so many other black artists of the sixties had based their careers; the Chi-Lites made Pickett's old bragging music sound fake. Pickett had told his audience that ninety-nine and a half won't do and made them believe it, but the Chi-Lites seemed ready to settle for a lot less—or to beg for something else altogether. The key to any black singer is in that old catch phrase about the way you talk and the way you walk; the Chi-Lites spoke softly and moved with great care.

This new music was a step back for a new look at black America; it was a finger pointed at Staggerlee and an attempt to freeze his spirit out of black culture. On many levels—direct, symbolic, commercial, personal—this music was a vital, conservative reaction to the radical costs Sly had shown that Staggerlee must ultimately exact. And since Stack was roaming virtually unchallenged in the new black cinema, this musical stance amounted to a small-scale cultural war.

All the new black movies—from *Hit Man* to *Trouble Man* to *Detroit* 9000 to *Cleopatra Jones*—were cued by the reality behind one very carefully thrown-away line from *The Godfather* (a movie, it is worth remembering, that attracted mil-

lions of black Americans, even though it had no black characters, let alone any black heroes).

"They're animals anyway," says an off-camera voice, as
the Dons make the crucial decision to dump all their heroin
into the ghettos. "Let them lose their souls."

The Mafia may have missed the contradiction in that
line, but Francis Coppola certainly did not; neither did the
black men and women in the theaters. They suffered it; in
Lady Sings the Blues, Diana Ross was stalking screens all over
the country showing just what it meant. That audience had a
right to revenge.

And so the fantasy went to work again. If that line had
opened up the abyss, the old black hero shot up from the
bottom and pushed in the white man instead. Stack slipped
through the hands of the white sheriff, won his fight, got his
girl, and got away.

Superfly summed up the genre; perhaps its first scene
did, more than it was meant to. The hero, cocaine dealer
Priest (played by Ron O'Neal, who looked uncomfortably
like a not-very-black Sean Connery) stirs in the bed of his
rich white mistress. Some black fool has made off with his
stash. Priest chases him through the alleys, up the side of a
building, and traps him in a tiny apartment. There, in full
view of the man's family, Priest beats him half to death. This
was John Hurt's Billy, but Lloyd Price's Stagger Lee.

Still, Priest is nervous. Hustling's all the Man has left
us, he tells his partner, who thinks that's just fine; Priest
wants out of the Life, but the invisible whites who run the
show want him in—or dead. He bets everything on one last
big deal. He turns on the pressure; one of his runners, Freddie, can't take it, and he panics and gets himself killed. Another man, a sort of father figure (who started Priest out peddling reefers when just a lad) is talked into the game, and he
too loses his life to Priest's bid for freedom. Priest's partner
weighs the odds and sells him out.

Moving fast, Priest penetrates the white coke hierarchy,
takes out a first-class Mafia contract on Mr. Big to cover his

bet, unmasks Mr. Big as a queer, and, with his money and his strong black woman, gets away clean. He turned up one movie later as a crusader for social justice in Africa, where life was simpler.

It was a fairy tale; but like most of the Staggerlee movies, *Superfly* had a soundtrack by an established soul singer, and in this case Curtis Mayfield's songs were not background, but criticism. (Mayfield had appeared in the picture singing in a dealers' bar, grinding out an attempted parody of his audience—but they thought it was a celebration.) His music worked against the fantasy, because to him one incident in the movie counted for more than all its triumphs: Freddie's dead. "Pushin' dope for *the Man!*" he sang, incredulous and disgusted. The movie hadn't even slowed to give Freddie an epitaph, but Mayfield clearly aimed his song at the hero as well.*

Superfly had a black director, Gordon Parks, Jr.; there was a surface ghetto realism, and there were touches of ambiguity, but the movie had Hollywood in its heart, and that was enough to smother everything else. Most of the pictures that followed simply shuffled *Superfly* clichés, but they kept coming.

Young black men began to imitate the movies, and real life put on its own endings. In the tiny black town of Brooklyn, Illinois, the mayor deputized a hustler named Bollinger to run a militant out of town (Priest had only contempt for black politics—not violent enough, he said, he'd deal with the Man his own way). With the competition out of business, Bollinger took over; he ran the town the way Capone ran Cairo, until another black man named Skinner—lacking the hustler's long coat and broad-brimmed hat—faced him down. Anyone doubting they had been to the movies can read the dialogue.

---

* Interestingly, these lyrics were not in the movie, even though the backing track was. Mayfield held off until the film was in the theaters, then wrote the words, released the record, and so took on the picture on his own turf: the radio. You could say he chickened out, and you could also say he was very smart.

" 'I guess you're lookin' for me,' said Bollinger calmly.

" 'That's right,' replied Skinner. 'I'm lookin' for you, man. I know you've heard I'm the police chief now.'

" 'I'm not giving up a goddamn thing,' said Bollinger."

Skinner shot Bollinger dead; then the hustler's girl stood over him. She said: "He lived like a man. He died like one too." *

The story out of Detroit was worse. A group of three young men—determined, like the heroes of so many new black movies, to clean the smack out of their neighborhood—began to lean hard on dealers and junkies. They were armed and violent. A run-in with STRESS (Stop Robberies Enjoy Safe Streets), the killer squad of the Detroit police, which the three men suspected had ties with the heroin trade, seemed inevitable. When it was over two cops were dead and the vigilantes were on the run. The youngest was caught in Detroit, and survived; his two comrades were tailed to Atlanta, set up, and executed. And all the while, in uptown movie houses across the country, Staggerlee killed and fucked and killed and fucked and white sheriff near died of envy and Billy died to let Stack kill and fuck another day.

One movie was different, but it never found its audience, not among blacks, or whites either. *Across 110th Street* (directed by Barry Shear, who earlier made *Wild in the Streets*, the most paradoxical youth exploitation picture; written by Luther Davis) looked enough like all the others to make it easy for nearly all critics to dismiss it. The film was almost unbelievably violent, which gave reviewers license to attack it. It began with the same clichés everyone else used, but intensified them mercilessly. It pumped so much pressure into the world of the new black movies that it blew that world apart.

Three black men—Jamaica, Superflake, and Dry Clean—murder a pack of black and white Mafia bankers and make off with the week's take for all of Harlem. They don't steal because they hate the mob; they steal because they want

---

* Dialogue quoted from "High Noon after Nightfall," *Time*, December 17, 1973.

the money. A Mafia lieutenant—played by Tony Franciosa—is sent out to bring back the money and execute the thieves, knowing full well he can forget his future if he fails. Anthony Quinn plays a bought cop caught in the middle. He has to take the case straight to make his pension, and a new black cop is keeping an eye on him, but he has to do it without losing his payoff—or his life—to the Mafia hirelings who control his district: a black man who runs a taxi company and looks like Fats Domino risen from the swamp of evil, and his bodyguard, a Staggerlee who watches over the entire film with the cold eyes of someone who sold his soul to the devil the day he was old enough to know he had one.

You paid for every bit of violence, perhaps because the film refused its audience the pleasures of telling the good guys from the bad guys, and because the violence was so ugly it exploded the violence of the genre. It wasn't gratuitous, but it wasn't "poetic" either. Every character seemed alive, with motives worth reaching for, no matter how twisted they might turn out to be; every character (save for Taxi Man and his gunman) fled through the story scared half out of his wits, desperate for space, for a little more time, for one more chance.

The thieves speed away from the litter of corpses, divide up the money, and go into hiding. Superflake is too proud of himself to stay holed up; good times are what it was all for, right? His best hustler's clothes—tasteless Sly Stone, but gaudy—have been hanging for this moment. Down at the best whorehouse in Harlem Superflake has a dozen women and he's bragging.

Franciosa picks up the scent, and with Taxi Man's Staggerlee at his side, his eyes glazing over with a sadism that masks his own terror, he rips Superflake out of the whorehouse bar. When Quinn finds Superflake crucified, castrated, and skinned alive, you realize that along with no heroes, this movie may offer no way out. It was made to take your sleep.

Jamaica and Dry Clean pass the word and panic; they know that Superflake had to finger them. Dry Clean shoves

his money into a clothes bag from his shop and hails a cab for
Jersey. The driver spots the markings on the bag, radios back
to Taxi Man, and delivers Dry Clean straight to Franciosa at
110th Street—the border of Harlem and the one line the
movie never crosses. Dry Clean breaks away; Franciosa traps
him on a roof, ties a rope to his leg, and hangs him over a
beam, dangling him into space. Staggerlee holds the rope; his
eyes show nothing as he watches the white man torture the
black. If Dry Clean talks, they say, they won't kill him; he is
so scared he believes them. He talks, and the rope shoots
over the side.

Jamaica and his girl meet in his wretched apartment
(there is a little torn-out picture of Martin Luther King taped
to the wall, a gray reminder of some other time) to plan an
escape, or a better hideout. And in one of the most extraordinary scenes in any American movie, a death's-head reversal
of every warm close-up you have ever seen, Jamaica begins
to talk—about green hills and a blue sky; about quiet, rest,
peace of mind; about going home. He has only killed nine
men to get there. His face is scarred by smallpox; his eyes
try hard to explain. Jamaica goes on; you don't hear him; the
camera stays in tight. Every few seconds his whole face
shudders, seems almost to shred, as a ghastly, obscenely
complex twitch climbs from his jaw to his temple, breaks,
and starts up again.

It is the visual equivalent of that last song on *Riot*,
"Thank You for talkin' to me Africa," another reach for a
home that isn't there. Like Sly's music, the scene is unbearably long, it makes you want to run, but each frame like each
note deepens the impact, until everything else in the world
has been excluded and only one artistic fact remains. Jamaica's twitch traces the fear of every character in the movie;
it is a map of the ambiguities the other movies so easily shot
away; and in this film, it is most of all the other side of
Staggerlee's face, which never moves.

Finally, Franciosa, Quinn, and their troops converge on
the abandoned tenement where Jamaica and his girl are hiding. Taxi Man gets word of the showdown. "Wanna watch,"

says Staggerlee. "No," says Taxi Man. "I know how it's gonna turn out."

A bullet cuts through the girl's forehead and pins her to the wall behind Jamaica. She stays on camera, standing up dead, a blank ugliness on her face. When Jamaica turns to see her you can feel the life go out of him, but he keeps shooting. Franciosa is killed; the cops take over. Jamaica flees to the roof with his gun and his bag of money, still firing. He kills more. Staggerlee, sent to cover for Taxi Man, watches from another rooftop. Jamaica falls, and in the only false moment in the picture, flings his money down to children in a playground. Staggerlee sets up a rifle, takes aim on Quinn, who has proved himself too weak to be worth the mob's time, and kills him.

In one way, then, this movie was like all the others: Staggerlee wins. But this time, the audience was not given the benefit of any masks; they had to take him as he came, and they were not about to pay money to see that.

Almost always, there is a retreat once something like the truth is out. Audiences respond to that moment of clarity, but they only want so much of it; scared of their own vision or not trusting their audiences, artists grow timid and hedge their bets. Follow hard rock with a ballad, follow a threat with reassurance. The O'Jays and their producers, Kenny Gamble and Leon Huff, put as much distance between themselves and "Back Stabbers" as they could with "Love Train" (the tough "992 Arguments" had died); the Temptations, as usual, copied themselves with the horrendous "Ghetto" ("Hmmm, life sure is tough here in the ghetto") and turned art into schlock in record time. The perfectly named Brighter Side of Darkness got a hit with "Love Jones," and made dope romantic. The restraint of the Chi-Lites became so stylized they went off the deep end with "We Need Order." The music seemed to lose its edge; it went bland, as if to prove that the only alternative to Stago-lee was an imitation of white middle-class respectability.

At the core of the attempt to make artistic and commercial sense out of the world *Riot* revealed—and in terms of black music, almost invented—was a new triumph of black capitalism and controlled craftsmanship, a kind of poetic efficiency. Most of the records discussed here were created by producers, not groups, and while the producers would take virtually any risk to break onto the charts, their real ambition seemed to be to stay on the charts without taking any risks at all.

The team of Gamble and Huff, working out of Philadelphia, epitomized the style. Their records featured beautifully intricate hooks, a sophisticated blend of R&B force and mainstream strings, and irresistible internal riffs that stood up under hundreds of listenings, which meant that when the records got on the radio they stayed there. The Spinners' "I'll Be Around" (produced by Gamble-Huff disciple Thom Bell) featured an up-and-down guitar line that could have carried a French lesson without losing any of its commercial force. But cultural force was something else again.

The new black hit factories—Willie Mitchell in Memphis with Al Green (who found his voice in the gap between Pickett's arrogance and the Chi-Lites' weakness), Lambert and Potter in Los Angeles with the Four Tops (whose "Keeper of the Castle" affirmed the family over hustling—or politics), and Gamble-Huff—spoke of consistency and stability as the crucial values. After that one burst of unity and vitality (which, if we call it a fad, will tell us how good fads can be), black music drifted back into something like a parallel of the most conventional black reality (save for Stevie Wonder and Marvin Gaye, who produced their records with their own money, and kept moving). This was a limit not only on violence and excess, but on real cultural ambition: a black version of "benign neglect." Daniel Moynihan thought if you removed the promise you would remove the threat; here, the threat submerged, but so did the promise, because the paradox that gives *Riot* its tension is that Sly knows that Staggerlee holds the key to vitality as well as disaster.

What makes *Riot* truly bleak, after all, is not that Sly

ever resists the role Staggerlee has carved out, not that he shrinks from its momentum, but that he cannot survive it. And it was this truth that made *Riot* so different from all the other records, no matter how good they were. The producers' singers moved easily from music that could have made history to music that merely reflected it; many even lost the energy that in popular music can usually be substituted for vision. They drifted, like all cultural reflections, into accommodation, into music for a new normalcy.

"An insufferable deadness had invaded our lives," Frank Kermode has written of the thirties, though his words do well enough for our own time. "We needed . . . to be violently stirred into life . . . intolerable social constraints grew daily upon us."

Nixon's rule made those lines seem quite familiar; their meaning has seeped down into our bones, like a secret second nature. It is a debilitating secret to which those who keep it can barely admit, because, in spite of all the clichés about how nothing can ever imprison an idea or a dream, dreams can be imprisoned inside those who once held to them.

Those dreams are worn down and dissolved as the world mocks them by its versions of reality; they are dissolved because the one who once felt alive because of them must live in that world. He or she does not conform to it, necessarily, but adjusts to it in a hundred ways every day: with every thought he turns away from, with every word she does not speak, with every fantasy of violence, liberation, or death that fades into the nightly dreams one does not understand and does not much want to.

Too much war and too much public crime has poisoned the country to be easily put to rest by any kind of reform or vengeance. There is simply too much to forget. Our politics have robbed the good words of ethics of their meaning; an impenetrable official venality has robbed the good ideas of the last few years of theirs. What, in the sixties, looked like a chance to find new forms of political life, has been replaced by a flight to privacy and cynicism; the shared culture that grew out of a love affair with the Beatles has collapsed (not without their help) into nostalgia and crackpot religion. The revisionists have already gone to work on the last decade—which was, no matter how smug, self-righteous, or naïve, a time of greater cultural and political freedom than most of us will likely know again. Those who, in Leslie Fiedler's words, "lived the mythic life of their generation," those who made it and were remade by it, can now hardly remember it.

Throughout the years of Nixon's ascendancy the *New Yorker* opened most issues with a page of unsigned commentary that tried to see through each week's dose of lies—the obvious lies told by those in power, and the more subtle, pathetic lies told by those who twisted to escape the first. It was something better than comforting to read that commentary every week, and something worse. There was satisfaction in knowing that someone had the will and the talent to work to find the truth no matter how pointless the effort seemed; there was a queasy disgust in knowing that someone else had to do that work for me. Whether my own talents were not up to the job, or my will too weak, didn't much matter. It was too easy to lose touch with rage, with a sense of what is good and evil, to lose touch with the idea that it is worth something to make, and try to live out, such a distinction.

These are politics of the freeze-out. They turn into a culture of seamless melancholy with the willful avoidance of anything—a book, some photographs, a record, a movie, even a newspaper—that one suspects might produce really deep feeling. Raw emotions must be avoided when one knows they will take no shape but that of chaos.

Within such a culture there are many choices: cynicism, which is a smug, fraudulent kind of pessimism; the sort of camp sensibility that puts all feeling at a distance; or culture that reassures, counterfeits excitement and adventure, and is safe. A music as broad as rock 'n' roll will always come up with some of each, and probably that's just as it should be.

Sometimes, though, you want something more: work so intense and compelling you will risk chaos to get close to it, music that smashes through a world that for all of its desolation may be taking on too many of the comforts of familiarity. Sly created a moment of lucidity in the midst of all the obvious negatives and the false, faked hopes; he made his despair mean something in the midst of a despair it is all too easy to think may mean nothing at all. He was clearing away the cultural and political debris that seemed piled up in mounds on the streets, in the papers, in the record stores; for all of the darkness of what he had to say and how he said it, his music had the kind of strength and the naked honesty that could make you want to start over.

A QUIET REBELLION

Sly clearly could not push *Riot* much farther, not without releasing a whole album of silence; and not, perhaps, without losing the audience he had worked to win. *Fresh*, the album that did follow, in 1973, showed Sly clicking his heels for Richard Avedon's camera, and the songs did their best to keep up with the title and the cover. "There's a mickie in the tastin' of disaster," was the first line of *Fresh*—Sly's instinctive paraphrase of Nietzsche's belief that he who gazes into the abyss will find the abyss looking back; that he who looks too long at monsters may well become one.

The music was good, but it lacked the fire of *Riot*, the tiny explosions of a bass riff or a horn part stuttering along vocal lines, ambushing words and transforming emotions. Save for "Que Sera, Sera," which Sly and Rosie Stone turned into a blues (this following months of bizarre rumors of a romance between Sly and Doris Day—"*Riot* or no *Riot*," said a friend, "he hasn't lost his sense of humor"), the music and the singing lacked risk. Most critics applauded Sly's step toward "a more positive" stance, but there was little on *Fresh* to prove that it was more than a stance.

Worse, the complexity of Sly's music, from *A Whole New Thing* to *Riot*—the tension between the individual and the group, the tension of politics orchestrated in personal terms—was overtaken by a straightforward presentation of

Sly's role, and the group now seemed little more than his servant. The album's hit, "If You Want Me to Stay," was a conventional comment on the ambiguities of stardom, and there were too many references to Sly's coke habit (switched to pep, he said), the time lag between LP's, and the like. Such subjects may have been meant to work outside the limited context of Sly's personal dilemma, but they did not connect. Still, there was "Que Sera"—and the album could be seen as an attempt to figure out how it would feel to live with honesty and energy in a country that had forced the recognitions of *Riot*, but that had more to show those who knew how to look.

A tour followed the release of *Fresh*—the first Sly and the Family Stone had made in two years (two original members had quit and been replaced)—and the show I saw in Berkeley in the summer of 1973 was both interesting and a fraud. It was Sly's homecoming concert, and he presented it as such; his last in the Bay Area had been a post-*Riot* shambles, with Sly walking off the stage after a few bitter minutes, shouting something about how the audience couldn't handle what he had to give them. He had played the Cow Palace then, which holds 16,000; the Berkeley Community Theatre was nearly full, but it seats only about 3,000.

Sly celebrated trumpet player Cynthia Robinson's birthday by bringing her mother out on stage; he talked quietly about his parents, smiling broadly, trying to get across how appropriate it seemed to him that his mother had given him the ideas for some of his best songs. That was interesting, and moving. It was the music that was a fraud.

The playing was mostly mechanical; as Dave Marsh, who walked out on a similar show on Long Island, put it, the songs were "a rehash of older, more frivolous material . . . also a rehash of the part of [the past] which is most insidious, bypassing the strength of songs like 'Everybody Is a Star' and 'Everyday People' for the relatively empty 'Stand!' and 'M'Lady.' " There was not a single tune from *Riot*; the only performance that had conviction was a stunning "Que Sera," which for a moment almost saved the show; and the concert ended, as all Sly's concerts ended back in the Woodstock days, with "I Want to Take You Higher," which was always facile and is now a stupid lie. It wasn't even an effective one; the audience probably wanted to go farther more than they wanted to be taken higher, and the old piece of frenzy fizzled out in three or four minutes, as if neither the audience nor the band had much heart for the deception.

"It's one thing to change on record, in private," Dave Marsh said to me when we compared notes on the tour. "It's something else to look all those people in the face and tell them the good old days are gone." Maybe so. Perhaps, if Sly had woven a new show out of *Riot* and *Fresh*, the next tour would have had him playing to empty seats. Neither record includes much of an obvious crowd pleaser, and something had already brought Sly down from the big arena to the theater.

Most of all, though, Sly seemed eager to say that *Riot* had been a bad dream best forgotten. But if the weakness and failure of nerve of the concert I saw is what really grows out of *Riot*, that only means that the world Sly discovered and made real on that record is as debilitating as he said it was.

Whether the retreat is one of vision, as I think it is in Sly's case, or of craftsmanship and accounting, as with many black record producers, Sly's truest work has its own momentum ("Never trust the artist, trust the tale," D. H. Lawrence wrote, noting that American artists, because they cannot escape their audiences, are always desperate to cover up whatever they reveal); Sly's work penetrates into black politics just as it changed black music and haunts black movies. The turnaround of the Black Panther party— from the politics of violent rhetoric and armed self-defense to the politics of elections and alliance with the black church— parallels the retreat of the black producers and of *Fresh*. The Panther retreat may produce the same kind of guarded success; it may also tell us how necessary such retreats are. But

it is worth remembering that Eldridge Cleaver and Huey
Newton fought a war over this change in politics—a very
strange war.

After a murderous shootout provoked by the Oakland
police in 1968, Cleaver was to be returned to prison as a
parole violator. He was willing to stand trial, but he was convinced he would be killed in jail; he would not go back. And
there was more to it. He told Gene Marine:

When I went back to prison before, it didn't matter, you know?
Nobody cared about me anyway, I was in the same prison, you
know? The prison of being alone. Out or in, it didn't matter. But
this time—this time I've found something, since I've been in the
movement and working with all these cats. I've found people who
really dig me, people I really dig. People care about me, people *like*
me. I've never had that before, never at all. I can't go back in there
now and leave that out here. I've got friends—I've got friends for
the first time in my life, and man, I just don't think I can do
without that anymore.*

Pushed into a corner, Cleaver jumped bail, escaped to
Cuba, and eventually set up headquarters in Algeria. There,
if the Panther newspaper is accurate, he terrorized his wife,
took a new mistress, murdered a rival, and tumbled into fantasies of sweeping across America at the head of a guerilla
gang. He denounced Newton, tried to seize the party from
exile, and ordered his followers on the East Coast and in Los
Angeles to put his vision into practice. The war for the party
commenced; bodies began to turn up.

Newton and Seale had founded the Black Panthers
(drawing up their statement of aims and demands while playing Dylan's "Ballad of a Thin Man" over and over) as a
local self-defense organization, but the idea was irresistible
and soon there were Panther chapters all over the country.
As Bobby Seale says so well, Staggerlee was crucial to these
new politics. A killer, a thief, setting himself up against his
own people, plundering them to get what he wanted—they

* From Gene Marine, *The Black Panthers* (New York: Signet, 1969).

began there. They seized the fact of criminal violence, and tried to turn that fact into a political threat. Since no one doubted the fact was real, the threat was taken seriously.

Newton's idea came down to a new kind of power, growing out of the barrel of a gun that was good only as long as it didn't have to be fired, because once it was fired, the other side was going to win. The Panthers walked that fine edge, threatened by their own rhetoric, which called for actions they could not afford to take; their rhetoric won them some of the space necessary for action, but the police also forced them to live up to it. Police raids on chapter after chapter decimated the party; many of those who were left were junkies, hoods, and spies. Both Newton and Seale had been off the street while murder raps, ultimately tossed out, were hung over their heads; the party had lost its center. Either it changed drastically or it died, and once Newton got out of jail he moved to quiet it down and clean it out.

Cleaver, a confessed rapist who had spent nine years in California prisons, had been valuable to the Panthers not only because he was a superb recruiter and a good theorist, but because their politics were rooted in the streets. Newton's genius had been to bring Staggerlee into politics and there transform him; that also meant Newton had to risk him. Newton's careful arrogance and perfect nerve under the guns of San Francisco cops had inspired Cleaver to join the party, but Newton is a man of tremendous self-discipline; the demands his politics made on all party members were in some ways too much of a reflection of his own unquestionable ability to live up to them. Staggerlee was a mask Newton could put on at will; Cleaver was not always under control, and the myth held more traps for him. But he could take it farther, even as politics: he really was Staggerlee, and the explosive threat of his performance was vital to his role in the party.

Cleaver's worth lay in his ability to balance that role between his exploitation of it and it of him. In Algeria, cut off from the people who had changed his life, that balance shattered absolutely, and his old nemesis roared back with a vengeance. He had been a political man whose politics were rooted in a vitality and rage that had once come out in crime, but he emerged a criminal once again, out for blood.

There were no politics. The balance broke down because the political space necessary to it had been taken away, and what was left was murder, not for a five-dollar Stetson hat, but the old story all the same. Cleaver fell back to Staggerlee; he went all the way into his hands, and it may be that the only way he will ever get out will be with the epitaph John Hurt gave to his Stag-o-lee, the cruelest epitaph of all:

> *Standing at the gallows*
> *Head way up high*
> *At twelve o'clock they killed him*
> *They was all glad to see him die.*

And that is the context of *Riot*.*

These events and Sly's understanding of his own career came together, as most likely they never will again, to form a music of extraordinary depth and power. Sly questioned his earlier music and our love for it; he implied that whatever the

* It was, I still believe, the context—but events have proved my comments on Newton and Cleaver more than a little naïve. At the least, an update is called for.

After a bizarre incident in which he "arrested" fellow-fugitive Timothy Leary in Algiers, Cleaver fled to Paris, where he renounced politics for haberdashery—to wit, "Cleavers," pants cut with an "appurtenance" for genital display. Unable to interest a distributor in the latest in rapists' fashions, Cleaver negotiated instead with prosecutors back in Oakland. He proclaimed himself a born-again Christian (it had worked for Charles Colson), returned to the U.S., and ultimately copped a plea to reduced charges stemming from the 1968 shootout—which, Cleaver now said, he had provoked. Free at last, Cleaver went on tour with various evangelists, worked as a shill for a right-wing, hard-money Mormon institute, and was last heard expounding the virtues of wife-beating—from the pulpit of his own "church."

Huey Newton's story is no prettier. Following the disintegration of the Black Panther Party in the early '70s, Newton took to cruising the streets of Oakland with his bodyguard. After a number of arrests for picking fights in bars, and rumors of his harassing women and attempting to shake down local black merchants, Newton was charged with murdering an Oakland prostitute (allegedly because she had refused his advances) and with pistol-whipping his tailor. Few thought him innocent: Newton escaped to China, then to Cuba. When he finally returned to stand trial, his tailor suffered a mysterious attack of amnesia, and an attempt was made to kill a witness to the murder with which Newton was charged. Newton beat both raps—but not a weapons charge that, unless a last appeal succeeds, will send him to prison.

beauty of "Everybody Is a Star," that may have been only another way of saying that everybody is a mark. Sly's work was deeply personal and inescapably political; innovative and tough in its music; literate and direct in its words; a parody of the past and an unflinching statement about the present that its present has hardly contained.

Sly returned to the pop arena at a time when black music had remade itself on terms he had defined; he damned those terms and invented new ones. He recognized the expectations of his audience, and moved to subvert them.

If after a time he allowed his audience to subvert his work, or simply played on and followed where his music led, *There's a riot goin' on* stands as a quiet, bitter, open act of rebellion. It is a rebellion the resolution of which depends as much on the audience as it does on Sly Stone, and a rebellion which as music or politics is not likely to work itself out for a long time. And if that musical insurrection can be captured in a line, it is probably a remark Josef von Sternberg once made: "Obviously, it is easier to kill than to create."

RANDY NEWMAN
Every Man Is Free

I believe . . . that to be very poor and very beautiful is most probably a moral failure much more than an artistic success. Shakespeare would have done well in any generation because he would have refused to die in a corner; he would have taken the false gods and made them over; he would have taken the current formulae and forced them into something lesser men thought them incapable of. Alive today he would undoubtedly have written and directed motion pictures, plays, and God knows what. Instead of saying, "This medium is not good," he would have used it and made it good. If some people called some of his work cheap (which some of it is), he wouldn't have cared a rap, because he would know that without some vulgarity there is no complete man. He would have hated refinement, as such, because it is always a withdrawal, and he was much too tough to shrink from anything.

RAYMOND CHANDLER, 1949,
from *Raymond Chandler Speaking*

POP

Chandler's statement, written in the midst of his failed attempts to do good work as a Hollywood screenwriter, tells us how completely he understood what it means to be an American artist. The momentum of democracy (of equality) (or conformity) that powers American life does not, as Tocqueville thought it might, bleed all the life out of culture; it has created a wholly new kind, with all sorts of new risks and possibilities. At its worst it an do just what Tocqueville expected, and there is always a good example around: *The Sound of Music* ("The audience," Pauline Kael wrote bitterly, "becomes the lowest common denominator of feeling—a sponge."); *Love Story;* the pop group "America" (Tocqueville smiling in his grave at the elegance of their conceit). There is, though, Chandler also wrote, "a vast difference between writing down to the public (something which always flops in the end) and doing what you want to do in a form that the public has learned to accept."

There have been great American artists who have worked beyond the public's ability to understand them easily, but none who have condescended to the public—none who have not hoped, no matter how secretly, that their work would lift America to heaven, or drive a stake through its heart. This is a democratic desire (not completely unrelated to the all-time number one democratic desire for endless wealth and fame), and at its best it is an impulse to wholeness, an attempt not to deny diversity, or to hide from it, but to discover what it is that diverse people can authentically share. It is a desire of the artist to remake America on his or her own terms.

This impulse powers the strongest popular artists as it powers pop culture itself. It is an urge to novelty and necessity; it exhausts most talents with terrific speed and goes on to something else.

The inability of the vital American artist to be satisfied with a cult audience, no matter how attentive, goes right

back to the instinctive perception that whatever else America
might be, it is basically *big;* that unless you are doing something big, you are not doing anything at all. The Beatles
("those imaginary Americans," Leslie Fiedler called them),
madly in love with American popular culture and living out
their own American dream, increased their ambitions as they
got closer to their goals: first they wanted to be Eddie
Cochran, then they decided they could be Elvis, and then
they were on their own. They understood, finally, that they
could affect the lives of kids all over the world. The fact that
they succeeded tells us how much big pop ambitions are
worth; everyone who might conceivably read this book has
been changed for the better because of what the Beatles did.

When it is alive to its greatest possibilities—to disturb,
provoke, and divide an entire society, thus exciting and
changing a big part of society—pop says that the game of a
limited audience is not really worth playing. It is as contra-
dictory and as American as a politician who can't stand dis-
sent, who gets and keeps his power by dividing the country
and turning the country against itself, and then wants everyone to love him.

This is not simply a matter of the depth of the artist's
idea, anymore than the contours of American history really
turn on how well Andrew Jackson understood macroeconom-
ics. What matters is the depth and breadth of response an
artist can evoke in an audience, and whether or not that artist
is really challenging the audience and not simply playing off
its fears and weaknesses. In the case of someone extraordinary like Elvis Presley, or the Beatles, this process becomes
its own idea—and a pretty deep one. But who knows if
"Eight days a week is not enough to show I love you" is a
deep idea, or a trivial one, or any kind of idea at all? And
who cares? The joy of pop is that it can deliver you from
such questions by its immediacy and provoke them by its impact.

Rock 'n' roll is a combination of good ideas dried up by
fads, terrible junk, hideous failings in taste and judgment,
gullibility and manipulation, moments of unbelievable clarity

and invention, pleasure, fun, vulgarity, excess, novelty and
utter enervation, all summed up nowhere so well as on Top
40 radio, that ultimate rock 'n' roll version of America. As
one writer put it, describing a classic radio segue of a pimple
commercial directly into Bob Dylan's "George Jackson":
"Right on."

We fight our way through the massed and leveled collective safe taste of Top 40, just looking for a little something
we can call our own. But when we find it and jam the radio
to hear it again it isn't just ours—it is a link to thousands of
others who are sharing it with us. As a matter of a single
song this might mean very little; as culture, as a way of life,
you can't beat it.

And what about Randy Newman, who is, unfortunately, somewhere else entirely (that is, buried on an occasional FM radio or in the back of someone's record collection)? "All combined," Newman is fond of saying, "my
records have sold as many copies as James Taylor's last album
sold in Des Moines. But I'm fantastically wealthy, so nothing
matters." Spoken like a pop master: only money counts. But
obviously if his public failure didn't bother him Newman
wouldn't complain about it. To the degree that he knows his
work is good he will want it to affect everyone in sight. And
more than that, a singer whose songs contain an astonishing
affection for every American from a middle-class couple
wasting away in Florida to a rapist preying on their daughter
cannot be satisfied with the attention of an elite, of critics and
a few more, because a cult contradicts the best impulses of
his work.

NEWMAN'S AMERICA, I

He is, all in all, one of the strangest performers to
emerge in rock 'n' roll since the heady days of *Sgt. Pepper*.
Born in New Orleans in 1944, and raised in Southern California, Newman was heir to both a family movie music dy-
nasty (the most famous member was his Oscar-winning Uncle
Alfred, whose credits are ubiquitous on late night TV), and

along with everyone else his age, to rock 'n' roll. Fats Domino was his man.

Newman took up the piano, was classically trained at
UCLA, and got a job with a music publishing company,
hacking out songs for money. He made a lot, as he says, but
since he didn't much like the way other people did his stuff,
he began recording it himself.

Since the release of his first album, in 1968, Newman's
singing has shifted from a style that could be called Jewish to
one that can only be called black. He has become, as his producer Lenny Waronker likes to call him, "The King of the
Suburban Blues Singers."

What Newman has taken from black singers is not what
most rock 'n' roll singers have taken: assertiveness, aggression, melancholy, sexual power. His somnambulant personality determined his choice of a lazy, blurred sound, where
words slide into each other, where syllables are not bitten
off, but just wear out and dissolve. The blues practice of
dropping a key word off the end of a line, to hint at ominous
sexual mastery or knowledge too strong to put into words,
becomes with Newman a wonderful throwaway, a surface
lack of seriousness that at first hides, and after a few listenings intensifies, a sense of Newman's commitment to his material. It is as if Randy's real blues hero wasn't Howlin' Wolf,
but Stepin Fetchit—and as if Randy had a pretty good idea
of what secrets were hidden in the shuffle.

The movie music side of Newman's songs grows out of
a tradition so well absorbed by generations of film fans that
by now it seems completely American, regardless of its
classy European antecedents. Listening to Newman, irrespective of the lyric of any particular song, you might see
John Wayne in Monument Valley, Charles Boyer in a final
clinch. Chances are it won't be anything so specific; you will
hear a hundred movies whose titles you just cannot recall.

Newman's music is stronger than any to be found in
those movies; his music is from a movie no one ever made,
the score that was never quite written. It is everything that

movie music aspired to, richer on his records because he is making records, not movies.

He uses the familiarity of the music to set us in the moods and situations the music automatically calls up; we respond in predictable ways to the music, and as we do, Newman's words and his singing pull us in other directions, or shift the story just enough to make it new. The music defines for us the way we want it to be, the way the movies have told us it is, and then Newman tells us how it looks to him. The tension that comes is almost never facile, because the movie dreams the music evokes are real to him too, and because he loves the music itself. It's not merely a device, but at the heart of the matter; not just half of his strategy, but half of his aesthetic.

When I saw Newman perform one night, I was startled by how many of his songs mattered to me. I was a casual fan, but after each number another came into my head that I had to hear. I hadn't been part of a rock 'n' roll audience that laughed so well since Dylan's tours in the mid-sixties (we forget how funny crowds found "Desolation Row," and how right they were).

Newman could put on the chill, too. He told an old man he ought to give it up and die; he made you feel, with "God's Song," that life is indeed a joke, and that all the laughs belong to its Author. Newman did his Southern California beach song—which must derive, somehow, from "Surf City"—about a girl who has fled from her graduation dance to offer herself to the gears of the beach-cleaning machine, which scoops her up along with the beer cans, candy wrappers, and condoms, like a California teenager hungry after a swim. He sang some of his easy-target tunes, like "Burn On," about the firetrap Cuyahoga River. Best of all was "Davy the Fat Boy," sung in the voice of "Davy's only friend," who has made a deathbed promise to the fat boy's parents to take care of the freak and keeps it by putting him into a sideshow. It reminded me of that unbearable climactic scene in von Sternberg's *Blue Angel*, where Emil Jannings—

the fallen professor forced to stand before his ex-students imitating a chicken—holds his body like one enormous club-foot, his face in a frozen mask of terror and madness, and produces a squawk that can shrivel the soul. As Davy's friend orders him to begin "his famous fat boy dance," Newman leaned back from his piano for a little ballet music, letting the audience see the scene as he did; and as the song ended, one of its lines echoed with a gruesome kind of love: *"You've got to let this fat boy in your life!"*

Newman had asked for requests, and I had yelled out for "Davy" because I had vaguely remembered being moved by it some years before. If I had remembered it better I probably would have kept my mouth shut.

Except in its weaker moments, this was not satire. It was a whole world, irresistibly funny and extremely uncomfortable, like W. C. Fields with the Hollywood varnish rubbed off. But the laughter was not smug, and the scariness of the songs was not smug on Newman's part, but simply presented as what he did for a living, what he did better than anyone else. When he sang his "Suzanne," the tale of a rapist picking a woman's number off a phone booth wall, you were caught up in the woman's terror and the rapist's crime. Both were real, both mattered.

The song was in the great rock 'n' roll tradition of answer records; in this case, an answer to Leonard Cohen's "Suzanne," the tender ballad of a river nymph, as erotic as a $500 book of pornographic etchings. Cohen's song screamed Poetry and Art; it virtually raped the listener with its mastery of the Higher Schlock. "This is not Leonard Cohen's 'Suzanne,' " Newman said. "It's on a somewhat lower moral plane, actually."

He said that with such modesty, fading his comment as if he were throwing away one of his best lines, that you had to think that sometimes, late at night when he couldn't make a song work, he might even believe it.

Newman is afraid of his sensibility, to the degree that he has to get it over to an audience. On one album he sang a version of that old Cotton Club favorite, "Underneath the Harlem Moon," all about the colored singing and dancing, summed up in the classic line: "That's why darkies were born." He sang it straight—beautifully, in fact—and you just couldn't tell. Where was he? Or more to the point, where did he put you? Here he was, a struggling singer whose only possible audience would be urbane, liberal rock 'n' roll fans, and he was unveiling . . . the charms of racism. He would not perform the song in front of an audience. "I was afraid someone might beat me up," he said. The night I saw him he sang his own "Yellow Man"; apparently no one had told him he was singing in a Chinese movie theater in the middle of the biggest Chinese community in the U.S.A. Or maybe he thought his height would save him. His distance from his material is always a bit uncertain.

If Newman's songs are the result of New Orleans R&B and an after-the-ball cul-de-sac of Hollywood movie music, they also grow out of a cul-de-sac pure and simple: Los Angeles, the Edge of America, the City of the Future. As an Angeleno, Randy Newman is something like Nathanael West on the verge of having a good time in spite of himself.

West thought Southern California was where America came to make its last stand, to reach for the last chance; inevitably betraying those hopes, Los Angeles became, to West and to Chandler and others, the place where those now resentful Americans would turn to fantasies of revenge, violence, and death. Looking for rebirth, dreamers found only that they felt older than they had seemed at home. These discrepancies—presented over and over again, in Chandler's *Big Sleep* and *Farewell, My Lovely*, in *Sunset Boulevard*, from a Holy Roller church in downtown L.A. to the Kirke Order of Dog Blood roaming the desert—created, against the backdrop of an industry based on the inexhaustibility of banal fantasy, a curious sort of moral ambivalence, a state of mind equally capable of producing commonplace boredom and uncommon crime. This ambivalence, I think, grows out of an attempt to come to terms with that sense of discrepancy: an aggressive and in many ways positive denial of the need for roots, a perception that everything that is old must be covered in neon and sandstone before anyone can be really free.

Once this is accomplished, of course, there is little left
on which to base an idea of what that freedom could be for.
People improvise; nothing seems completely out of the question. Some can endure, and use, this kind of freedom. Some
can't; they lust after authority, and there are always too
many to provide it: pimps, the Children of God, organized
crime, weird figures of extraordinary charisma walking the
street devouring souls.

Such a story is familiar enough. The same scared and
lustful Americans who changed their names and killed for
new lives in Chandler's books crawl through Ross Mac-
Donald's; the rubber horse clumped at the bottom of a
swimming pool in *Day of the Locust* was dumped into a bed in
The Godfather. But because such a vision of Los Angeles
pushed West and Chandler into a queer sort of Puritanism,
they never noticed something else that matters about Southern California: its incredible exuberance, the talent of Southern Californians for enjoying themselves. It's a little too easy
to look at the movement of the place and call it hysterical,
too easy to quote Thoreau and pronounce that "the mass of
men lead lives of quiet desperation," and think that you have
told the whole truth. Put the Beach Boys of the early sixties
up against West, and *he* sounds hysterical; there isn't a hint
of their warmth and friendliness in his "definitive" book, but
no one can tell me that "Fun, Fun, Fun" is a lie. The Beach
Boys don't wipe out Chandler's world, but they enlarge it;
and if finally the Beach Boys held hands with Charlie Manson as the sixties ended, that only meant that they were
as vulnerable to the L.A. of West and Chandler as they
might have been to the Beach Boys'. You can say that the
energy and pride the Beach Boys found cruising the strip in
"I Get Around" was never meant to last, that it hardened
and cracked like cheap Santa Monica stucco when they found
out it was not enough and embraced the authority of the
dread Maharishi. You can write their delight off to sun and
money, but its value is still strong, still full of life. They felt
free to enjoy themselves in every way imaginable, and that

freedom from tradition, the freedom to invent, cuts deeply and all across the board. There's no way to separate the Beach Boys' smiling freedom from Manson's knife. Because this new world is a rich one, Randy Newman, as an artist, can work in it—he can laugh well and realize his fantasies of violence and death. "Suzanne" really is the other side of "Surf City"—or part of it.

Nathanael West was an Easterner; in spite of the fact that "West" was a name he chose, he was never at home in California—he was unable to imagine that anyone could be. But many Southern Californians, were they to be told that murder was the price of a way of life based on fun and fantasy, might still pay it. Newman accepts the deal because L.A. provides the indolence that suits his personality, and the risk that suits his art.

As an American artist, Newman represents some kind of opening up of the classic archetype of the keeper of the American imagination; and this too has a lot to do with the peculiar freedoms of Los Angeles. Most American critics—Nathaniel Hawthorne, say—throw up all sorts of horror and pretend they do so only to condemn it. If West, through his transplanted Easterner hero Tod Hackett, admitted complicity in the L.A. nightmare, he had to satisfy the guilt such a confession produced by destroying the city in a private apocalypse. Since Newman takes the moral shapelessness of his hometown as a given, such fantasies would be ridiculously melodramatic for him (they're more than a little ridiculous in West, too). Like the Beach Boys, Newman builds freedom out of what he's got; his humor is his version of the Beach Boys' open naïveté. Newman laughs all around his world, never at it. He is too at home in the place to feel guilty about it, and anyway, he is a rock 'n' roll singer, and such attitudes are not in the rock 'n' roll style. As with almost any popular art, the moment rock 'n' roll tries to criticize something, it becomes hopelessly self-righteous and stupid. It effectively criticizes by rendering a situation with such immediacy, or by affirming it to the point of such absurdity, that you can no longer take it straight. That is why there is no tougher antidrug song than the Velvet Underground's "Heroin," which also risks creating new addicts.

Perhaps because of the ambivalence of Southern California, Newman can sing with the same insulated force. He always writes, and what is harder, sings, in the voices of his characters (except when they are women, but he will manage that someday); no matter what grotesquerie is involved, he does not sing about, he sings *as*. He feels this is dangerous, which it is.

The imagination has fallen upon sorry days in post-Beatle rock 'n' roll. Audiences are no longer used to the idea that someone might make something up, create a persona and effectively act it out, the way Chuck Berry and Bob Dylan used to do. Audiences take everything literally, partly because sensitive personal confession, "honesty," and one-to-one communication between the singer and whoever is listening is so attractive and reassuring in times when pop culture and politics have lost their grander mythic dimensions, when there are no artists and no politics to create community, and every fan is thrown back on himself. Let me quote from a typical ad for a troubled troubador, supposedly appropriate to such times, presumably addressed to a troubled audience:

A few rare performers immediately become your friend the first time you listen to them. Jonathan Edwards is about to become your friend.

His songs are sensitive and warm, containing feelings and recollections which are sure to remind you of things in your life as well.

Jonathan Edwards. A new friend.

Courtesy Atlantic Records and Tapes, a Division of Warner Communications, the friendly giant conglomerate.

Note the style of the ad. The cadence is wonderfully smooth, caressing. The grammar is perfect, proper. The voice is fatherly. The whole thing is absolutely unbearable.

But it's always fun to fill in the blanks. Let's say:

A few rare performers immediately become your friend the first time you listen to them. Mick Jagger is about to become your friend.

His songs are loud, brutal, and mean, containing feelings you like to pretend you do not have, recollections you would like to forget, and temptations that up until now you have wisely avoided.

Mick Jagger. A new friend.

Courtesy Rolling Stones Records and Tapes, distributed by Atlantic Records and Tapes, a Division of Warner Communications . . . rock 'n' roll may have no center, but it is nothing if not pluralistic. Newman records for the same company, naturally.

Rock 'n' roll is suffering from that old progressive school fallacy that says if what you write is about your own feelings, no one can criticize it. Truth telling is beginning to settle into a slough where it is nothing more than a pedestrian autobiography set to placid music framed by a sad smile on the album cover. This is about as liberating as thinking typecast movie stars are "really like" the roles they play. In many cases, though, this *has* come to be true in rock 'n' roll: singers have dispensed with imagination and songs are just pages out of a diary, with nothing in them that could give them a life of their own. A good part of the audience has lost its taste for songs that are about something out there in the world that the singer is trying to make real—usually by convincingly assuming the burden of that reality; replacing such songs are tunes that desperately deny the world by affirming the joys of solipsism. The success of this genre, represented by no one so well as James Taylor (along with the Rowan Brothers, Shawn Phillips, "America," and many others who will no doubt be forgotten by the time this book is published), only reminds me of an old philosophy student joke: "Solipsism is great, everyone should try it." That was, actually, the cornerstone of Nixon's Second Inaugural: "What can I do for myself?"

As the members of an audience grow older, they lead

less public lives. Their deepest affections shift from a multiplicity of friends—from the idea of friendship itself—to husbands, wives, children; they exchange the noisy heterogeneity of school for the quiet homogeneity of a job. They travel less freely, act less impulsively. If politics once meant the fellowship of the street or the political community of a campus for those who were lucky enough to have known such things, more and more politics comes to mean voting—the most solitary political act there is—or, at best, talk with a few friends. A life that was fluid with possibility can solidify into loneliness. One looks harder for the comforts of similarity, and shies from the risks of diversity. It becomes easy to think that nothing is new under the sun, or that if there is, that one can no longer be a part of what is new. Too much is settled.

If at its best rock 'n' roll *is* a kind of public life (" 'School's Out' is my favorite song and I've been out of school for ten years!" my friend Simon Frith wrote. "What does that mean?"), the cults that have fragmented an audience potentially as big and broad as America itself speak for a less open life, as do the names of some successful post-Beatles record companies: Island, Shelter, Haven, Chrysalis, Asylum. Newman works against the limits of privacy, domesticity, and solipsism with his fantasies and the role playing of his songs, and yet he lacks the obsessive pop ambition to do more than that. Against the ideal community of music he feels the emotional and imaginative poverty of an America where men and women live estranged. But to drive the aesthetic of his fantasies into our heads would require him to value his music more than anything else, to be on the road constantly, to risk the collapse of his own family life, the shelter of his own privacy, and even—after the rock 'n' roll deaths of the last years I don't feel very romantic saying this—his sanity and his life.

"If I couldn't perform I'd give up," said Rod Stewart. "It's not a question of the money side of it. I don't have to work for the rest of my life. I don't want to. But not having that ninety minutes up there anymore. Phew. I don't like to think about it. It frightens me." And he went on: "I'm not willing to get married, because I think there are some people who just shouldn't get married. Elvis Presley should never have been married." He's not talking about the fall-off in a movie star's mail when he takes the sacred vows, but about the freedom to act in the midst of an audience. To be the kind of rock 'n' roll star Stewart is is to be like a politician who campaigns every moment of his life.

"In America," Newman sings, "every man is free/ To take care of his home, and his family." But no more than that, is the bitter, unsung line. And that may not be enough, even if it is all most of us see.

The constriction of vision produced by that kind of life points to why Newman is right when he feels it is risky to get up on stage and sing from inside the soul of a rapist. It's not just a matter of what people will think of Newman; what if someone heard the song and went looking for a woman to rape? Oh, ridiculous, we might say. That's like pretending someone could listen to the Beatles sing a good old rock 'n' roll fuck song like "Helter Skelter" and take it as a sign to go out and murder seven people.

Good art is always dangerous, always open-ended. Once you put it out in the world you lose control of it; people will fit it into their lives in all sorts of different ways. If so much of the rock 'n' roll of the post-Beatle era is closed off and one-dimensional, like the politics it serenades and reinforces, if the aesthetic of solipsism is freezing the imagination and our ability to respond openly, it is Newman's risk taking that makes him so valuable. As a rather lazy Southern Californian who just wants a good life with his wife and his kids, his sense of risk makes him shrink from his audience; but as an artist, that sense makes him reach for bigger risks.

NEWMAN'S AMERICA, II

To introduce his greatest song, Randy will tell a little story about a movie he almost made, with all the big stars: " 'Van,' that's Van Morrison, Elton, you know Elton. . . ."

The joke of this small-time rock 'n' roller up there with the big guns is more than obvious, but still funny. It would be even better if Newman made the whole thing up; it would somehow add to the charm of a song he will do later, "Lonely at the Top." It was written for Frank Sinatra, who, most likely thinking it was a slur on his need for a toupee, turned it down.

Up on stage Newman is still entranced by his tale of the silver screen stardom he might have had. Each singer will be given fifteen minutes to prepare and perform any kind of scenario he wants—do it all. And Newman has a wonderful idea. He will dress himself in a pure white planter's suit, white shoes, white hat—perhaps a red string tie, for color. As the camera zooms in for its opening shot, Newman is poised on the quarterdeck of a great clipper ship, testing his profile against the wind. What's he doing there? He's a recruiter for the slave trade, naturally.

His profile suitably established, Newman steps ashore. He is met by a hushed crowd of Africans, who hang on his every word. (Finally, Newman is a star.) He begins to sing, in a voice that combines the lazy drawl of the black man (something his audience will invent in their new land) with the gentle assurance of the holiest rabbi. The music, as Newman ultimately recorded it, comes in on the soundtrack (in the theater, Newman begins the song on his piano), and it is awesomely beautiful. And the slaver sings:

> *In America*
> *You'll get food to eat*
> *Won't have to run through the jungle*
> *And scuff up your feet*
> *You'll just sing about Jesus and drink wine all day*
> *It's great to be an American*

We are back in Harmonica Frank's medicine show, and it is the softest sell of all. "By the second verse," Randy confides, "they're already running for the boat."

Climb aboard little wog
Sail away with me

And if they are caught up in Newman's vision, the pure feel of it, so am I. "Sail away," he sings, "Sail away," and the grace of his singing conquers the last resistance. It is majestic. You can see the glassy waters, the birds hovering over the ship as the last glimpse of Africa drops over the horizon.

We will cross the mighty ocean into Charleston Bay *

You can dredge through all the antebellum fantasies kicked up to defend the peculiar institution and you will never find an image of slavery as lovely as this one.

This peaceful, quiet song is more outrageous than anything the Rolling Stones have ever done—or would be, if the nation heard Newman do it on the radio every day. Scary, astonishing, Newman has presented an American temptation—tempting not only the Africans, who became Negroes, and went on to create the music that finally tossed up Elvis Presley, rock 'n' roll, Newman, and his audience, but tempting America to believe that this image of itself just might be true.

"Sail Away" moves on one of the most seductive melodies ever to grace a popular song. It is just out of reach, with a fabulous edge of déjà vu, calling up the classic Ray Charles records of the early sixties—"Born to Lose," "You Don't Know Me," "That Lucky Old Sun"—calling up a thousand songs and a thousand happy endings.

The power of the song is in the simple, perfectly accomplished idea that something as horrible and charged with guilt as slavery could take on such real beauty. The focus is not on those who are to be enslaved, but on the singer, the confidence man. Of course he is lying. He has seen babies thrown into the sea, smelled the death and excrement in the

* Words and Music by Randy Newman. © 1972 WB Music Corp. & Randy Newman. All rights reserved. Used by permission of Warner Bros. Music.

hold, watched the brand burn into the flesh. He has looked
without flinching into the bewildered eyes that are perhaps
the most terrible of all. But for the moment, he believes himself. A secret ambivalence of four hundred years of American
life finds a voice in this song. It is not particularly liberating;
too strange for that, it is like a vision of heaven superimposed
on hell.

Y'all gonna be an American

Rock 'n' roll has always specialized in racial paradoxes,
but none as queer as this. It has virtually nothing to do with
"rock 'n' roll" as a musical form (save that Newman's singing
owes so much to the blues) and everything to do with the
rock 'n' roll audience. Newman offers it a vision its members
have spent years driving from their minds, bringing them
back to a home that was never there.

The song transcends its irony. It is, in the end, what
America would like to believe about itself, and what ten
years of a war across the ocean and ten years of bitter black
faces will never let it believe, even in secret: that everything
America did was for the good. Better than good: that God's
work really was our own and meant to be. That we brought
something new and precious into the world, a land even the
most miserable slaves would recognize as Eden.

For if they did not, how could we believe it?

Sailing across the ocean, the slaver and his slaves are in
love.

NEWMAN'S FAILURE

"Every great artist must create for a great audience,"
Bob Christgau pronounced one night when we were delving
into The Great Randy Newman Mystery (Why isn't this genius as big as he deserves to be?). Christgau meant an aggressive, critical audience, with a conscious sense of itself *as* an
audience, but he also meant a big, broad audience, one

whose complexity and diverse needs can push an artist beyond comfortable limits.

When a single like the O'Jays' "Back Stabbers" rams home the result of years of shifting black consciousness and takes over the charts, it creates a cultural moment shared by a good part of the country, shoving a particular sensibility through all sorts of ordinary barriers that grow up between audiences. The passion and clarity of the song can connect a black pimp, whose life it was virtually meant to define, to a middle-class white kid, who just digs the beat and will find his or her place in the lyrics soon enough. When a movie like *The Godfather* becomes the national pastime, you can feel, as you sit for perhaps the first time in a theater half black and half white, that for better or for worse America's fantasies are at last becoming common property; that artists and audiences have come to a verge, that the stakes of American life have been raised.

If *The Godfather* had succeeded merely as a genre classic, it would have been a very different movie—the response it provokes changes how we see and understand it. Like "Back Stabbers," it matters, has its particular meanings, partly *because* it is a hit. Without massive public response, we would not even get close to two crucial democratic questions, questions worth asking about any interesting work of popular culture: How far can this work take its audience? How far can its audience go with it? Only works that can't be ignored—liking them is hardly the point—raise such questions and bring them to life. In one way or another we are all affected by hits, and are forced to define ourselves in terms of our response to them, just as we are all, for good or ill, affected by the romantic heroism of the Westerns, and not necessarily by, say, the chaotic heroism that is the subject of Orson Welles' movies. Certainly we are caught up in these things that impelled Welles, but his version of them, the shape of his vision, has not inevitably become part of us; we don't have to live in the world as he tried to define it, as we helplessly live out and respond to the nostalgia of John Ford or

Howard Hawks. The life of a whole generation is authentically quickened and brightened by the Beatles, but it is not disturbed and sharpened by Randy Newman. The point is not that it would be "good for people" if the radio were playing "Sail Away" all day long, but that such exposure might be the only way to find out how strong the song really is. But Newman is quite different from Orson Welles, who lost a great fight with Hollywood in his attempt to get his movies made, because Newman is barely on the battlefield.

His quandary is not unlike the one the Kinks fell into in the late sixties. After a string of post-Beatle Invasion hits based on a chopped and channeled version of "Louie, Louie," the sensibility of Ray Davies, their resident ex-art-student genius (every British band had one in those days), began to take over the group. The Kinks became less of a band, less a bundle of ambition and lust for money, fame, and fun, and more of a means to Davies's fantasies. He became a social critic, or more appropriate for rock 'n' roll, a social complainer. He squeezed a few hits out of this stance, but the last chart success he got in the sixties crystallized his new view of the world and dropped the commercial bottom out of the group. "Sunny Afternoon" (1966) could have been another put-down of the English middle class, but instead the hunter was captured by the game. This was an ode to upper-class boredom. The Kinks became a classy little outfit, neurotic, long on intelligence and short on raunch, and their album sales dropped into the low thousands. They were idolized by the critics and ignored by everybody else.

You couldn't call Davies's world dark, exactly; it was dimmed. Like Newman's, it was completely idiosyncratic, if generally a lot less compelling. An anthem Davies wrote to himself defined it best: a fearsome, ferocious piece of hard rock he slipped onto the flip side of "Sunny Afternoon," and which didn't surface on an American album until seven years later—"I'm Not Like Everybody Else."

Davies opened the song as a sickly kid pushed up against the wall by a gang of thugs (that is, everybody else), and then broke wide open with a rage that negated the whole world he wouldn't serve, that he wouldn't and couldn't change into. By the last fiery choruses he was free, as free to ignore his listeners as they had always been to ignore him. It was a great record.*

Davies commenced to delineate the subtleties of nostalgia, the quirks of inadequacy, the aesthetics of oddball. For a time his insulation produced appropriate fantasies, and also his best songs (such as "Waterloo Sunset," an unbearably lovely tune about an old man who watches lovers from his window). Artistic privacy also produced terrible self-indulgence and embarrassing cuteness. The critics cheered the good and the bad, as they do with Newman, but finally even they began to weary in their proselytizing. Paul Williams, an original Kinks booster, reviewed their last bomb "for those who love the Kinks," formally ending the great struggle to spread the word.

But not quite. Davies had written *Arthur*, an "opera" about a post-Victorian lost in a twentieth-century world; some of it was brilliant and some of it was crap, as with all Kinks albums, which shouldn't have made any difference one way or the other. But an extraordinary push by two *Rolling Stone* reviewers (one of whom, I confess, was me), and its release at the same time as the Who's *Tommy* (suddenly nothing was as salable as the concept of Opera, which is to say, Art), made *Arthur* a decent success. The Kinks stumbled back to America for their first tour in years, and eventually got another hit, a big one, with "Lola," the tender tale of a shy country boy meeting up with a big-city transvestite— superb rock 'n' roll and a pop masterpiece.

The Top 40 audience, which had grabbed for the record, not "the Kinks," settled back, but as happens whenever a group gets a hit, the band picked up enough new fans to make them successful, seventies-style. Instead of a little cult, they had a big cult. Davies's insulation was gone, and the sharp edge of his feel for being different collapsed into

* And I swear I hear a hint of the closet Davies later came out of; doesn't he scream, "I won't go to bed like everybody else?"

gross parody of the big bad world. His songs became either hysterically unfunny (the next album was called *Lola v. the Power-Mad Money Men*, or something like that) or merely dull. An uncritical audience—a cult—was even worse for the band than uncritical critics. Davies's outsider stance, which had given his work what strength and vitality it had, was vitiated by the presence of an automatic audience.

And yet the echo of that wonderful statement, "I'm Not Like Everybody Else," is still there—not in Davies's work, but in Newman's: the idea that communication is failure, because if you get what you have to say across to a mass audience, that means what you have to say is not deep enough, or strong enough, to really matter. Newman has said he feels his songs are disturbing; that his lack of success is due to the weight of his material and the discomfort of his version of the truth. He is not surprised by his small audience, just frustrated by it, because if he cannot get his work across he is failing his work. That is, he can't win.

Newman's most accessible songs (as he performs them, which is all that concerns me, and all I think really concerns Newman) are generally his sledge-hammer ironies like "Political Science" (Let's drop the bomb on all our snotty so-called allies) or "Burn On." The genre only parodies the depth of Newman's talent, and it is impossible that he doesn't know it. If his thinnest, weakest work gets the most applause, what's he to think? That his audience isn't good enough for him? That he panders to his audience? This genre may expand anyway, because one part of Newman wants the great audience because he knows his work deserves it. And what often happens to the American popular artist, who feels he must grab the country itself and fails to even scratch it, is that he tries so desperately and honestly to alter his work in order to make it matter (not even compromising to make it palatable, though the line is hard to draw, especially for the artist), that he loses all sense of what impelled him in the first place. Either his career declines, and he is forgotten, or he hits, and decides that he has betrayed himself—and his audience. Someday this may happen to Newman; his music will lose its subtleties, even his humor will fall flat. Then he will be easier to accept, and useless as an artist.

Well, he knows all this, puttering around the house watching *Secret Storm* and vaginal deodorant commercials just like I do when I'm trying to avoid doing some *serious work* like writing this book, but in one sense none of it matters—in *his* case—because the deepest thing keeping Randy Newman from the American audience is his own sensibility.

There is something to Newman's idea that his marginal status in the rock 'n' roll world is a matter of the darkness and perversity of his vision, but I think it has more to do with the ambivalence that underlies that vision. Pop careers are not gifts of the muse, they are won, and Newman, finally, is all doubt as to whether or not the fight is worth it. There is one song he has written that captures his ambivalence so perfectly I can hardly believe he ever cranked himself up to write another one; it's called "My Old Kentucky Home." Imagine one of those automatic L.A. country backing tracks, straw on the studio floor, anything that helps set the scene, and then Randy (not Jewish or black this time, just drunk), warbling a timeless tribute to nothingness, negating the ambition rock 'n' roll demands just as Davies wiped out his audience:

> *Turpentine and dandelion wine*
> *I've turned the corner and I'm doin fine*
> *Shooting at the birds on the telephone line*
> *Pickin' em off with this gun a mine*
>
> *Brother Gene he's big and mean*
> *And he don't have much to say*
> *He had a little woman who he whupped each day*
> *But now she's gone away*
> *He got drunk last night*
> *Kicked mama down the stair*
> *But I'm alright so I don't care*

You can't get any farther into ambivalence than that. The connection between Newman's sense of himself, and the way the world looks to him, could hardly be more exact. He might turn into a homosexual someday, he told Susan Lydon, get religion, find a God. Maybe his entire generation would. Maybe the whole world will turn upside down and Newman will say Yes to all of it. Or something.

He's not particularly ambiguous; his meanings, though they expand if you keep his songs in your head, are clear enough—even if some singers have willfully deluded themselves into recording "Sail Away" as if it were a rewrite of "Born Free" (changing that disagreeable line about "Climb aboard, little wog" to "little child," which I suppose means they know quite well what the song is about after all).

But if his meanings are clear, their value is something else. We know what the slavemaster has in mind and what will happen to his audience as soon as he gets it on the ship, but who knows how to take it? You can't get out from under, that music just washes over you and makes you feel clean. When beauty and evil are so perfectly intertwined, what choices are really possible?

There are no cheap thrills in "Davy the Fat Boy," because Newman's performance is strong enough to force the listener into all its roles: purveyor, victim, and drooling carny audience. His best songs implicate the listener. He goes far enough to wonder if everything might not be worth doing, which means he is far enough gone to wonder if any-thing *is* worth doing—such as pursuing an audience. If God, as Newman likes to see Him, is something worse than am-bivalent in His heaven, how could *man* be any better? Since man is cursed anyway ("I recoil in horror," says Newman's God, "from the foulness of thee . . . / How we laugh up here in heaven at the prayer you offer Me/ That's why I love mankind"), wouldn't any act of will lead straight to that realm of folly and sin that is Newman's garden—so far lim-ited to his art, not yet taking over his life? Isn't it almost true by Newman's definition of how the world works that desire and action produce disaster at worst and failure at best? If Newman is necessarily ambivalent about the ambitions of his

characters, how could he regard his own ambitions any differently?

The answer is that he could be filled with such rage at
the world for being the way it is that nothing could stop him
from conniving against it. Herman Melville's view of the
world was not so different, and when he finally understood
the trap God had set for man (and he was no older than
Newman), he had the time of his life trying to write his way
out of it. Even though he saw clearly enough to know he
would never make it, he was caught up in a vision of what a
remarkable fight it would be.

But if such a perception of the nature of things was
enough to set an American's teeth on edge more than a
hundred years ago, it may not be anymore. America is tired;
Newman is not a driven artist like Melville, or for that matter a sixties Bob Dylan (hero of another young America, itself grown weary by the time Newman arrived to stake a
claim to it)—perhaps he cannot afford to be. Newman is am-
bivalent even about his own talent; as a factual matter of
daily life, he cannot decide if it is worth writing a song, let
alone recording it once it is written. He lacks what Chandler
called "the hard core of selfishness necessary to exploit talent
to the full"—the aggression and insanity that lie beneath the
pop version of the Alger dream. Newman is very distant
from that, and close enough to see it for what it is; he is a
Bartleby, the man who would prefer not to.

Newman skirts the rock 'n' roll audience, but he and a
few others keep the margins of possibility open. Aesthetically a figure of real genius and culturally a born cult hero,
his America does not come across quite as readily as that of
Chuck Berry, the Rolling Stones, or the Band. In his own
peculiar way, Randy Newman is much closer to the Sly
Stone of *Riot*.

Newman's rock 'n' roll is short on musical force, vocal
exuberance, and the promise of good times no matter what
(everything Sly willfully removed from *Riot*); his work lacks

the undeniable satisfaction we get from Mick Jagger roaring he can't get none. *That* kind of satisfaction is what we ask from rock 'n' roll; but if Norman Mailer is right when he says that the worst American promise is the promise of an unearned freedom from dread, Randy Newman's songs may give us some of what we need.

Laconic, funny, grim, and solitary, Randy Newman is a typical figure in the American imagination: the man who does not like what he sees but is wildly attracted to it anyway, a man who keeps his sanity by rendering contradictions other people struggle to avoid. For the moment, he carries the weight of one version of America on his shoulders—not that anyone has asked him to, as audiences have asked Bob Dylan, Elvis Presley, and Sly Stone—but his real task is to make his burden ours.

And then Randy Newman got the chance to do just that.

Newman's cult status was deceptive. Over the years, he had won more and more fans and more and more rave reviews; as a sort of antipop pop star, he had become more and more hip. His work had grown stronger; the more listeners he attracted, it seemed, the more ambitious he became. In 1974, two years after "Sail Away," he brought out *Good Old Boys:* nothing less than a portrait of the South from the 1920s to the present, as seen through the eyes of a redneck. Newman's cult was, sort of, ready to explode into the pop mainstream. *Good Old Boys* was a small hit—for Newman, it was a big hit—and it hung onto the charts for almost half a year. Newman toured seriously for the first time; at a few concerts, he performed with a full orchestra conducted by his Uncle Lionel. Then, three years later, came the shock. Newman had a national hit—and a national scandal.

"Short People," six-foot-plus Randy tried to convince his interviewers, was a joke: a satire on, you know, bigotry. With its unforgettable tag line—"Short people got no reason to live"—the song went to number two on the *Billboard* charts. It was number one on others, and banned from nu-

merous radio stations: program directors claimed the song
was "disturbing to little children," but one suspected little
disc jockeys were more to the point. *Little Criminals*, the album that contained "Short People," hit the top ten. Suddenly, Newman was, well, not a star, exactly, but something
other than he had been. The effect of all this on his music
was very odd.

In pop terms, Newman had already been received as a
star on the *Good Old Boys* tour. His fans had given him abso-
lution; he could do no wrong. Applauding wildly for every
number, the crowds weren't responding to the songs, but
cheering Newman himself. He was "a genius"; he knew.

Newman was being celebrated as someone who was
more than, other than, an entertainer; this made him want to
entertain, to please, to flatter his audience. The number that
made this indelibly clear was "A Wedding in Cherokee
County," the most affecting cut on *Good Old Boys*: an almost
impossible song about a backwoods farmer, his wedding day,
and his impotence.

The man has always been laughed at; no one has considered the woman he is marrying worth laughing at. On record, Newman took a listener to the edge of laughter, but
never allowed the listener to cross it; singing as the farmer,
his touch was never more delicate. "Lord, help me if you
will," he pleaded, anticipating failure; you shared a bit of the
man's suffering, knowing there was no help.

It may have been that, in a concert hall, there was nothing Newman could have done to keep an audience from
laughing at the people in this song. Newman's audience may
have been too smug, and Newman at his best too subtle—
and performance, after all, requires a certain level of dramatization. But on stage, Newman made it impossible for a
crowd not to laugh at the people in his song. Introducing "A
Wedding in Cherokee County" as the surviving remnant of
a discarded "rock opera about Albania"—thus distancing
himself and his audience from the tune to the most extreme
extent—Newman did not merely fail to put the song across,
he destroyed it. He promised that the song was a joke, that
its characters were jokes, and that their predicament was

something those smart enough to buy tickets to a Randy Newman concert could take as a freak show staged for their personal amusement. The farmer and his bride truly became "morons," as one reviewer approvingly called them. On *Good Old Boys*, Newman made a listener respect his characters; in concert, he had the crowd in the aisles before the first verse was over. He turned his audience into the people who paid to see Davy do his famous fat-boy dance, and himself into the carny barker who egged them on. Face to face with the Northern, white, liberal, well-educated audience whose preconceptions about the redneck South *Good Old Boys* was meant to change, Newman—himself born a Southerner—stepped back from the complexity of his song, and offered instead a postcard of an old Kentucky moonshiner with flies buzzing around his head.

If Newman's trashing of the man and woman in "Cherokee County" indicated a lack of trust in the ability of his audience to catch the subtleties of his music, it also made the rest of *Good Old Boys*—the autobiography of a Birmingham steelworker and, perhaps, of one of his forebears—seem anything but subtle. It made the disc sound like a liberal fantasy about the goodness of the white South, a fantasy generated more by fears that Richard Nixon and Spiro Agnew were right about the "Silent Majority" than by anything else. The statements Newman made about himself in concerts across the country indicated a more serious insecurity—and allowed his audience a deeper smugness.

Sold-out halls notwithstanding, Newman was appearing as a cult figure; his fans were thus defined as those in the know. So on stage, in the midst of his first full-scale national tour, Newman made much of the fact that—with his album rising to the lower reaches of the top of the charts—he was "selling out" to the mass audience. "I want Shea Stadium!" he cried—the ironic point being that the audience was not to take Newman's rising mass popularity all that seriously. Deep down, Newman was assuring the crowd, he would remain theirs, unsullied by the mob. The audience liked this, and they got the joke.

What the fans missed was the truth—Newman did want Shea Stadium. He thought his work deserved it, and, maybe, needed it. But playing cult hero on the verge of success, Newman found it necessary to speak coyly: to pretend he didn't want the mass audience, and that his fans weren't part of it. His use of the Shea Stadium line at every concert he gave in 1974 made it seem as if he were always selling out *tomorrow* night; his talk allowed even arriviste ticket-buyers admission to his cult. The implicit idea was that Newman's cult could grow bigger and bigger, until it really did become something like a mass, national audience—at which point, still maintaining the cult cachet that was its reason for being, it would have to feel superior to itself. But Randy Newman had not sold out to the mass audience; he had only sold out to his cult.

These contradictions were buried at the time, but they surfaced in 1977 with "Short People" and *Little Criminals.* Released concurrently with the stunning debut of Elvis Costello, whose songwriting showed that he had learned much from Newman, the record was bland; Newman's edge was off, as if he were afraid he might lose his new fans if he challenged them. "Short People" was not that far from such earlier headbangers as "Political Science" or "Burn On," but it had a better melody, a better hook, and a catchier idea— and so it became a hit. Newman's burgeoning cult had nothing to do with the song's chart success; in terms of his career, it was clearly a fluke. What counted was the emptiness of *Little Criminals*, a record that did not connect.

Newman had, far more perfectly than anyone could have expected, fallen into the trap of acclaim: the audience he had won with *Good Old Boys* disarmed him. But the fury over "Short People" made him think; he understood that he, like the Monotones with "Book of Love," was likely destined for one ride on the charts, and one only. And so, as he told the reporters who flocked to him in the wake of the protests against "Short People," he went back to work on "a broader insult."

And he got it. Released in 1979, the prescient *Born*

Again opened with a ditty called "It's Money that I Love."
Digging in with a rumble of New Orleans piano, Newman
tossed off a mad inversion of the Moral Majority's new
American agenda: he performed as a good liberal, born-again
as a saint dedicated to greed. "I used to worry about the
black man/Now I don't worry about the black man," Randy
sang. "Used to worry about the starving children of
India/You know what I say now about the starving children
of India?"

What did Randy Newman say now?

He said, "Oh, mama."

He was back at the margin, scheming.

ELVIS
Presliad

FANFARE

Elvis Presley is a supreme figure in American life, one whose presence, no matter how banal or predictable, brooks no real comparisons. He is honored equally by long-haired rock critics, middle-aged women, the City of Memphis (they finally found something to name after him: a highway), and even a president.* Beside Elvis, the other heroes of this book

* Richard Nixon had Elvis over to the White House once, and made him an honorary narcotics agent. Nixon got his picture taken with the King. An odd story, though, from rock critic Stu Werbin: "It seems that the good German who arranges the White House concerts for the President and his guests managed to travel the many channels that lead only in rare instances to Col. Tom Parker's phone line. Once connected, he delivered what he considered the most privileged invitation. The President requests Mr. Presley to perform. The Colonel did a little quick figuring and then told the man that Elvis would consider it an honor. For the President, Elvis's fee, beyond traveling expenses and accommodations for his back-up group, would be $25,000. The good German gasped.

seem a little small-time. If they define different versions of America, Presley's career almost has the scope to take America in. The cultural range of his music has expanded to the point where it includes not only the hits of the day, but also patriotic recitals, pure country gospel, and really dirty blues; reviews of his concerts, by usually credible writers, sometimes resemble biblical accounts of heavenly miracles. Elvis has emerged as a great *artist*, a great *rocker*, a great *purveyor of schlock*, a great *heart throb*, a great *bore*, a great *symbol of potency*, a great *ham*, a great *nice person*, and, yes, a great American.

In 1954 Elvis made his first records with Sam Phillips, on the little Sun label in Memphis, Tennessee; then a pact was signed with Col. Tom Parker, shrewd country hustler. Elvis took off for RCA Victor, New York, and Hollywood. America has not been the same since. Elvis disappeared into an oblivion of respectability and security in the sixties, lost in interchangeable movies and dull music; he staged a remarkable comeback as that decade ended, and now performs as the transcendental Sun King that Ralph Waldo Emerson only dreamed about—and as a giant contradiction. His audience expands every year, but Elvis transcends his talent to the point of dispensing with it altogether. Performing a kind of enormous victory rather than winning it, Elvis strides the boards with such glamour, such magnetism, that he allows his audience to transcend their desire for his talent. Action is irrelevant when one can simply delight in the presence of a man who has made history, and who has triumphed over it.

Mark now, the supreme Elvis gesture. He takes the stage with a retinue of bodyguards, servants, singers, a band, an orchestra; he applies himself vaguely to the hits of his past, prostrates himself before songs of awesome ickiness; he acknowledges the applause and the gasps that greet his every

'Col. Parker, nobody gets paid for playing for the President!'

'Well, I don't know about that, son,' the Colonel responded abruptly, 'but there's one thing I do know. Nobody asks Elvis Presley to play for nothing.' "
(*Creem*, March, 1972).

movement (applause that comes thundering with such force you might think the audience merely suffers the music as an excuse for its ovations); he closes with an act of show-biz love that still warms the heart; but above all, he throws away the entire performance.

How could he take it seriously? How could anyone create when all one has to do is appear? "He *looks* like Elvis Presley!" cried a friend, when the Big E stormed forth in an explosion of flashbulbs and cheers, "What a burden to live up to!" It is as if there is nothing Elvis could do to overshadow a performance of his myth. And so he performs from a distance, laughing at his myth, throwing it away only to see it roar back and trap him once again.

He will sing, as if suffering to his very soul, a song called "This Time, You [God, that is] Gave Me a Mountain," which sums up his divorce and his separation from his little girl. Having confessed his sins, he will stand aside, head bowed, as the Special Elvis Presley Gospel Group sings "Sweet, Sweet Feeling (In this Place)." Apparently cleansed of his sins, he will rock straight into the rhythm and blues of "Lawdy, Miss Clawdy" and celebrate his new-found freedom with a lazy grin. But this little melodrama of casual triumph will itself be a throwaway. As with the well-planned sets, the first-class musicians, the brilliant costumes, there will be little life behind the orchestration; the whole performance will be flaccid, the timing careless, all emotions finally shallow, the distance from his myth necessitating an even greater distance from the musical power on which that myth is based.

Elvis gives us a massive road-show musical of opulent American mastery; his version of the winner-take-all fantasies that have kept the world lined up outside the theaters that show American movies ever since the movies began. And of course we respond: a self-made man is rather boring, but a self-made king is something else. Dressed in blue, red, white, ultimately gold, with a Superman cape and covered with jewels no one can be sure are fake, Elvis might epitomize the worst of our culture—he is bragging, selfish, narcissistic, condescending, materialistic to the point of insanity.

But there is no need to take that seriously, no need to take anything seriously. "Aw, shucks," says the country boy; it is all a joke to him; his distance is in his humor, and he can exit from this America unmarked, unimpressed, and uninteresting.

"From the moment he comes out of the wings," writes Nik Cohn, "all the pop that has followed him is made to seem as nothing, to be blown away like chaff." That is exactly what that first moment feels like, but from that point on, Elvis will go with the rest of it, singing as if there are no dangers or delights in the world grand enough to challenge him. There is great satisfaction in his performance, and great emptiness.

It is an ending. It is a sure sign that a culture has reached a dead end when it is no longer intrigued by its myths (when they lose their power to excite, amuse, and renew all who are a part of those myths—when those myths just bore the hell out of everyone); but Elvis has dissolved into a presentation of his myth, and so has his music. The emotion of the best music is open, liberating in its commitment and intangibility; Elvis's presentation is fixed. The glorious oppression of that presentation parallels the all-but-complete assimilation of a revolutionary musical style into the mainstream of American culture, where no one is challenged and no one is threatened.

History without myth is surely a wasteland; but myths are compelling only when they are at odds with history. When they replace the need to make history, they too are a dead end, and merely smug. Elvis's performance of his myth is so satisfying to his audience that he is left with no musical identity whatsoever, and thus he has no way to define himself, or his audience—except to expand himself, and his audience. Elvis is a man whose task it is to dramatize the fact of his existence; he does not have to create something new (or try, and fail), and thus test the worth of his existence, or the worth of his audience.

Complete assimilation really means complete acceptance. The immigrant who is completely assimilated into

(at the end of his life) or after his death

America has lost the faculty of adding whatever is special about himself to his country; for any artist, complete assimilation means the adoption of an aesthetic where no lines are drawn and no choices are made. That quality of selection, which is what is at stake when an artist comes across with his or her version of anything, is missing. When an artist gives an all-encompassing Yes to his audience (and Elvis's Yes implicitly includes everyone, not just those who say Yes to *him*), there is nothing more he can tell his audience, nothing he can really do for them, except maybe throw them a kiss.

Only the man who says No is free, Melville once wrote. We don't expect such a stance in popular culture, and those who do might best be advised to take their trade somewhere else. But the refusal that lurks on the margins of the affirmation of American popular culture—the margins where Sly Stone and Randy Newman have done their best work—is what gives the Yes of our culture its vitality and its kick. Elvis's Yes is the grandest of all, his presentation of mastery the grandest fantasy of freedom, but it is finally a counterfeit of freedom: it takes place in a world that for all its openness (Everybody Welcome!) is aesthetically closed, where nothing is left to be mastered, where there is only more to accept. For all its irresistible excitement and enthusiasm, this freedom is complacent, and so the music that it produces is empty of real emotion—there is nothing this freedom could be for, nothing to be won or lost.

At best, when the fans gather around—old men and women who might see their own struggles and failures ennobled in the splendor of one who came from the bottom; middle-aged couples attending to the most glamorous nightclub act there is; those in their twenties and thirties who have grown with Elvis ever since he and they created each other years ago (and who might have a feeling he and they will make their trip through history together, reading their history in each other)—at best, Elvis will confirm all who are there *as* an audience. Such an event, repeated over and over all across the land, implies an America that is as nearly complete as any can be. But what is it worth?

When Elvis sings "American Trilogy" (a combination of "Dixie," "The Battle Hymn of the Republic," and "All My Trials," a slave song), he signifies that his persona, and the culture he has made out of blues, Las Vegas, gospel music, Hollywood, schmaltz, Mississippi, and rock 'n' roll, can contain any America you might want to conjure up. It is rather Lincolnesque; Elvis recognizes that the Civil War has never ended, and so he will perform The Union.

Well, for a moment, staring at that man on the stage, you can almost believe it. For if Elvis were to bring it off— and it is easy to think that only he could—one would leave the hall with a new feeling for the country; whatever that feeling might be, one's sense of place would be broadened, and enriched.

But it is an illusion. A man or woman equal to the song's pretension would have to present each part of the song as if it were the whole story, setting one against each other, proving that one American really could make the South live, the Union hold, and slavery real. But on the surface and beneath it, Elvis transcends any real America by evading it. There is no John Brown in his "Battle Hymn," no romance in his "Dixie," no blood in his slave song. He sings with such a complete absence of musical personality that none of the old songs matter at all, because he has not committed himself to them; it could be anyone singing, or no one. It is in this sense, finally, that an audience is confirmed, that an America comes into being; lacking any real fear or joy, it is a throw-away America where nothing is at stake. The divisions America shares are simply smoothed away.

But there is no chance anyone who wants to join will be excluded. Elvis's fantasy of freedom, the audience's fantasy, takes on such reality that there is nothing left in the real world that can inspire the fantasy, or threaten it. What *is* left is for the fantasy to replace the world; and that, night after night, is what Elvis and his audience make happen. The version of the American dream that is Elvis's performance is blown up again and again, to contain more history, more people, more music, more hopes; the air gets thin but the bubble does not burst, nor will it ever. This is America when it has outstripped itself, in all of its extravagance, and its emptiness is Elvis's ultimate throwaway.

There is a way in which virtually his whole career has been a throwaway, straight from that time when he knew he had it made and that the future was his. You can hear that distance, that refusal to really commit himself, in his best music and his worst; if the throwaway is the source of most of what is pointless about Elvis, it is also at the heart of much of what is exciting and charismatic. It may be that he never took *any* of it seriously, just did his job and did it well, trying to enjoy himself and stay sane—save for those first Tennessee records, and that night, late in 1968, when his comeback was uncertain and he put a searing, desperate kind of life into a few songs that cannot be found in any of his other music.

It was a staggering moment. A Christmas TV special had been decided on; a final dispute between Colonel Parker (he wanted twenty Christmas songs and a tuxedo) and producer Steve Binder (he wanted a tough, fast, sexy show) had been settled; with Elvis's help, Binder won. So there Elvis was, standing in an auditorium, facing television cameras and a live audience for the first time in nearly a decade, finally stepping out from behind the wall of retainers and sycophants he had paid to hide him. And everyone was watching.

In the months preceding Elvis had begun to turn away from the seamless boredom of the movies and the hackneyed music of the soundtrack albums, staking out a style on a few half-successful singles, presenting the new persona of a man whose natural toughness was tempered by experience. The records—"Big Boss Man," "Guitar Man," "U.S. Male"—had been careful, respectable efforts, but now he was putting everything on the line, risking his comforts and his ease for the chance to start over. He had been a bad joke for a long time; if this show died, little more would be heard from Elvis Presley. Did he still have an audience? Did he still have anything to offer them? He had raised the stakes himself, but he probably had no idea.

Sitting on the stage in black leather, surrounded by friends and a rough little combo, the crowd buzzing, he sang and talked and joked, and all the resentments he had hidden over the years began to pour out. He had always said yes, but this time, he was saying no—not without humor, but almost with a wry bit of guilt, as if he had betrayed his talent and himself. "Been a long time, baby." He told the audience about a time back in 1955, when cops in Florida had forced him to sing without moving; the story was hilarious, but there was something in his voice that made very clear how much it had hurt. He jibed at the Beatles, denying that the heroes who had replaced him had produced anything he could not match, and then he proved it. After all this time he wanted more than safety; he and the men around him were nervous, full of adventure.

"I'd like to do my favorite Christmas song," Elvis drawls—squeals of familiarity from the crowd, the girls in the front rows doing their job, imitating themselves or their images of the past, fading into an undertone of giggles as the music begins. Elvis sings "Blue Christmas," a classically styled rhythm and blues, very even, all its tension implied: a good choice. He sings it low and throaty, snapping the strings on his guitar until one of his pals cries, "Play it dirty! Play it dirty!"—on a Christmas song! All right! But this is re-creation, the past in the present, an attempt to see if Elvis can go as far as he once did. Within those limits it works, it is beautiful. The song ends with appropriate, and calculated, screams.

"Ah think Ah'll put a strap around this and stand up," Presley says. AHAHAHAHAHAHAHAAHAHA! God, what's that? Nervous laughter from a friend. Slow and steady, still looking around for the strap no one has bothered to hook onto the guitar, Elvis rocks into "One Night." In Smiley Lewis's original, it was about an orgy, called "One Night of Sin" (with the great line, "The things I did and I saw/ Would make the earth stand still"); Elvis cleaned it up into a love story in 1958. But he has forgotten—or remembered. He is singing Lewis's version, as he must have always wanted to. He has slipped his role, and laughing, grinning, something is happening.

> . . . *The things I did and I saw, could make* . . .
> these dreams—*Where's the strap?*

Where's the strap, indeed. He falls in and out of the two songs, and suddenly the band rams hard at the music and Elvis lunges and eats it alive. No one has ever heard him sing like this; not even his best records suggest the depth of passion in this music. One line from Howlin' Wolf tells the tale: "When you see me runnin', you know my life is at stake." That's what it sounds like.

Shouting, crying, growling, lusting, Elvis takes his stand and the crowd takes theirs with him, no longer reaching for the past they had been brought to the studio to reenact, but responding to something completely new. The crowd is cheering for what they had only hoped for: Elvis has gone beyond all their expectations, and his, and they don't believe it. The guitar cuts in high and slams down and Elvis is roaring. Every line is a thunderbolt. *AW, YEAH!*, screams a pal—he has waited years for this moment.

> *UNNNNNNH! WHEW! When* . . . I ain't nevah did no wrong!

And Elvis floats like the master he is back into "One night, with you," even allowing himself a little "Hot dog!", singing softly to himself.

It was the finest music of his life. If ever there was music that bleeds, this was it. Nothing came easy that night, and he gave everything he had—more than anyone knew was there.

Something of that passion spilled over into the first comeback album, *From Elvis in Memphis;* into "Suspicious Minds," the single that put him back on top of the charts; into his first live shows in Las Vegas; and then his nerves steadied, and Elvis brought it all back home again. You can still hear the intensity, the echo of those moments of doubt, in the first notes of most songs Elvis sings on stage—just before he realizes again that the crowd cares only that he is before them, and that anyway, the music would be his if he wanted it, that his talent is so vast it would be demeaning to apply it. So he will revel in his glory, acting the part of the King it has always been said he is; and if that is a throwaway, it is at least thrown at those who want it. A real glow passes back and forth between Elvis and his audience, as he shares a bit of what it means to transcend the world of weakness, failure, worry, age and fear, shows what it means for a boy who sprung from the poor to be godly, and shares that too.

I suppose it is the finality this performance carries with it that draws me back to Elvis's first records, made when there was nothing to take for granted, let alone throw away. Those sides, like "One Night," catch a world of risk, will, passion, and natural nobility; something worth searching out within the America of mastery and easy splendor that may well be Elvis's last word. The first thing Elvis had to learn to transcend, after all, was the failure and obscurity he was born to; he had to find some way to set himself apart, to escape the limits that could well have given his story a very different ending. The ambition and genius that took him out and brought him back is there in that first music—that, and much more.

HILLBILLY MUSIC

"This is the mystery of democracy," intoned Woodrow Wilson (dedicating the log cabin where Abraham Lincoln was born, in words ponderous enough to suit the mayor of Tupelo, Mississippi, when he dedicated the birthplace of Elvis Presley), "that its richest fruits spring up out of soils which no man has prepared and in circumstances where they are least expected. . . ."

I like those words. The question of history may have

been settled on the side of process, not personality, but it is not a settlement I much appreciate. Historical forces might explain the Civil War, but they don't account for Lincoln; they might tell us why rock 'n' roll emerged when it did, but they don't explain Elvis any more than they explain Little Peggy March. What a sense of context does give us, when we are looking for someone in particular, is an idea of what that person had to work with; but for myself, it always seems inexplicable in the end anyway. There are always blank spots, and that is where the myths take over. Elvis's story is so classically American (poor country boy makes good in the city) that his press agents never bothered to improve on it. But it is finally elusive too, just like all the good stories. It surrounds its subject, without quite revealing it. But it resonates; it evokes like crazy.

Now, the critical (and least tangible) point in the biography of any great man or woman is just that place where that person's story begins to detach itself from those of countless others like it. Take Lincoln again; was it that famous hike when he brought the borrowed book back? The moment on the stand facing Douglas when he knew he had him licked and loved it?

ELVIS ECHOES: Introducing a series of interruptions of Presley-Presence that, occuring while this chapter was written, are an essential part of its context, but do not fit anywhere else.

✳ EE #1. Elvis is to perform at the Oakland Coliseum in 1972. Back in the Dark Ages, two San Francisco high school girls win a "Why I Love Elvis" contest and are flown to Hollywood to be kissed. *Their principal expels them:* "We don't need that kind of publicity," he explains. Now, some babies and divorces later (for Elvis, too), the winners return. The word is passed; they are ushered backstage; they are kissed once more. It is a link to the past, but I am willing to bet that most of those in the hall (16,000) are meeting Elvis in the flesh for the first time, as am I. I have a bad seat, and the fortyish woman next to me passes her binoculars. I trade off with her preteen daughter. I notice that the best seats are occupied by couples who look old enough to substitute for El's grandparents. A thought from my friend Mary Clemmey comes to mind: In his present-day audience, Elvis sees the ghost of his mother, and the family life he has had to give up in order to be what he is. Behind me, a hippie pulls furiously on a joint. Is he performing an act of rebellion? Against Elvis? Or affirming that, in a bouffant utopia, he alone keeps the true Presley spirit alive?

The day he was born? You can't answer such questions, not computer-style, but you have no claim on the story unless you risk a guess.

They called Elvis the Hillbilly Cat in the beginning; he came out of a stepchild culture (in the South, white trash; to the rest of America, a caricature of Bilbo and moonshine) that for all it shared with the rest of America had its own shape and integrity. As a poor white Southern boy, Elvis created a personal culture out of the hillbilly world that was his as a given. Ultimately, he made that personal culture public in such an explosive way that he transformed not only his own culture, but America's.

It was, as Southern chambers of commerce have never tired of saying, A Land of Contrasts. The fundamental contrast, of course, could not have been more obvious: black and white. Always at the root of Southern fantasy, Southern music, and Southern politics, black Americans were poised in the early fifties for an overdue invasion of American life, in fantasy, music, and politics. As the North scurried to deal with the problem, the South would be pushed farther and farther into the weirdness and madness its best artists had been trying to exorcise from the time of Poe on down. Its politics would dissolve into night-riding and hysteria; its fantasies would be dull for all their gaudy paranoia. Only the music got away clean.

The North, powered by the Protestant ethic, had set men free by making them strangers; the poor man's South that Elvis knew took strength from community.

The community was based on a marginal economy that demanded cooperation, loyalty, and obedience for the achievement of anything resembling a good life; it was organized by religion, morals, and music. Music helped hold the community together, and carried the traditions and shared values that dramatized a sense of place. Music gave pleasure, wisdom, and shelter.

"It's the only place in the country I've ever been where

you can actually drive down the highway at night, and if you listen, you hear music," Robbie Robertson once said. "I don't know if it's coming from the people or if it's coming from the air. It lives, and it's rooted there." Elegant enough, but I prefer another comment Robbie made. "The South," he said, "is the only place we play where everybody can clap on the off-beat."

Music was also an escape from the community, and music revealed its underside. There were always people who could not join, no matter how they might want to: tramps, whores, rounders, idiots, criminals. The most vital were singers: not the neighbors who brought out their fiddles and guitars for country picnics, as Elvis used to do, or those who sang in church, as he did also, but the professionals. They were men who bridged the gap between the community's sentimentalized idea of itself, and the outside world and the forbidden; artists who could take the community beyond itself because they had the talent and the nerve to transcend it. Often doomed, traveling throughout the South enjoying sins and freedoms the community had surrendered out of necessity or never known at all, they were too ambitious, ornery, or simply different to fit in.

The Carter Family, in the twenties, were the first to record the old songs everyone knew, to make the shared musical culture concrete, and their music drew a circle around the community. They celebrated the landscape (especially the Clinch Mountains that ringed their home), found strength in a feel for death because it was the only certainty, laughed a bit, and promised to leave the hillbilly home they helped build only on a gospel ship. Jimmie Rodgers, their contemporary, simply hopped a train. He was every boy who ever ran away from home, hanging out in the railroad yards, bumming around with black minstrels, pushing out the limits of his life. *He* celebrated long tall mamas that rubbed his back and licked his neck just to cure the cough that killed him; he bragged about gunplay on Beale Street; he sang real blues, played jazz with Louis Armstrong, and though there was melancholy in his soul, his smile was a

good one. He sounded like a man who could make a home
for himself anywhere. There's so much *room* in this country,
he seemed to be saying, so many things to do—how could an
honest man be satisfied to live within the frontiers he was
born to?

Outside of the community because of the way they
lived, the singers were tied to it as symbols of its secret
hopes, of its fantasies of escape and union with the black
man, of its fears of transgressing the moral and social limits
that promised peace of mind. Singers could present the extremes of emotion, risk, pleasure, sex, and violence that the
community was meant to control; they were often alcoholic
or worse, lacking a real family, drifters in a world where
roots were life. Sometimes the singer tantalized the community with his outlaw liberty; dying young, he finally justified
the community by his inability to survive outside of it. More
often than not, the singer's resistance dissolved into sentiment. Reconversion is the central country music comeback
strategy, and many have returned to the fold after a brief
fling with the devil, singing songs of virtue, fidelity, and
God, as if to prove that sin only hid a deeper piety—or that
there was no way out.

By the late forties and early fifties, Hank Williams had
inherited Jimmie Rodgers' role as the central figure in the
music, but he added an enormous reservation: that margin of
loneliness in Rodgers' America had grown into a world of
utter tragedy. Williams sang for a community to which he
could not belong; he sang to a God in whom he could not
quite believe; even his many songs of good times and good
lovin' seemed to lose their reality. There were plenty of jokes
in his repertoire, novelties like "Kaw-Liga" (the tale of
unrequited love between two cigar store Indians); he traveled
Rodgers' road, but for Williams, that road was a lost highway. Beneath the surface of his forced smiles and his light,
easy sound, Hank Williams was kin to Robert Johnson in a
way that the new black singers of his day were not. Their
music, coming out of New Orleans, out of Sam Phillips'
Memphis studio and washing down from Chicago, was loud,

fiercely electric, raucous, bleeding with lust and menace and loss. The rhythmic force that was the practical legacy of Robert Johnson had evolved into a music that overwhelmed *his* reservations; the rough spirit of the new blues, city R&B, rolled right over his nihilism. Its message was clear: What life doesn't give me, I'll take.

Hank Williams was a poet of limits, fear, and failure; he went as deeply into one dimension of the country world as anyone could, gave it beauty, gave it dignity. What was missing was that part of the hillbilly soul Rodgers had celebrated, something Williams' music obscured, but which his realism could not express and the community's moralism could not contain: excitement, rage, fantasy, delight—the feeling, summed up in a sentence by W. J. Cash from *The Mind of the South*, that "even the Southern physical world was a kind of cosmic conspiracy against reality in favor of romance"; that even if Elvis's South was filled with Puritans, it was also filled with natural-born hedonists, and the same people were both.

To lie on his back for days and weeks [Cash wrote of the hillbilly], storing power as the air he breathed stores power under the hot sun of August, and then to explode, as that air explodes in a thunderstorm, in a violent outburst of emotion—in such a fashion would he make life not only tolerable, but infinitely sweet.

In the fifties we can hardly find that moment in white music, before Elvis. Hank Williams was not all there was to fifties country, but his style was so pervasive, so effective, carrying so much weight, that it closed off the possibilities of breaking loose just as the new black music helped open them up. Not his gayest tunes, not "Move It on Over," "Honky Tonkin'," or "Hey Good Lookin'," can match this blazing passage from Cash, even if those songs share its subject:

To go into the town on Saturday afternoon and night, to stroll with the throng, to gape at the well-dressed and the big automobiles, to bathe in the holiday cacaphony . . . maybe to have a drink, maybe to get drunk, to laugh with the passing girls, to pick

them up if you had a car, or to go swaggering or hesitating into the
hotels with the corridors saturated with the smell of bicloride of
mercury, or the secret, steamy bawdy houses; maybe to have a
fight, maybe against the cops, maybe to end, whooping and god-
damning, in the jailhouse. . . .

The momentum is missing; that will to throw yourself
all the way after something better with no real worry about
how you are going to make it home. And it was this spirit,
full-blown and bragging, that was to find its voice in Elvis's
new blues and the rockabilly fever he kicked off all over the
young white South. Once Elvis broke down the door, dozens
more would be fighting their way through. Out of nowhere
there would be Carl Perkins, looking modest enough and
sounding for all the world as if he was having fun for the first
time in his life, chopping his guitar with a new kind of
urgency and yelling: "Now Dan got happy and he started
ravin'—He jerked out his razor but he wasn't shavin' "—

> *He hollered* R-R-RAVE ON *chillen, I'm with ya!*
> RAVE ON CATS *he cried*
> *It's almost dawn and the cops're gone*
> *Let's alllllllll get dixie fried!*

Country music (like the blues, which was more damned
and more honestly hedonistic than country had ever been)
was music for a whole community, cutting across lines of
age, if not class. This could have meant an openly expressed
sense of diversity for each child, man, and woman, as it did
with the blues. But country spoke to a community fearful of
anything of the sort, withdrawing into itself, using music as
a bond that linked all together for better or for worse, with a
sense that what was shared was less important than the crucial fact of sharing. How could parents hope to keep their
children if their kids' whole sense of what it meant to live—
which is what we get from music when we are closest to it—
held promises the parents could never keep?

The songs of country music, and most deeply, its even,
narrow sound, had to subject the children to the heartbreak

of their parents: the father who couldn't feed his family, the wife who lost her husband to a honky-tonk angel or a bottle, the family that lost everything to a suicide or a farm spinning off into one more bad year, the horror of loneliness in a world that was meant to banish that if nothing else. Behind that uneasy grin, this is Hank Williams' America; the romance is only a night call.

Such a musical community is beautiful, but it is not hard to see how it could be intolerable. All that hedonism was dragged down in country music; a deep sense of fear and resignation confined it, as perhaps it almost had to, in a land overshadowed by fundamentalist religion, where original sin was just another name for the facts of life.

RAISED UP

Now, that Saturday night caught by Cash and Perkins would get you through a lot of weekdays. Cash might close it off—"Emptied of their irritations and repressions, left to return to their daily tasks, stolid, unlonely, and tame again"— and he's right, up to a point. This wasn't any revolution, no matter how many cops got hurt keeping the peace on Saturday night. Regardless of what a passport to that Southern energy (detached from the economics and religion that churned it up) might do for generations of restless Northern and British kids, there is no way that energy can be organized. But the fact that Elvis and the rest could trap its spirit and send it out over a thousand radio transmitters is a central fact of more lives than mine; the beginning of most of the stories in this book, if nothing near the end of them.

For we are treading on the key dividing line that made Elvis "King of Western Bop" (they went through a lot of trouble finding a name for this music) instead of just another country crooner or a footnote in someone's history of the blues: the idea (and it was just barely an "idea") that Saturday night could be the whole show. You had to be young and a bit insulated to pull it off, but why not? Why not trade pain and boredom for kicks and style? Why not make an es-

cape from a way of life—the question trails off the last page
of *Huckleberry Finn*—into a way of life?

You might not get revered for all time by everyone from
baby to grandma, like the Carter Family, but you'd have
more fun. Reality would catch up sooner or later—a pregnant girlfriend and a fast marriage, the farm you had to take
over when your daddy died, a dull and pointless job that
drained your desires until you could barely remember
them—but why deal with reality before you had to? And
what if there was a chance, just a chance, that you *didn't* have
to deal with it? "When I was a boy," said Elvis not so long
ago, "I was the hero in comic books and movies. I grew up
believing in a dream. Now I've lived it out. That's all a man
can ask for."

Elvis is telling us something quite specific: how special
he was; how completely he captured and understood what
for most of us is only a tired phrase glossing the surfaces of
our own failed hopes. It is one thing, after all, to dream of a
new job, and quite another to dream of a new world. The
risks are greater. Elvis took chances dreaming his dreams; he
gambled against the likelihood that their failure would betray
him, and make him wish he had never dreamed at all. There
are a hundred songs to tell that story, but perhaps Mott the

❋ EE #2. May 1972. I read in *Modern Screen* that top GOP politicos
are giving *serious consideration* to placing Elvis's name in nomination for the
vice-presidency (a plot to get around that $25,000 fee?). The article is illus-
trated by fifteen-year-old shots of girls waving ELVIS-FOR-
PRESIDENT banners. Elvis, the story says, thinks this is a good idea,
and has recently addressed a group of Black Panthers in order to test his
forensic skills. He told them, and I quote: "Violence is not where it's at.
It's a real turn-off, man." I do not know how to take this, especially as I
recall it a year later when a TV trailer announces, "Tonight, immediately
following the President's speech on Watergate, see Elvis further the cause
of rock 'n' roll in *Roustabout*." I am more disoriented by the idea that Elvis
could further the cause of *anything* in a movie like *Roustabout* than I am by
the missed chance of his involvement in the Watergate scandal. But then,
he would have known how to handle it. To Elvis, Watergate would have
been something like a cosmic paternity suit.

Hoople, chasing the rock 'n' roll fantasy Elvis made of the American dream, said it best: "I wish I'd never wanted then/ What I want now twice as much."

Always, Elvis felt he was different, if not better, than those around him. He grew his sideburns long, acting out that sense of differentness, and was treated differently: in this case, he got himself kicked off the football team. Hear him recall those days in the midst of a near-hysterical auto-biography, delivered at the height of his comeback from the stage at the International Hotel in Las Vegas: ". . . Had pretty long hair for that time and I tell you it got pretty weird. They used to see me comin down the street and they'd say, 'Hot dang, let's get him, he's a squirrel, he's a squirrel, get him, he just come down outta the trees.' "

High school classmates remember his determination to break through as a country singer; with a little luck, they figured, he might even make it.

Out on the road for the first time with small-change country package tours, though, Elvis would plot for something much bigger—for everything Hollywood had ever shown him in its movies.

On North Main in Memphis, as Harmonica Frank recalls Elvis, this was nothing to put into words. Talking trash and flicking ash, marking time and trying to hold it off, what did Elvis really have to look forward to? A year or so of Saturday nights, a little local notoriety, then a family he didn't quite decide to have and couldn't support? It would be all over.

Elvis fancied himself a trucker (if there weren't any Memphis boys in the movies, there were plenty on the road), pushing tons of machinery through the endless American night; just his version of the train whistle that called out to Johnny B. Goode and kept Richard Nixon awake as a boy. If it is more than a little odd that what to Elvis served as a symbol of escape and mastery now works—as part of his legend—as a symbol of everything grimy and poor he left behind when he did escape, maybe that only tells us how much his success shuffled the facts of his life—or how much he raised the stakes.

You don't make it in America—Emerson's mousetrap to the contrary—waiting for someone to come along and sign you up. You might be sitting on the corner like a Philly rock 'n' roller and get snatched up for your good looks, but you'll be back a year later and you'll never know what happened. Worst of all, you may not even care. What links the greatest rock 'n' roll careers is a volcanic ambition, a lust for more than anyone has a right to expect; in some cases, a refusal to know when to quit or even rest. It is that bit of Ahab burning beneath the Huck Finn rags of "Freewheelin' " Bob Dylan, the arrogance of a country boy like Elvis sailing into Hollywood, ready for whatever kind of success America had to offer.

So if we treat Elvis's words with as much respect as we can muster—which is how he meant them to be taken—we can see the first point at which his story begins to be his own. He took his dreams far more seriously than most ever dare, and he had the nerve to chase them down.

Cash's wonderful line—"a cosmic conspiracy against reality in favor of romance"—now might have more resonance. Still, if the kind of spirit that romance could produce seems ephemeral within the context of daily life, you would not expect the music it produced to last very long either. Not even Elvis, as a successful young rocker, could have expected his new music to last; he told interviewers rock 'n' roll was here to stay, but he was taking out plenty of insurance, making movies and singing schmaltz. You couldn't blame him; anyway, he liked schmaltz.

Within the realm of country music, the new spirit dried up just like Saturday fades into Monday, but since rock 'n' roll found its own audience and created its own world, that hardly mattered. Rock 'n' roll caught that romantic conspiracy on records and gave it a form. Instead of a possibility within a music, it became the essence; it became, of all things, a tradition. And when that form itself had to deal with reality—which is to say, when its young audience began to grow up—when the compromise between fantasy and reality that fills most of this book was necessary to preserve the possibility of fantasy, the fantasy had become part of the reality that had to be dealt with; the rules of the game had changed a bit, and it was a better game. "Blue Suede Shoes" had grown directly into something as serious and complex, and yet still offhand, still take-it-or-leave-it-and-pass-the-wine, as the Rolling Stones' "You Can't Always Get What You Want," which asks the musical question, "Why *are you* stepping on my blue suede shoes?"

✳ EE#3. Elvis's 1973 TV special, *Aloha from Elvis in Hawaii*, was beamed by satellite to one-third of the world's population. Or so his publicity men announced. Perhaps it was that if the one-third of the world—principally the heathen part—had TV sets, it could have watched. It doesn't matter: the conceit of the concept is what matters.

You can see him now, Col. Thomas Andrew Parker, ex-carny barker, the great medical menagerist, tossing helplessly on his bed, scheming—after all these years, still peddling Elvis pens at press conferences, hustling glossies in the aisles at concerts, Colonel Parker does not rest—and what keeps him awake is that *even now there are people who do not know about Elvis Presley!* There are worlds to be conquered! There is work to be done!

Finally, he drops off to sleep. Yes, there are poor beggars somewhere in the Amazon jungle who have yet to get the word (perhaps the King would succeed where dozens of casseroled missionaries have failed—make a note of that), but the Colonel will deal with that tomorrow . . . wait for tomorrow.

Parker dreams.

It is perhaps 1990. Elvis is in his middle fifties now, still young, still beautiful. His latest single—"Baby Let Me Bang Your Box," backed with "My Yiddishe Mama"—has topped all charts. Parker has had his third heart transplant. The world has received the long-awaited actual communication from intelligent beings beyond the solar system. Earth's greatest scientists have assembled in Japan to decipher the message, and after years of error they have succeeded. It consists of only one word, one question on which the fate of ten billion people may rest:

"ELWIS?"

So Colonel Parker rests easy. Age has mellowed him, and his expectations do not go beyond the Milky Way.

Echoing through all of rock 'n' roll is the simple demand for peace of mind and a good time. While the demand is easy to make, nothing is more complex than to try to make it real and live it out. It all sounds plain, obvious; but that one young man like Elvis could break through a world as hard as Hank Williams', and invent a new one to replace it, seems obvious only because we have inherited Elvis's world, and live in it.

Satisfaction is not all there is to it, but it is where it all begins. Finally, the music must provoke as well as delight, disturb as well as comfort, create as well as sustain. If it doesn't, it lies, and there is only so much comfort you can take in a lie before it all falls apart.

The central facts of life in Elvis's South pulled as strongly against the impulses of hedonism and romance as the facts of our own lives do against the fast pleasures of rock 'n' roll. When the poor white was thrown back on himself, as he was in the daytime, when he worked his plot or looked for a job in the city, or at night, when he brooded and Hank Williams' whippoorwill told the truth all too plainly, those facts stood out clearly: powerlessness and vulnerability on all fronts. The humiliation of a class system that gave him his identity and then trivialized it; a community that for all its tradition and warmth was in some indefinable way not enough; economic chaos; the violence of the weather; bad food and maybe not enough of that; diseases that attached themselves to the body like new organs—they all mastered him. And that vulnerability produced—along with that urge to cut loose, along with that lively Southern romance— uncertainty, fatalism, resentment, acceptance, and nostalgia: limits that cut deep as the oldest cotton patch in Dixie.

Vernon Presley was a failed Mississippi sharecropper who moved his family out of the country with the idea of making a go in the city; it's not so far from Tupelo to Memphis, but in some ways, the journey must have been a long one—scores of country songs about boys and girls who lost their souls to the big town attest to that. Listen to Dolly Parton's downtown hooker yearning for her Blue Ridge mountain boy; listen to the loss of an America you may never have known.

They don't make country music better than that anymore, but it's unsatisfying, finally; too classical. This country myth is just one more echo of Jefferson pronouncing that, in America, virtue must be found in the land. I like myths, but this one is too facile, either for the people who still live on the land or for those of us who are merely looking for a way out of our own world, for an Annie Green Springs utopia. The myth is unsatisfying because the truth is richer than the myth.

"King Harvest (Has Surely Come)," the Band's song of blasted country hopes, gives us the South in all of its earthly delight and then snuffs it out. All at once, the song catches the grace and the limbo of the life that must be left behind.

The tune evokes a man's intimacy with the land and the refusal of the land to respond in kind. The music makes real, for the coolest city listener, a sense of place that is not quite a sense of being at home; the land is too full of violence for that. One hears the farmer's fear of separating from the land (and from his own history, which adhering to the land, is not wholly his own); one hears the cold economic necessities that have forced him out. The melody—too beautiful and out of reach for any words I have—spins the chorus into the pastoral with a feel for nature that is *really* hedonistic—

> *Corn in the field*
> *Listen to the rice as the wind blows cross the water*
> KING HARVEST HAS SURELY COME *

—and a desperate, ominous rhythm slams the verses back to the slum streets that harbor the refugees of the pastoral disaster: "Just don't judge me by my shoes!" Garth Hudson's organ traces the circle of the song, over and over again.

The earliest picture of Elvis shows a farmer, his wife, and their baby; the faces of the parents are vacant, they are set, as if they cannot afford an unearned smile. Somehow, their faces say, they will be made to pay even for that.

You don't hear this in Elvis's music; but what he left out of his story is as vital to an understanding of his art as what he kept, and made over. If we have no idea of what he left behind, of how much he escaped, we will have no idea what his success was worth, or how intensely he must have wanted it.

Elvis was thirteen when the family left Tupelo for Memphis in 1948, a pampered only child; ordinary in all respects, they say, except that he liked to sing. True to Chuck Berry's legend of the Southern rocker, Elvis's mother bought him his first guitar, and for the same reason Johnny B. Goode's mama had in mind: keep the boy out of trouble. Elvis sang tearful country ballads, spirituals, community music. On the radio, he listened with his family to the old music of the Carter Family and Jimmie Rodgers, to current stars like Roy Acuff, Ernest Tubb, Bob Wills, Hank Williams, and to white gospel groups like the Blackwood Brothers. Elvis touched the soft center of American music when he heard and imitated Dean Martin and the operatics of Mario Lanza; he picked up Mississippi blues singers like Big Bill Broonzy, Big Boy Crudup, Lonnie Johnson, and the new Memphis music of Rufus Thomas and Johnny Ace, mostly when no one else was around, because that music was naturally frowned upon. His parents called it "sinful music," and they had a point—it was dirty, and there were plenty of blacks who would have agreed with Mr. and Mrs. Presley—but Elvis was really too young to worry. In this he was no different from hundreds of other white country kids who wanted more excitement in their lives than they could get from twangs and laments—wanted a beat, sex, celebration, the stunning nuances of the blues and the roar of horns and electric guitars. Still, Elvis's interest was far more casual than that of Jerry Lee Lewis, a bad boy who was sneaking off to black dives in his spare time, or Carl Perkins, a musician who was consciously working out a synthesis of blues and country.

The Presleys stumbled onto welfare, into public housing. Vernon Presley found a job. It almost led to the family's eviction, because if they still didn't have enough to live on, they were judged to have too much to burden the county with their troubles. Elvis was a loner, but he had an eye for flash. He sold his blood for money, ushered at the movies, drove his famous truck, and divided the proceeds between his mother and his outrageous wardrobe. Looking for space, for a way to set himself apart.

Like many parents with no earthly future, the Presleys, especially Gladys Presley, lived for their son. Her ambition must have been that Elvis would take all that was good in the family and free himself from the life she and her husband endured; she was, Memphian Stanley Booth wrote a few years ago, "the one, perhaps the only one, who had told him throughout his life that even though he came from poor country people, he was just as good as anybody."

On Sundays (Wednesdays too, sometimes) the Presleys went to their Assembly of God to hear the Pentecostal ministers hand down a similar message: the last shall be first. This was democratic religion with a vengeance, lower class and gritty. For all those who have traced Elvis's music and his hipshake to his religion (accurately enough—Elvis was the first to say so), it has escaped his chroniclers that hillbilly Calvinism was also at the root of his self-respect and his pride: the anchor of his ambition.

His church (and the dozens of other Pentecostal sects scattered throughout the South and small-town America) was one part of what was left of the old American religion after the Great Awakening. Calvinism had been a religion of authority in the beginning; in the middle-class North, filtered through the popular culture of Ben Franklin, it became a system of tight money, tight-mindedness, and gentility; in the hillbilly South, powered by traveling preachers and their endless revivals, the old holiness cult produced a faith of grace, apocalypse, and emotion, where people heaved their deepest feelings into a circle and danced around them. Momentum scattered that old authority; all were sinners, all were saints. Self-consciously outcast, the true faith in a land of Philistines and Pharisees, it was shoved into storefronts and tents and even open fields, and no less sure of itself for that.

Church music caught moments of unearthly peace and desire, and the strength of the religion was in its intensity. The preacher rolled fire down the pulpit and chased it into the aisle, signifying; men and women rocked in their seats, sometimes onto the floor, bloodying their fingernails scratching and clawing in a lust for absolute sanctification. No battle against oppression, this was a leap right through it, with tongues babbling toward real visions, negating stale red earth, warped privvies, men and women staring from their sway-backed porches into nothingness. It was a faith meant to transcend the grimy world that called it up. Like Saturday night, the impulse to dream, the need to escape, the romance and the contradictions of the land, this was a source of energy, tension, and power.

Elvis inherited these tensions, but more than that, gave them his own shape. It is often said that if Elvis had not come along to set off the changes in American music and American life that followed his triumph, someone very much like him would have done the job as well. But there is no reason to think this is true, either in strictly musical terms, or in any broader cultural sense. It is vital to remember that Elvis was the first young Southern white to sing rock 'n' roll, something he copied from no one but made up on the spot; and to know that even though other singers would have come up with a white version of the new black music acceptable to teenage America, of all that did emerge in Elvis's wake, none sang as powerfully, or with more than a touch of his magic.

Even more important is the fact that no singer emerged with anything like Elvis's combination of great talent and conscious ambition, and there is no way a new American hero could have gotten out of the South and to the top— creating a whole new sense of how big the top was, as Elvis did—without that combination. The others—Perkins, Lewis, Charlie Rich—were bewildered by even a taste of fame and unable to handle a success much more limited than Presley's.

If Elvis had the imagination to come up with the dreams that kept him going, he had the music to bring them to life and make them real to huge numbers of other people. It was the genius of his singing, an ease and an intensity that has no parallel in American music, that along with his dreams separated him from his context; and for the rest of this chapter, we can try to discover what that singing was all about.

THE ROCKABILLY MOMENT

There are four of them in the little studio: Bill Black, the bass player; Scotty Moore, the guitarist; in the back, Sam Phillips, the producer; and the sexy young kid thumping his guitar as he sings, Elvis Presley, just nineteen. 1954.

Sam Phillips is doing all right for himself. He has been among the first to record men who will be giants in the world of postwar blues: B. B. King, Junior Parker, and the Howlin' Wolf himself. The names on Phillips' roster show his willingness to try anything: wonderful names like Big Memphis Ma Rainey, the Ripley Cotton Choppers, Dr. Ross, Hard-rock Gunter, Rufus "Bear Cat" Thomas, Billy the Kid Emerson, the Prisonaires (a vocal group from the state pen), the immortal Hot Shot Love. There are plenty more knocking on the door, and with no more than this, Phillips' place in the history of American music would be assured—not that a place in history is quite what he is looking for.

In the records Phillips makes you can discern something more than taste, something like vision. He has cooked up a sound all his own: hot, fierce, overbearing, full of energy and desire, a sound to jump right out of the jukebox. But Phillips wants money, a lot of it, and he wants something new. Deep down in a place not even he sees clearly, he wants to set the world on its ear.

The kid with the guitar is . . . unusual; but they've

been trying to put something on the tape Sam keeps running back—a ballad, a hillbilly song, anything—and so far, well, it just doesn't get it.

The four men cool it for a moment, frustrated. They share a feeling they could pull something off if they hit it right, but it's been a while, and that feeling is slipping away, as it always does. They talk music, blues, Crudup, ever hear that, who you kiddin' man, dig this. The kid pulls his guitar up, clowns a bit. He throws himself at a song. *That's all right, mama, that's all right* . . . eat shit. He doesn't say that, naturally, but that's what he's found in the tune; his voice slides over the lines as the two musicians come in behind him, Scotty picking up the melody and the bassman slapping away at his axe. Phillips hears it, likes it, and makes up his mind.

All right, you got something. Do it again, I'll get it down. Just like that, don't mess with it. Keep it simple.

They cut the song fast, put down their instruments, vaguely embarrassed at how far they went into the music. Sam plays back the tape. Man, they'll run us outta town when they hear it, Scotty says; Elvis sings along with himself, joshing his performance. They all wonder, but not too much.

Get on home, now, Sam says. I gotta figure what to do with this.

They leave, but Sam Phillips is perplexed. Who is gonna play this crazy record? White jocks won't touch it 'cause it's nigger music and colored will pass 'cause it's hillbilly. It sounds good, it sounds sweet, but maybe it's just . . . too weird? The hell with it.

Sam Phillips released the record; what followed was the heyday of Sun Records and rockabilly music, a moment when boys were men and men were boys, when full-blown legends emerged that still walk the land and the lesser folk simply went along for the ride.

Rockabilly was a fast, aggressive music: simple, snappy drumming, sharp guitar licks, wild country boogie piano, the music of kids who came from all over the South to make records for Sam Phillips and his imitators. Rockabilly came and it went; there was never that much of it, and even including Elvis's first Sun singles, all the rockabilly hits put together sold less than Fats Domino's. But rockabilly fixed the crucial image of rock 'n' roll: the sexy, half-crazed fool standing on stage singing his guts out.

Most important, the image was white. Rockabilly was the only style of early rock 'n' roll that proved white boys could do it all—that they could be as strange, as exciting, as scary, and as free as the black men who were suddenly walking America's airwaves as if they owned them. There were two kinds of white counterattack on the black invasion of white popular culture that was rock 'n' roll: the attempt to soften black music or freeze it out, and the rockabilly lust to beat the black man at his own game.

Sam Phillips had the imagination to take in a country folksinger like Johnny Cash and a Stan Kenton fan like Charlie Rich; he was commercial enough to get rock 'n' roll out of both of them. Phillips gave a funny-looking kid named Roy Orbison the chance to growl that no girl had the style to match him, and the music to prove it. Sun tossed up Warren Smith, who claimed he had a girl who looked like a frog; Sonny Burgess, who dyed his hair red to match his red suit and his red Cadillac and told anyone who would listen he wanted to boogie with a red-headed woman; Sun offered us Billy Lee Riley, who blithely argued that rock 'n' roll was so strange it had to come from Mars. The little green men taught him how to do the bop, was the way he put it.

Carl Perkins found greatness here, and nowhere else; Jerry Lee Lewis simply took greatness as his due. ("*I* played on 'em," Jerry Lee told an interviewer who had asked the names of the musicians who had played on his records, "what else do you need to know?") Jerry Lee stormed his way through the whorehouse rock of "Deep Elem Blues" like Elmer Gantry moonlighting from the revival tent (celebrating the Dallas red light district that crawled with sin and blues piano); he tumbled into "Big Legged Woman," leering at an

imaginary audience with the arrogance that would bring him
down.

Let me tell ya, tell ya, tell ya something
WHAT I'M TALKIN' ABOUT
I bet my bottom dollar there ain't a cherry in this house *

While it lasted, Sun was a space of freedom, a place to
take chances. The music Sun produced was ominous, funny,
kicking up rhythm and bursting with exuberance, determination, and urgency, full of self-conscious novelty and experi-
ment. Most of the first rock 'n' roll styles were variations on
black forms that had taken shape before the white audience
moved in and forced those forms to turn its way; rockabilly
was almost self-contained, a world of its own, and as authentically new as any music can be.

Back in those days I knew some country kids who captured the spirit of the music as well as any 45: farm boys,
long, lean, tough, and good-humored. They flashed me my
first picture of Little Richard, kicked raccoons to death with
their bare feet, rustled sheep, chased Indian girls into the
bushes, and made it into town on Saturday night to watch
the razor fights. They were easy to idolize; one night they
got drunk, drove their car to the railroad tracks, and got
themselves blown to pieces.

Rockabilly was squeaky Charlie Feathers, a country
singer of no special talent or even much drive, trekking up to
Cincinnati, after failures at Sun, for the chance to yell, "Aw,
turn it *loose!*" and then disappear. He reached once, and he
missed, but these lines have stayed with me ever since a
scratchy tape of his one great song arrived in the mail:

Well, I'm a tip-top daddy an' I'm gonna have my way
Dontcha worry 'bout me baby, dont worry what they say
I got one hand, baby, let it swing by my side
Just gimme one hand loose, and I'll be satisfied
Satisfied! †

* Copyright © P. Donald White. Used by permission.
† Copyright © 1956 by Fort Knox Music Company.

"Maybe someday your name will be in lights," Chuck
Berry promised the young rockers, and most of them never
got past the "maybe." There was a price for all that unex-
pected vitality and flash. Carl Perkins, still billing himself
"The King of Rock 'n' Roll" on the thin line of one hit and a
score of failures, sunk into alcohol; Johnny Cash nearly killed
himself on pills; Gene Vincent found himself exiled to England, where some still remembered, and died of a bleeding
ulcer before he was forty. Johnny Burnette, Eddie Cochran,
Buddy Holly, chasing after Elvis's pot of gold, died in ac-
cidents, in fast cars and chartered planes. Most simply vanished and were forgotten—if they were lucky enough to have
been known at all. They fell back into the predictability of
country music or the day-to-day sameness they had meant to
escape. All they left behind was rock 'n' roll, and an audience
that twenty years later was still acting out their fantasies and
seeking novelty and amusement in their ghosts.

It was an explosion, and standing over it all was Elvis.
In the single year he recorded for Sam Phillips—August
1954 through August 1955—ten sides were released (four
more were used by RCA to fill up Elvis's first album); about
half derived from country songs, the rest took off from blues.
His music stands to the rest of rockabilly as genius does to
talent.

The blues especially have not dated at all. Not a note is
false; their excitement comes through the years intact, unburdened by cuteness, mannerism, or posturing.* Nothing is
stylized. The music is clean, straight, open, and free.

That's what these sides are about: finding space in the

---

*For most of us, the songs are unburdened by any sort of nostalgia as well. In
their time, they were little heard outside of the South, and they turned up on
albums only when Elvis was off in the army and RCA had to scrape its vaults for
something to release. None ever made the national pop charts. Today they are
rarely played on the radio (though spinning the dial on Elvis's thirty-eighth
birthday, I picked up "That's All Right"—on a country station). Until 1976,
Colonel Parker, or Elvis himself, deemed it vital that the King be protected from
his past, so the songs were not, as with most classic rock, reissued in a package
that might attract an audience. Given the publicity that has come with Elvis,
these sides remained almost invisible, the result of a prepop moment; but *their*
result is as public as rock 'n' roll. From one point of view they are the basis of
the whole show. So there is a lot of power packed into these records, and not all
of it is musical.

crunch of the worn-out and overfamiliar; finding a way to feel free in that space and finding the voice to put that feeling across.

The best evidence of Sam Phillips' spirit is in the sound of the records. Each song is clear, direct, uncluttered, and blended into something coherent. There is that famous echo, slapping back at the listener, and a bubbling tension that is never quite resolved; no comforts of vocal accompaniment, but the risk of one young man on his own. The sound is all presence, as if Black and Moore each took a step straight off the record and Elvis was somehow squeezed right into the mike. "I went into the studio," Sam Phillips recalled years later, "to draw out a person's innate, possibly unknown talents, present them to the public, and let the public be the judge. I had to be a psychologist and know how to handle each artist and how to enable him to be at his best. I went with the idea that an artist should have something not just good, but totally unique. When I found someone like that, I did everything in my power to bring it out." *

The sides Phillips cut with Elvis might have worked in the twenties, and they might do for the eighties; not simply as listenable music—there is no doubt about that—but as music that still sounds new, that still breaks things open.†

---

* From an interview with John Pugh, *Country Music*, November 1973.
† Even the lyrics evade any possibility of camp—unlike so much of fifties rock 'n' roll, including Elvis's RCA material, which was made with a trendy commercial ear. The blues and country motifs of the Sun sides are as lively today as they were old in 1954; if it takes little effort to trace "That's All Right" and "Milkcow Blues Boogie" back to Son House's epic "My Black Mama," cut in 1930, it takes even less to follow the trail forward to the Rolling Stones or the Allman Brothers.

Not surprisingly, on the album that today features House's masterpiece (*Really! The Country Blues*), there is an ancient, quiet statement of the theme Elvis brought home with such force. Made in 1928, it comes deadpan, spoken over a pretty little guitar line by one William Moore—an old, old mood, there too in Harmonica Frank or the Allmans' "Pony Boy," but to modern ears, *about* what Elvis *was*. This is "Old Country Rock": "Come on, Bill, let's take them for an old country rock. Let's go back down the Rappahanock, down Tappahanock way. Look at Bill while everybody rocks. Get that old rock, Bill. Everybody rock. Old folks rock. Young folks rock. Boys rock. Girls rock. Trot back, man, and let me rock. Rock me, sis, rock me. Rock me till I sweat. Trot back, folks, let your pappy rock. Pappy knows how. Children rock. Sister Ernestine, show your pappy how you rock. Mighty fine, boys,

Elvis can tell us what was new and distinctive about his time without being trapped by it, and without trapping us. He can do it because to a great degree ELVIS PRESLEY was the distinctive item. For all the writers who have found a neat logic to the development of the music Elvis made, and have lost his genius in a process, that is not what I hear; I hear a whole world of music that by no means had to crystallize as it did. "I heard the news," Elvis would sing in "Good Rockin' Tonight"—but he was the news.

Elvis's Memphis records—"Milkcow Blues Boogie," "You're a Heartbreaker," "Good Rockin' Tonight," "Baby Let's Play House"—might be his best; a choice between the Sun sides and "Hound Dog," "Don't Be Cruel," "All Shook Up," "Reconsider Baby," "Suspicious Minds" and "Long Black Limousine" is not one I ever want to make. Elvis's first music deserves a close and loving attention not simply because it represents all that Elvis and those he has sung for have lost—youthful exuberance, innocence, haven't we tired of that story?—but because this is unquestionably great music, fun to think about, and because this music foreshadows, and contains, the entire aesthetic Elvis has worked out over the twenty years of his career. This is emotionally complex music that can return something new each time you listen to it. What I hear, most of the time, is the affection and respect Elvis felt for the limits and conventions of his family life, of his community, and ultimately of American life, captured in his country sides; and his refusal of those limits, of any limits, played out in his blues. This is a rhythm of acceptance and rebellion, lust and quietude, triviality and distinction. It can dramatize the rhythm of our own lives well enough.

---

rock it, rock it till the cows come home. Whip that box, Bill, whip it. Too sad, I mean too sad for the public. Now up the country, back down the country again on that old rock. Rappahanock. Tappahanock. Cross the river, boys, cross the river. Man, it's sporty. Play it, Bill, play it till the sergeant comes." No one could ask for a better statement than that.

ELVIS MOVES OUT

Elvis first went into Sam Phillips's studio in early 1954, and though it took him months of work to get to the point where he could make his first record, it is impossible to imagine a more natural sound. There's more here than anyone could have guessed, he seems to be saying: more soul, more guts, and more life.

"That's All Right" was one of three Arthur Crudup tunes Elvis recorded. Crudup had cut many sides for RCA's Bluebird outlet in the forties and early fifties; he wrote good songs, pointed little messages of loss fitted to bright blues melodies, but he was a minimal guitarist and an erratic singer, a bit one-dimensional. Only on numbers that verged on country or pop styles (as with his lovely "So Glad You're Mine," which Elvis recorded in a disinterested manner soon after reaching RCA) does Crudup seem to hit his stride.

Elvis reduces the bluesman's original to a footnote. He takes over the music, changing words and tightening verses to suit himself, hanging onto the ends of lines as Scotty Moore chimes in with pretty high-note riffs. Elvis sounds very young, sure of himself, ready to win; he turns Crudup's lament for a lost love into a satisfied declaration of independence, the personal statement of a boy claiming his manhood. His girl may have left him, but nothing she can do can dent the pleasure that radiates from his heart. It's the blues, but free of all worry, all sin; a simple joy with no price to pay.

Phillips put out the record on August 6, 1954, and it soon earned its place on the Memphis R&B charts, along with new hits by Muddy Waters and Johnny Ace. *Cashbox*, oblivious to Presley's color, reviewed the side as a blues; *Billboard*, prophetically, saw potential in all markets. It was an event, to some a scary one, but if "That's All Right" brought home the racial fears of a lot of people, it touched the secret dreams of others; if it was a threat, it was also another ride on the raft. "It was like a giant wedding ceremony," said Marion Keisker, Sam Phillips's working partner, and the one

who first heard in Elvis's voice everything Phillips was after.
"It was like two feuding clans who had been brought together by marriage."

"That's All Right" was a tremendous hit with teenagers, and in
Memphis, where the record broke first, the current greeting among
the teenagers is still a rhythmical line from the song: "Ta dee dah
dee dee dah."

The Memphis Press-Scimitar, 1954

You can't get that kind of success in *Billboard;* "Sun's
Newest Star," as the *Press-Scimitar* called Elvis, wasted no
time taking advantage of it. He tried out his material in the
local clubs, drew three thousand people to the opening of a
shopping center, and busted up a big country review when
he sang a song called "Good Rockin' Tonight." Phillips, for
his part, wasted no time getting Elvis back into the studio
and a new record into the stores.

"That's All Right" was an easy ride. "Good Rockin' " is
a cataclysm; it reflects the new confidence of a young man
who knows what it means to satisfy an audience, to take
them beyond their expectations. The record is charged with
an authority that no other country rocker ever approached.

Roy Brown, the most influential blues singer of the forties, wrote the tune, and Wynonie Harris made it a hit in
1949. Harris was a sophisticated uptown R&B vocalist; his
"Good Rockin' " is a conventional jump blues, lacking real
tension or drama. He seems unable to exploit the stomping
promise of the lyrics in rhythm or phrasing; he bumps words
into each other and sometimes trips on them. He's too removed from the country revel the song is all about, and too
cool.

Elvis opens with a high, wild "WELLLLLLLLL . . ."
and pulls fast and hard into the first verse before the echo of
his shout has had a chance to fade. His voice is raw, pleading and pushing, full of indescribably sexy asides, the
throaty nuances that would flare up into "All Shook Up" and
"Burning Love." Elvis slows for a second in the middle of a

line, drawling softly, over his shoulder, as if he can't quite bring himself to say out loud how good the party's going to be; and then suddenly he is out of breath, as if he's run for miles to tell his story, but there's good rockin' tonight and everybody *has* to know—how could they live if they miss it? Tonight his girl will get everything *she's* been missing. "We're gonna rock—ALL OUR BLUES AWAY!" He can't tell it fast enough, he can barely keep up with himself. Near to bursting, the song slams home.

"Milkcow Blues Boogie" came out in January 1955, with writer's credit on the label going to Kokomo Arnold, a Georgia-born blues singer who recorded "Milk Cow Blues" in Chicago in 1934. One always reads that Elvis re-created Arnold's song, though apparently no one has bothered to listen to both men—Elvis takes all of one verse from the bluesman. Presley's style might well owe something to Arnold; they share a fast, nervous delivery, full of unpredictable swoops and moans, a flair for crazy-quilt tempo changes of tremendous excitement, and the ability to come down with a great force on a key line. But "Milkcow" was a song held in common long before Elvis was born, recorded by more blues and country singers than anyone has bothered to count. What Elvis did, in fact, was to throw a bit of Arnold—who perhaps Phillips played for him—into Bob Wills' western swing hit, "Brain Cloudy Blues," which was cut in 1946. "Brain Cloudy," highlighted by Wills' fiddle and a tough guitar solo, featured the straight, insulated vocal of Tommy Duncan up against Wills' patented cornball asides, which worked very effectively to bleed the punch out of every line. Elvis started with Wills' second verse, dropping the "brain cloudy" motif; faded to Arnold; and then finished off with Wills' words, changing lyrics when Duncan's crisp, almost effete diction threw him off.

I go into the musicology of this song in some detail because of what it can tell us about how these first records came about. The book on Elvis's early music is that it was "spontaneous," "without any evident forethought," "unselfconscious." In other words, Elvis was the natural (and, the implicit assumption is, likely unthinking) expression of a folk culture. I've tried to present some hints of the culture Elvis came out of as a set of forces that could have held him back and worn him down as easily as they gave him life; to build a context that puts us in touch with will and desire, not just smug sociology. Researching his biography of Elvis, Jerry Hopkins dug back into the world Elvis left behind in Memphis, and he found that nearly every record Elvis made with Sam Phillips was carefully and laboriously constructed out of hits and misses, riffs and bits of phrasing held through dozens of bad takes. The songs grew slowly, over hours and hours, into a music that paradoxically sounded much fresher than all the poor tries that had come before; until Presley, Bill Black and Scotty Moore had the attack in their blood, and yes, didn't have to think about it. That's not exactly my idea of "spontaneity" or "unself-consciousness."

Elvis had the nuance of cool down pat—the pink pants-and-shirt outfit he wore to his audition, the carelessness of his swagger, or the sneer around the edges of his smile—because the will to create himself, to matter, was so intense and so clear. He strolled into the studio and didn't leave until every note was perfect. Even later at RCA, still on the way up and wavering between complete self-confidence and a lingering doubt, he would demand thirty takes on "Hound Dog," pleading for one more try long after everyone else was satisfied.

Try to wash the images of success from your mind and picture a twenty year old in a tacky studio on perhaps his fifteenth take of a song that is coming together out of fragments of memory, old 78's, and pure instinct. Everything was riding on each new release: whether Elvis could really take his career beyond the commonplace expectations of those around him; whether he could top that last record; whether he could find a sound that would give him room to breathe and yet hold the fans he had won and spread the word. The little success he had achieved was fragile; each new record risked it. He had to take that energy of desire and distance himself from it, throw it into the song so that it would be coherent and powerful *as* a song; so that when he sang, "Tonight she'll know I'm a mighty mighty man," it would sound like an obvious, thrilling statement of the facts. Whatever strain there might have been in his voice or his hopes—that unpleasant hint of the small time that you can hear so plainly in Bill Haley and so many of Elvis's imitators—it had to go. The talent was there, and it was extraordinary, but it was complex, and it needed a form. They were in the studio a long, tiresome time to catch the spirit of a boy who, on record, sounded as if he flew in, stopped long enough to blow the walls back, and exited through the unhinged back door with a grin.

With "Milkcow Blues Boogie" we are back to the image Cash chose as the essence of the soul of the back country South: hot heavy air bursting all over the sky in lightning and rain. No music of any kind captures it better than this record.

Wills and Arnold move right into the song; Elvis lingers over the first lines, and his voice drips an erotic tension that must have melted the mike. "Oh well, Ah woke up . . . this moanin'—An' Ah looked out . . . the doah—." He has you;

✳ EE #4. At a DJ convention early in 1973, I sit drinking with Bobby Vee and Brian Hyland, veterans of the Now-That-Elvis-Is-in-the-Army-We-Can-Cash-in-on-the-Vacuum-Era. I am interviewing Bob (he has changed his name back to Veline and is a folksinger now) in order to pen six thousand words of liner notes to a greatest hits package, an essay that will no doubt be the only extended critical discussion of his *oeuvre*. Bob tells me that, yes, for him it all began with Elvis—and suddenly the whole tone of the conversation is different. Professional cool drops away and we are shameless fans, awed by our subject. Vee and Hyland have met Elvis: he got drunk with Hyland (so Brian says) and was surly to Vee (I believe that). Well, they are outcasts in the rock 'n' roll world now, two very ordinary looking men; for all their triviality as rock singers, they once did their best to live up to Elvis and keep the faith. You can almost feel them gazing at Elvis as he is today, as if in his comeback they still see a glimmer of a future for themselves, just as they did when he started out years ago.

you're hungering for whatever comes next, but he cuts you off. "Hold it fellas!" he shouts. "That don't *move* me!" Soft and sultry again: "Let's get real . . . *real* gone, for a change." It's too perfect; you think he must be reading lines, as if this is a scene from one of his movies; and it is, I guess, even if at this point the dreams were only in his head.

Elvis charges the song, shooting that boundless *Welllllllllll* out ahead of himself, and the three of them are off. Elvis spurs the changes with his guitar, flying all over the story he is telling—his woman is gone and he wants her back but she's got about five minutes to make up her mind— singing with the crazy shifts from high to low that with Buddy Holly sounded funny and with Elvis sound frightening. In two and a half minutes he carries his listener through anger, loss, bemusement, melancholy, violence, defiance, fatalism, menace, delight, freedom, and regret. The song is as sure and tough a tale of breaking loose as any there is.

Yodeling, roaring his anger, yelling out to Scotty Moore—"Let's *milk* it!"—he comes off the guitar solo in a new mood, almost reflective now, meditating, this is all moving very fast but his guitar has somehow settled the music, and if his girl is gone, if that milkcow is never coming home, he still has time to step back and bring us into the song with a little blues philosophy:

> *Wellll, good evenin'*
> *Don' that sun look good goin' down*
> *Wee-eee-ell, good evenin'*
> *Don' that sun look good goin' down*
> *Well, dont that old moon look lonesome*
> *When your bay-ay-ayby's not around?*

And then rage pours back over his acceptance. He calls back his woman and faces her down, the song picking up momentum, his voice shimmering and shaking through night air:

> *Well I tried everything*
> *To git along with you*

Now I'm gonna tell you what I'm gonna do
I'm gonna quit my crying
I'm gonna leave you alone

and suddenly driving even harder, cursing with two of the most perfect lines in blues:

If you dont believe I'm leavin'
YOU CAN COUNT THE DAYS I'M GONE

Again, it is his authority that is so astounding. Scores of singers, black and white, have sung those lines, but few if any have ever made them seem so real, so *final*. The fatalism that is written right into the song, in that lovely image of the setting sun and the rising moon, will not do for Elvis, and he sings those last hard lines with an intensity that wipes out everything that has come before. A blues singer would use this verse as balance, to dramatize the rise and fall of his spirit, translating the circle the natural world draws around him into a metaphor for his inability to master his life. For Elvis, young and on his way, feeling his growing power over audiences, the growing space between himself and everything he should have taken for granted, there comes a point where he cannot settle for what others have made of this song, and the balance tips to fury. Our boy will get what he deserves; everyone else can get out of the way.

THE BOY WHO STOLE THE BLUES

I slicked myself up,
Till I looked like a guinea!
                CARL PERKINS, "Put Your Cat Clothes On"

For Carl Perkins and the rest of the rockabilly heroes, the liberation of the new music must have been a bit like a white foray into darktown, a combination of a blackface minstrel show and night riding—romantic as hell, a little dangerous, a little ridiculous. At the start, Elvis sounded black to

those who heard him; when they called him the Hillbilly
Cat, they meant the white Negro. Or as Elvis put it, years
later: ". . . made a record and when the record came out a
lot of people liked it and you could hear folks around town
saying, 'Is he, is he?' and I'm going, 'Am I, am I?' "

Well, I can't hear that anymore. I hear a young man,
white as the whale, who was special because in his best
music he was so much his *own* man, one who took the musical and emotional strengths of the blues as a natural and necessary part of the world he was building for himself—one
part of that world, no more, but clearly the finest stuff
around at the time.

True as it is in an historical or commercial sense, too
much has been made of Elvis as "a white man who sang
black music credibly," as a singer who made black music acceptable to whites. This and too many whites trying to do
the same thing have corrupted any sense of what Elvis did
do, of what was at stake in his personal culture. Most white
blues singing is singing at the blues; what comes out is either
entirely fake, or has behind it the white impulse to become
black: to ask for too much without offering anything in return.

Real white blues singers make something new out of the
blues, as Jimmie Rodgers, Dock Boggs, Elvis, and Bob
Dylan have; or, they sing out of a deep feeling for the blues,
but in a musical style that is not blues—not formally, anyway. But we can trace their strength to the blues; what links
their music to the blues is an absolute commitment to the
material, an expressive force open to some whites because
they have been attracted to another man's culture in a way
that could not be denied. This is the music of whites not so
much singing the blues as living up to them.

Van Morrison's "Listen to the Lion" would have to be
my best example, but Rod Stewart and Charlie Rich have
done their work here too, singing as if the fate of the whole
world rested on their ability to reach deeply enough into
their souls to get all the way into ours. I saw Rich do it not
so long ago, in a setting so anachronistic he came near to

leaving his audience behind him, because they were in a mood to be confirmed, not moved.

It was in August 1973, at a country music affair sponsored by Columbia Records, attended mostly by record industry heavies and hangers-on. Singer after singer took the stage, offering songs that made pain trivial and good times bland; music as sterile as it was predictable as it was (within a tight, well-regulated country market) commercially effective. The producers and song publishers and publicists sat near the stage, waiting for the singers to humble themselves before them, and as each did, I thought the humility might be worth a lot more if it were cynical than if it were real. It was that kind of day; I yearned for some rock 'n' roll arrogance, no matter how fake *that* might be.

Charlie Rich, who has always had too much of the blues in his style to fit easily into the country music market, was riding a number one country single that had, because it was more than country, crossed over into the upper reaches of the pop charts. He closed the show. Forty years old, a big man with white hair and lines deep in his face, he took his seat behind the piano and sang a harmless tune from his current album. After almost twenty years in the music business he had only three hits to show for it; even as "Behind Closed Doors" was climbing, the clerk in the record store marked up my Charlie Rich album under "nostalgia." A song Rich's wife Margaret Ann wrote about him, a haunting ballad of failure called "Life's Little Ups and Downs," tells the truth of Rich's career, but that day at the convention the crowd's truth was that Rich was on top and would stay there. Right as they may have been, I could not believe it was more than a public moment in an invisible career, and that made each song more precious and each missed chance that much more depressing.

Rich sang his hit, and it had grown for him. It meant more now than it had when it was just another throw of the dice, and it was a triumph. Because Rich was the star of the day, the men running the show gave him an encore. Staring into the keys, trying to balance the moment, Rich introduced his song. "I wrote this for Peter Guralnick," he said, "who wrote the book *Feel Like Going Home.*" Named for the most terrifyingly lonely of all Muddy Waters' songs, it is probably the most loving book ever written about American music; Charlie Rich is the subject of its finest chapter.

"Today," Rich said, "I would like to dedicate this song to the President of the United States." And so for Nixon, just then slipping over the line to the point where his whole existence would become a national joke, Rich sang,

> *I tried and I failed*
> *And I feel like going home.*

The words stayed in my mind throughout the strange, difficult song; they didn't change the president, or the country, or the world, but they changed how a few of us who were there to listen understood those things. They cut through everything I believe to uncover a compassion that I never, never wanted to feel.

We won't find Elvis here. The idea that the blues is a feeling and not a form can bring us closer to what Rich did that afternoon—but for Elvis, the blues was a style of freedom, something he couldn't get in his own home, full of roles to play and rules to break. In the beginning the blues was more than anything else a fantasy, an epic of struggle and pleasure, that he lived out as he sang. Not a fantasy that went beneath the surface of his life, but one that soared right over it.

Singing in the fifties, before blacks began to guard their culture with the jealousy it deserved, Elvis had no guilty dues to pay. Arthur Crudup complained his songs made a white man famous, and he had a right to complain, but mostly because he never got his royalties. Elvis sang "That's All Right" and "My Baby Left Me" (one of his first sides for RCA, and the only one in the Sun rockabilly style) with more power, verve, and skill than Crudup did; his early records were more than popular with blacks; but still the implication, always there when Crudup or Willie Mae

Thornton (who made the first version of "Hound Dog") looked out at the white world that gave them only obscurity in exchange for their music and penned them off from getting anything for themselves, is that Elvis would have been nothing without them, that he climbed to fame on their backs. It is probably time to say that this is nonsense; the mysteries of black and white in American music are just not that simple. Consider the tale of "Hound Dog."

Jerry Leiber and Mike Stoller were Jewish boys from the East Coast who fell in love with black music. Hustling in Los Angeles in the early fifties, they wrote "Hound Dog," and promoted the song to Johnny Otis, a ruling R&B bandleader who was actually a dark-skinned white man from Berkeley who many thought was black. Otis gave the song to Thornton, who made it a number one R&B hit in 1953; Otis also took part of the composer's credit, which Leiber and Stoller had to fight to get back. Elvis heard the record, changed the song completely, from the tempo to the words, and cut Thornton's version to shreds.

Whites wrote it; a white made it a hit. And yet there is no denying that "Hound Dog" is a "black" song, unthinkable outside the impulses of black music, and probably a rewrite of an old piece of juke joint fury that dated back far beyond the birth of any of these people. Can you pull justice out of *that* maze? What *does* Huck owe Jim, especially when Jim is really Huck in blackface and everyone smells loot? All you can say is this was Elvis's music because he made it his own.

Here's a better story. In 1955 the Robins (a black vocal group that had passed through seven labels with no real success) and Richard Berry (a black singer with two duds to his name) were brought together by Leiber and Stoller. Together they made the classic "Riot in Cell Block #9," which helped change the Robins into the Coasters and brought Berry his first notoriety. Leiber and Stoller went on to fame and fortune and the Coasters at least to fame; Berry, after losing out with "The Big Break," an outrageous follow-up to "Riot," made "Louie, Louie" in 1957, but though it was his biggest hit, it never made the pop charts.

In 1962 a white group called the Kingsmen unearthed "Louie, Louie," and their version hit number two in the country. Paul Revere and the Raiders, then a local Seattle band, rode the tune into a gold mine on the West Coast. As rock records, these discs were virtually definitive: hard rhythm, harder lead guitar, and a vocal that made no sense whatsoever. Within months every high school band in the country was playing "Louie, Louie," and every other person you met had a copy of the *real* lyrics, which were reputedly obscene. Some highlights I recall from locker room days: "Gonna make her again," "Gotta rag on," "Fuck that girl across the sea." (Not much, I admit, but those were thin years for rock 'n' roll.) Soon even Congressmen got into the act; they investigated the tune, duly played it (at 45, 33, 78, and 16 rpm), and charmingly pronounced the song "indecipherable at any speed." By this time, everyone but the man who owned the copyright—and likely he too—had forgotten all about Richard Berry, whose original lyrics would have been beside the point anyway.

Ten years later a white New York group called Stories released a single called "Brother Louie," and the record went to number one. "Louie, Louie, Loo-aye," went the chorus—familiar, to say the least. Obviously, the chorus was what caught your attention; it always had been. Since rock 'n' roll had been around long enough for its fans to develop a sense of history, a few people remembered Richard Berry. And what was this new "Louie, Louie" about? A black girl and her white boyfriend—Louie—and his mean racist parents. "Ain't no difference if you're black or white," Stories sang. "Brothers, you know what I mean." But this time, the "brother" was white; and finally the old song contained the racial contradictions that had sustained it.

If Elvis drew power from black culture, he was not exactly imitating blacks; when he told Sam Phillips he didn't sing like nobody, he told the truth. No white man had so deeply absorbed black music, and transformed it, since Jimmie Rodgers; instead of following Rodgers's musical style, as so many good white singers had—Lefty Frizzell, Ernest Tubb, Tommy Duncan, and, in his more personal way, Hank Williams, following that style until it simply wore out—Elvis followed Rodgers' musical strategy and began the story all over again.

Elvis didn't have to exile himself from his own community in order to justify and make real his use of an outsider's culture (like the Jewish jazzman Mezz Mezzrow, who would claim that his years on the streets of Harlem had actually darkened his skin and thickened his lips; like Johnny Otis and so many real white Negroes); as a Southerner and white trash to boot, Elvis was already outside. In 1955 he had at least as much in common with Bobby Bland as he did with Perry Como. Which is to say that Elvis was also hellbent on the mainstream, and sure enough of himself to ignore the irony that it would be his version of the backdoor freedoms of black music that would attract the mainstream to him, giving him the chance to exchange his hillbilly strangeness for acceptability.

Elvis's blues were a set of sexual adventures, and as a blues-singing swashbuckler, his style owed as much to Errol Flynn as it did to Arthur Crudup. It made sense to make movies out of it.

THE PINK CADILLAC

By the time "Baby, Let's Play House" came out in May 1955, the rockabilly singers were coming out of the swamps. Phillips was shifting his company from black to white, setting up an outbreak of rock 'n' roll that would follow hard on Presley's already discussed and taken-for-granted move up to a national label. Phillips had Malcolm Yelvington (a Memphis country singer endowed with false teeth and the best rockabilly name outside of Elvis's) cut the first of many country rock versions of Stick McGhee's 1949 R&B classic, "Drinkin' Wine Spo-Dee-O-Dee," and its message summed up the new mood: drinkin' and fightin' are what life is all about, and if anybody argues, give 'em a drink or lay 'em out.

Elvis had finished his early tours, ranging from Texas to Florida; he was set for San Francisco—alien territory, crucial to proving himself outside the South—and he was booked into the Cow Palace, the biggest arena in Northern California. The Colonel had made his initial connections. In Lubbock, Texas, a kid named Charles "Buddy" Holley bowed to the East every night and began getting a band together. There was, to put it mildly, excitement in the air.

Elvis's dive into "Baby, Let's Play House"—a wild crash of hiccups, gulps, and baby-baby-babys—measured perfectly the distance he had traveled since he broke into tears at the sight of his first record. There is a new spirit here, a lightness and a sense of fun, as if his whole little career has suddenly hit him as a wonderful joke. The dreams are coming true; that drive and secret ambition can afford to open up. He knows now that his mother was right, and he is safe. That throwaway superiority for which he has worked so hard can blossom out into arrogance, humor, and pure good times.

What was it his mother told him? That he was just as good as anybody? Or did she whisper, late at night when no one else was there to hear, that her boy could never lose?

Arthur Gunter, a black singer working for the Excello label in Nashville, wrote and recorded "Baby, Let's Play House," and got a hit with the black market in early 1955. He used a tight acoustic band and walked right through, vaguely interested in telling his girl that she might think she's hot stuff, but she'd better come on back and get down to it, or there'd be, you know, trouble. It was all very low-key (that splendid intro was all Elvis); Gunter's lack of concern was his charm. Still, he didn't sound very convincing.

Elvis wailed. He turned the song into a correspondence course in rock 'n' roll, and it was by far the most imitated of his first records. For pure excitement, he may never have matched it.

The rhythm was heavy, the syncopation astonishing—a fast, ominous bass tromping over a cottonmouth guitar—the band drove hard into every chorus and cut out for all the best lines. "Aw, let's play house," Elvis shouted, and Scotty punched out a few riffs; "HIT IT!" Elvis cried, and Moore and Black rammed home music so tough it wasn't touched until Elvis pushed them into the earthquake that was "Hound Dog."

Elvis made one crucial change in the lyrics. The girl he's after in this song is high-class stuff: she might go to college, he sings, she might go to school, but she'll never really get away, never be so sure of herself she can get along without the loving only he can give her. She might even get religion, Gunter had added, which won't help her either; but Elvis threw in a faster, flashier image that was more to his own point: "You may have a pink Cadillac/ But dontcha be nobody's fool!" Elvis had just bought one for himself.

Now, the obvious thing to say here is that the Pink Cadillac and All that it Implied proved Elvis's undoing: out there in mass culture America, Elvis would lose his talent in its reward. Dontcha be nobody's fool? The poor boy should have taken his own advice.

Well, we should be careful about this sort of thing. There is a deep need to believe that Elvis (or any part of American culture one cares about) began in a context of purity, unsullied by greed or ambition or vulgarity, somehow outside of and in opposition to American life as most of us know it and live it. Even RCA first presented Elvis as "a folksinger" (claiming, in the notes to his second album, that the simple-country-boy-with-guitar stance pictured on the cover was "most appropriate" for him). A writer as tough and sensitive as Stanley Booth can write (in a piece that seems to miss the point of its own title, "A Hound Dog, to the Manor Born"): "All that was really necessary was that [Elvis] stop doing his thing and start doing theirs. His thing was 'Mystery Train,' 'Milkcow Blues Boogie.' Theirs was 'Love Me Tender,' 'Loving You,' 'Jailhouse Rock,' 'King Creole.' " Charlie Gillett, author of *The Sound of the City*, as definitive a history of rock 'n' roll as we are likely to get, complains that Elvis sold out his true culture when he let RCA put *drums* on his records. It is virtually a critical canon that Elvis's folk purity, and therefore his talent, was ruined by (a) his transmogrification from naïve country boy into corrupt pop star (he sold his soul to Colonel Tom, or Parker just stole it), (b) Hollywood, (c) the army, (d) money and soft living, (e) all of the above.*

This approach may contain some figures, but not Elvis. "Milkcow Blues" was not "his thing"—it was one of many—so much as it was Sam Phillips'. Phillips loved money and he loved the blues, the basic pop combination; pairing a blues and a country tune on Elvis's first record gave him a successful commercial formula, and he stuck to it on every subsequent Presley release and on most of the records he cut by other rockabilly singers. But when Elvis left Memphis to confront a national audience as mysterious to him as he was to it, he had to define himself fully, and he did so by presenting his authentic multiplicity in music. I am, he announced, a house rocker, a boy steeped in mother-love, a true son of the church, a matinee idol who's only kidding, a man with too many rough edges for anyone ever to smooth away. Something in me yearns for a settling of affairs, he said with his pale music and his tired movies; on the other hand, he answered with his rock 'n' roll and an occasional blues, I may break away at any time. You never know. At RCA, where the commercial horizons were much broader than they were down at Sun, Elvis worked with far more "artistic freedom" than he ever did with Sam Phillips.

Two things did happen that led to the collapse of Elvis's music. His multiplicity opened up the possibility that he could be all things to all people, but his eagerness to prove it, with records like *Something for Everybody*, destroyed his abil-

---

*This Faustian scenario is an absolutely vital part of Elvis's legend, especially for all those who took part in Elvis's event and felt bewildered and betrayed by his stagnation and decline. We could hardly believe that a figure of such natural strength could dissolve into such a harmless nonentity; it had to be some kind of trick. Even a decade after the fact, Phil Spector was convinced that Colonel Parker hypnotized Elvis.

ity to focus his talent. He wound up without a commitment to any musical style; his music lost that dramatic shape Sam Phillips helped give it. And his ambition, the source of so much of the intensity and emotion he put into his early music, plainly outstripped itself. Two years after making his first record he had won more than anyone knew was there; he had achieved a status that trivialized struggle and made will obsolescent. His success turned his life upside down; from this point on, he would have in his hands what he set out to get, but he would have to reach for the energy and desire that had made his triumph possible.

The Pink Cadillac was at the heart of the contradiction that powered Elvis's early music; a perfect symbol of the glamor of his ambition and the resentments that drove it on. When he faced his girl in "Baby, Let's Play House" (like Dylan railing at the heroine of "Like a Rolling Stone," or Jagger surveying the upper-class women who star in "19th Nervous Breakdown," "Play With Fire," and "You Can't Always Get What You Want"), Elvis sang with contempt for a world that had always excluded him; he sang with a wish for its pleasures and status. Most of all he sang with delight at the power that fame and musical force gave him: power to escape the humiliating obscurity of the life he knew, and power to sneer at the classy world that was now ready to flatter him. Not the real upper class, of course; it would be years before socialites set out in pursuit of the Rolling Stones and academics began to fawn over the Beatles. Still, the jump Elvis made from the woods and welfare to simple respectability was far more epic. Girls who had turned up their noses in high school were now waiting in line, just as today men and women who are barely hanging on to the edge of the middle class wait in line to see a man who has achieved an eminence class can never bring.

Elvis sang out his song with a monumental disdain for all those folk who moved easily through a world that had never been easy for him (anyone who had ever shown the Presleys *exactly who they were*); he grinned at the big car he had dreamed about, because finally it was within reach, and he could take it, on his terms.

A bit farther into the image of the Pink Cadillac, something more interesting was going on. If Elvis was looking down on his smart girl's Caddy from the vantage point of his own, he was implicitly presenting his new successful self as a target for his own resentments, and singing with more than enough emotion to hit the bullseye. He was the Star; not asserting, in the conventional Uriah Heep country style, that all his wealth don't buy him happiness (it does, it does), but burlesquing and damning the complacency of the rich and powerful by flaunting *his* power and riches, and getting away with it. Somehow taking both sides, Elvis could show his listeners just how much, and how little, that Pink Cadillac was worth: more and less than anyone would have guessed.*

This is a kind of rock 'n' roll drive—the vitality that endows the artifacts of materialism with life—that is captured perfectly in *The Harder They Come*, a movie about the Jamaican version of the American pop dream, when Jimmy Cliff steals a white Cadillac and spins it over a golf course with an unbeatable smile on his face. He's a refugee from the most terrifying poverty, a reggae-singing people's outlaw with reflexes instead of politics. "You can get it if you really want," he sings. "The harder they come, the harder they fall, one and all." He wants that car and the whole world it stands for; he doesn't want it, he wants to smash it all up. He hasn't made the connections; he hasn't worked it all out any

---

* In America, after all, the final proof of grace is *economic* sanctification; which is to say, Elvis can have the piety of the poor along with the ease of the rich and know that since he never lost the first, he deserves the last. Still full of the energy of his comeback in early 1969, Elvis went back to Memphis and sang a song called "Long Black Limousine"—the tale of a hometown girl punished for her sins and her fancy city ways, mourned and damned by the poor country boy who has waited all these years for a better ending than the car crash that did his sweetheart in. The tension as the song opens is almost unbearable, and Elvis never lets go of the song. He is completely convincing. And yet of course he is the country boy captured by the city if there ever was one; he's that girl, riding in her long black limousine on her way to the graveyard, as surely as he is King Elvis, speeding away from the studio in his own black limousine. When he smashes through the contradictions of his career with such music, we have Elvis at his greatest.

more than a twenty-year-old Elvis did. But he knows that car belongs to him because he can take more pleasure from it than anyone else.

What is most remarkable is that Elvis was able to laugh at the persona he drew from "Baby, Let's Play House" as convincingly as he acted it out—as if a combination of the freedom to realize his desires and a freedom to ignore them was what freedom really meant. He was less into the music than on top of it, feigning toughness, feigning anger, finding it, for the famous lines

> *I'd rather see you dead little girl*
> *Than to be with another man*

and then all fun again, as if the venom he'd put into those words struck him at once as ludicrous, and maybe a little frightening. He put even more of himself into the song, and still parodied his menace, lowering his voice to a rumble, getting out of the tune with a chuckle that gave it all away: deep down he was just a good boy, out for a real good time.

Put it together and you may have the quintessential performance of Elvis's career: an overwhelming outburst of real emotion and power, combined with a fine refusal to take himself with any seriousness at all. Finding that power within himself, and making it real, was part of the liberation he was working out in this music; standing off from that power, with a broad sense of humor and amusement, was another.

This was the saving grace of Elvis's ambition, and a necessary counter to it. It allowed him to transcend his success and his public image just as his ambition allowed him to achieve and enjoy his success; that casual élan would let him see at least part of the way through the unprecedented adulation he received, just as his ambition would ultimately make it impossible for him to be satisfied with anything less. And if that lack of seriousness today distances Elvis not only from the absurdity of his reward but from his talent too, gives us a throwaway and a man virtually unable to take anything seriously, this side of Elvis has also brought a marvelous warmth to his best music, no matter if it's in the records he made back in Memphis, or the show he's sure to be putting on tonight.

ELVIS AT HOME: THE COUNTRY SIDES

Elvis's blues are music of drama, humor, and risk; the country tunes are very different. At their most vital, they capture the kind of beauty and peace of mind that can be found only within limits, when a lot has been given up, and you know exactly how far you can go.

Elvis gives us respect—for the musical form, for the established country music audience these songs were aimed at, for his mother, who was sure to be listening to *this* music—in place of resentment and personal authority. The music flows with the kind of grace the Allman Brothers found in their incandescent "Blue Sky": a sense of value that seems to come not from a feel for the open possibilities of life, but from a pretty deep understanding of its fragility.

There is a modesty of spirit. In this world you will hope for what you deserve, but not demand it; you may celebrate your life, but not with the kind of liberation that might threaten the life of someone else. The public impulse of the music is not to break things open, but to confirm what is already there, to add to its reality and its value.

This is the kind of freedom D. H. Lawrence had in mind when he wrote about America in an essay called "The Spirit of Place."

Men are free when they are in a living homeland, not when they are straying and breaking away. Men are free when they are obeying some deep, inward voice of religious belief. Obeying from within. Men are free when they belong to a living, organic, *believing* community, active in fulfilling some unfulfilled, perhaps unrealized purpose. Not when they are escaping to some wild west. The most unfree souls go west, and shout of freedom. Men are freest when they are most unconscious of freedom. The shout is a rattling of chains, always was.

Men are not free when they are doing just what they like. The moment you can do just what you like, there is nothing you care about doing.*

So speaks the stern English father to his rowdy American children; it's not a message America has ever had much time for. We much prefer Elvis's shout of freedom, sure that what chains there are in our world must be applied by other men. Something close to Lawrence's idea, though, that sense of staying at home in a place where one belongs, is part of what Elvis has always offered America—on the flipside, as it were.

Elvis's country sides, like his later gospel records for RCA, reveal how deeply he felt a pull at odds with the explosions of his new rock 'n' roll and the frenzy of his first stage shows. They let us in on the secret that his little drama of breaking loose could take on the extremes that gave it power because he knew he had a home to which he could always return; even as he set out to win his independence, he prepared his accommodation. The America that Elvis brings to life in this music grew out of his willingness to accept the limits of a community, and his desire for the pleasures of familiarity. It's a place of gentleness, and restraint.

In the least of this music, though—"I Forgot to Remember to Forget," "I Don't Care If the Sun Don't Shine," "Just Because," "I Love You Because," "I'll Never Let You Go (Little Darlin')"—it is the sound of a young man confined by his community that is most striking. Elvis is faceless, indistinguishable from a hundred others; he sounds less like a man who has been defeated than like one who has never wondered what it might mean to try to win. There's no real warmth in the music, only an imitation of it; if on the blues sides he took on the originals and outclassed them, here he defers. The emotional tone seems contrived, almost secondhand; this is the music of someone doing what he has always been told to do.

"I Don't Care If the Sun Don't Shine" has energy, but

* From *Studies in Classic American Literature* (New York: Viking, 1964).

not soul; "Just Because" has a little bounce, but no passion.
"I Love You Because" (actually the very first song Elvis recorded professionally) is truly painful to hear; he's so polite
to the material he can't even sing it. There is certainly nothing that could give that "believing community" any strength.

Here Elvis embodies exactly that world his blues fantasy
let him escape. If murder—the face of Charley Starkweather
imposed on Elvis's, the edge of sadism in Presley's music that
made one producer tag him as just right for *In Cold Blood*—
was the dark side of rockabilly flash and the flight from limits, then a death of possibility and a stupefying ordinariness
was the dark side of this music, the first version of Elvis's
empty Yes.

You can't have a community that grows and renews all
who are a part of it without the tension that comes from the
need to break away, without the resentment produced by the
tendency of any community to grow in on itself and shut out
the rest of the world. Tom Sawyer's fooling around won't
give us that tension; you need Huck's nerve and his suffering, perhaps an edge of Ahab's obsessions, and, in America,
you probably need Nigger Jim too.

Elvis was a rebel in the music that made him famous.
But he knew, and has always told anyone willing to listen,
how hard it is to break away, and how much you have to
give up to make it—more than he has been willing to part
with. So Elvis lives out his story by contradicting himself,
and we join in when we take sides, or when we respond to
the tension that contradiction creates. The liveliness of that
tension is as evident in the best of Elvis's country sides as it
is in his blues.

When Elvis sings Bill Monroe's "Blue Moon of Kentucky" as if he's going to jump right over it, he isn't, as has
always been said, singing the blues on a country song, any
more than he was really singing hillbilly on a blues with
"That's All Right." What Elvis is doing is both more complex and more coherent.

When I listened to an early take of "Blue Moon of Kentucky" (on a rockabilly bootleg that includes studio dialogue

as well as music *), I heard Elvis lost in the song, touching each line gently, playfully, bringing every word to life. The singing is rough, even though Elvis is clearly a long way past the first tries; Scotty Moore has trouble following the vocal. Scotty drops back, and then there is just Elvis, drawing out an unbelievably sensual portrait of his Southern landscape.

It sounds so primitive to me; music out of the Mississippi woods, a hundred years gone. Sam Phillips hears something else.

PHILLIPS: Fine, *fine*, man, hell, that's different! That's a *pop song* now, little guy! That's good!

SCOTTY MOORE: Too much vaseline!

Elvis laughs, nervously, proudly.

MOORE: I had it too!

ELVIS: Y'ain't just a-*woofin'*!

MOORE (imitating an eye-rolling black falsetto): Please, *please*, please—

ELVIS: What?

MOORE: *Damn*, nigger!

By the time Elvis reached the fast, confident version that appeared on the flip of his first record, most of the primitive feeling had disappeared, but not the vaseline; Elvis was celebrating a classic piece of white country music, but more than that he was celebrating himself. He was keeping the old song alive by bringing something new to it, putting some life back into his community by telling an old story in a way that no one had heard before—and he was reaching beyond his community, with the "pop song" Sam Phillips knew he had to make.

There is a delight in adventure and novelty here that we can't touch with pure musicology: Elvis's affection for a song he's heard for years, combined with the exuberance and satisfaction of a kid who's worked for months to make a record, and who is now actually pulling it off. And there are the new rhythms of "That's All Right," cut a few nights before—not

* *Good Rocking Tonight;* see Discography for details.

"blues" now, but Elvis's music, Scotty Moore's music—Southern energy that blacks had trapped and put into the air where anyone could get it.

✳ EE #5. I know a woman, black and about sixty, who loves old country blues. The albums I have given her are mostly unplayed, though, because she lives with her mother, a devout woman in her eighties, who forbids her to play them. The mother, who is blind, spends much of her time listening to the TV set, and once I found her attending to a kind of blues she apparently considered innocuous enough to tolerate: Elvis's film *G.I. Blues*.

I didn't know what to make of that. It seemed to represent a double dead end of American cross-culture, but there was something I liked about it. Partly, it was the movie itself. Elvis, as usual, plays a good-natured stud who breaks into song about every ten minutes and makes all the women snap their fingers (though curiously, none of them can keep time). The Sergeant Bilko-reject plot has to do with El's attempt to raise a stake for the nightclub he and his two army accompanists want to open when they get back in mufti. It comes down to rival platoons placing bets on which can field a man to seduce Juliet Prowse, the biggest glacier in Germany. Elvis, naturally . . .

He walks through the flick with the same air of What-Am-I-Doing-Here bemusement he employs in most of his other movies. When he strums his acoustic guitar, an electric solo comes out. When bass and guitar back him, you hear horns and electric piano. When he sings, the soundtrack is at least half a verse out of sync. These films are the throwaways of a man—perhaps I ought to say an industry—who doesn't even need to title his product as long as he can put his name on it, much like Elvis's post-comeback albums (randomly constructed out of leftover recordings, unmixed live tapes, plastered with shoddy composite promo photos and ads for old LP's), all of which seem to be called simply "E L V I S," in fact. The movies are so tacky no one else could possibly get away with them—and still make money.

Someday, French film critics will discover these pictures and hail them as a unique example of *cinema discrepant;* there will be retrospectives at the *Cinemateque*, and five years after that Harvard students will cultivate a lopsided grin and Elvis movies will be shown on U.S. educational TV, complete with learned commentary deferring to the French discovery and bemoaning America's inability to appreciate its own culture. Elvis will be touring the People's Republic of China and during an audience with Chairman Mao will be drawn into a discussion of the conflicting aesthetics of "Milkcow Blues Boogie" and "No Room to Rhumba in a Sportscar." The Chairman, being a staunch advocate of "The Folk," will cite James Agee's famous essay on the corruption of folk art by the nature of reality;

Elvis could not have sung "Blue Moon of Kentucky" as he did without the discoveries of "That's All Right"—but what he discovered was not his ability to imitate a black blues singer, but the nerve to cross the borders he had been raised to respect. Once that was done, musically those borders dissolved as if they had never existed—for Elvis. He moved back and forth in a phrase. But Scotty Moore might well have been speaking for the audience waiting outside the studio when he called Elvis a nigger—for many, it was the *fact* of a white boy singing a black man's song without clothing it in fiddles and steel guitar that they heard, not the strange ambiguities of the music. Perhaps if Phillips had put out the "country" side without the "blues," it would have warmed the community; the combination thrilled some and threatened others. There were country stations that refused to play any Elvis records, no matter how white they seemed to be. He was too complicated, this Presley boy; you couldn't tell what he might be slipping over, could you?

Yet "You're a Heartbreaker," another country side, is a

Elvis will reply that while he has never read the piece, he once saw some pictures from *Let Us Now Praise Famous Men* in a copy of *Life* he picked up on an airplane, and thought they were all right. "My 'folk' can be summed up very easily," he will tell Mao with a knowing smile. " 'The short and simple annals of the poor.' "

All right, then—where does all this fit in with an old woman hardening her heart against Skip James and passing her time with Elvis? Only in that at its blandest, the American mainstream has no limits at all; even Mao could get his hand caught in this tar-baby. It contains everyone from moment to moment, covering over and melting down and seducing the best along with the worst, until the toughest, wisest pessimist is defeated by his secret yearning for a happy ending and the cheap tears it brings to his eyes. And that mainstream—which could turn "Bartleby" into a musical as easily as it allowed Elvis to turn himself into *Tickle Me*—provides such a perfect antithesis to the realities of American life that inevitable discrepancies come out of the woodwork, come with enormous force—a surprise, again—and with them come the resentment and the humor that keep the soul of the place hanging onto life.

Big words? Heavy stakes? Too much to drop on a vitiated country boy and an old lady who in all probability was just too bored to change the channel? Well, if that's not America, I'll never recognize it.

masterpiece of reassurance. It is one of the most affecting records Elvis ever made; it gives us a young man who takes comfort, and pleasure, from a sure sense of all that he has to fall back on when something goes wrong: his self-respect (the rounded edge of the new superiority of the blues-boy); the steady, ongoing patterns of life that never range too far in one direction or the other. If the impulses of community were at odds with the extremes of Southern life, here Elvis captures the soul of the one just as he acted out the other side. It is a tribute to his range and his honesty that he can do this without making one feel he is offering less than the whole story.

How would you act if you lived in a community that *did* enclose extremes without making life banal and dull? You might act as Elvis sounds on this song, with a delicate grace and a modest affection. Flip the record over to "Milkcow Blues Boogie," and the same story—Elvis's girl has left him—is a matter of life and death. And yet, despite the apparent lack of struggle, of intensity, a certain truth is being told here; a balance is being worked out; and the song is satisfying, leaving any listener richer than before.

With "Trying to Get to You," the boy who always seemed bent on escape in the blues now has his eyes turned toward home. I got your letter and I came a-runnin' is the plot—"I've been traveling over mountains," Elvis sings, and you believe him. The passion is there (also humility—Elvis remembers to thank the Lord for helping him along), but what is interesting is how controlled the feeling is. This is an elegant record. The arrangement is very professional, very strict; Elvis sings beautifully, but he submits to the music. He never really takes it over. Some emotions, he might be saying, are authentic only when they are restrained—just as some emotions are authentic only when they are utterly free.

"I'm Left, You're Right, She's Gone" is cut from the same mold. It brings together a superb vocal, an unforgettably clean guitar solo, and a good rhythm—no rave-up, but just over the line into rock 'n' roll. There is a happy ending— Elvis finds a new girl—and maybe that's the real clue to these sides. Everything works out, in the lyrics, in the music (even the guitar parts are neatly resolved, while those in the blues tempt chaos), in the commercial and cultural context the singer can take as close to a given. What is missing is the suspense of a man creating himself, by the pure force of his will and desire, that one can hear in Elvis's blues.

There is an alternate version of "I'm Left," usually called "My Baby Is Gone," that shows how naturally Elvis's flair for this kind of material evolved into his later—and present-day—ballad style. All the mannerisms are there.* The performance is stunning: every line is measured out as if it costs the singer his soul to confess his loss. Elvis drops down so low on the scale he can barely get the words out; he blows up the subtleties of his phrasing into shameless melodrama, and it works. The song tells us what Elvis was after and where he was going as well as anything. The tune was written as a conventional country tear-jerker, but in this version Elvis stepped gently away from his community even as he gave that community something it could accept: a Hollywood movie, a Valentino love scene complete with heavy breathing. "Blue Moon" takes this blending of cultures even farther; it's more like "pre-Elvis" pop music than any of these sides, and queerer, too. "Blue Moon" comes with clippity-clop hoofbeats worthy of Gene Autry, and with a bit of Elvis's acoustic guitar; he sings like a swamp-spirit, making his way through the fog to that lamp post Frank Sinatra used to cart out for all his album covers. Whining and wailing between the lyrics—which, as Elvis sings them, sound quite surreal—he turns this old standard into a combination of a supper club ballad and an Appalachian moan.

This music is good enough, committed enough, to make you almost forget Elvis's Wild West. He played both ends against the middle; in the good moments, he escaped the deadening artistic compromise the middle demands. This

---

* The mannerisms of his great ballads, like "I Was the One," "Is It So Strange," "Don't," "Fame and Fortune," "Anyway You Want Me," "If I Can Dream," or "Suspicious Minds," and the awful ones, like "Tonight's Alright For Love," "Fool," "It's Impossible," and a couple of hundred others.

seems to have worked because both sides of his character, at this point in his career, were pulling so hard.

Jerry Lee Lewis, second in the hierarchy of white Southern rockers, had talent and drive that stopped just short of Presley's, but he gained only a fraction of Presley's success, perhaps because he lacked the broad scope of Elvis's ambition and Elvis's sure sense of where he meant to go—not to mention Elvis's understanding of how to act once he got there. If Elvis had a bit of grace to him, Jerry Lee seemed possessed; and Jerry Lee, far more than Elvis, came to represent all the mythical strangeness of the redneck South: lynch-mob blood lust, populist frenzies, even incest. When Jerry Lee made it onto national TV, Steve Allen didn't bother squeezing him into white tie or chaining him to the floor: in a

---

✳ EE #6. One night in 1973 we went out to catch El's latest movie; the theater was almost empty. There were a few couples in their late twenties, an elderly pair who left almost immediately, an old black man sitting alone, maybe just looking for a roof in the rain. The film was *Elvis on Tour*, a documentary of his post-comeback apotheosis—with gestures toward History.

There are kinescopes of the first triumph: Elvis rocking out on the Ed Sullivan Show with "Ready Teddy." The performance is astounding, otherworldly, and it is hard to believe anyone now living was really around to see such a sight (though, of course, *we* were). "That's All Right" plays under a shot of a train running on down the line, as Elvis talks about his childhood. "Never saw a git-tar player was worth a damn," he remembers his Daddy telling him. "I was born about ten thousand years ago," Elvis sings in one of his recent songs, and that seems to say it all, to sum up the jumbled sense of time that governs the movie, and us; the beginning of it all seems at least that distant, and brings home just how long Elvis and we have been caught up with each other.

Somewhere near the end of the flick is a wonderful sequence of Elvis-movie kisses, a perfect critical attack on the aggressive meaninglessness of the movie years: like dominoes, one starlet after another falls into Elvis-arms. Ah, Elvis says to us here, this is what I *became*, but this is not the *real me*. Well, what is? That pudgy flyer up on the screen, filmed live in concert after concert, mechanically grinding out the same songs and choreographed karate chops (the seventies equivalent of swiveling hips?) as if his life were a tape loop? The kiss sequence is meant to parody the past, but it only parallels the present.

vain attempt to parody the excess that made Jerry Lee Lewis great, tables and chairs were thrown across the stage while Jerry Lee pounded out "Whole Lotta Shakin'." Elvis's early music has drama because as he sang he was escaping limits, testing them, working out their value; unlike Jerry Lee, he at least knew the limits were there. With Southern power in his music, Elvis had mainstream savvy in his soul.

The problem was that the shallowness of the poorest of the music that captured Elvis's restraint, and the inoffensiveness of the best of it, opened up the I-Walked-Like-a-Zombie saga that Elvis would act out in the long years before his comeback in 1968—a saga that, in a much more extravagant way, he acts out today.

Elvis was very comfortable with his country music, and with the romantic ballads that were its mainstream equivalent; so were his first teenage fans. This was mother's milk; the responses the music elicited were virtually automatic. Elvis's ability to sing this music and to like it—to put it across without lying to himself or to anyone else—would never have brought him fame nor burst any limits. But that ability was crucial to his power to hold onto his success, and to keep at least that part of his original audience (and to attract so many more) who didn't grow with the musical culture Elvis founded: those who, all through the sixties, lived in an America that was ignored or damned by the Rolling Stones and the counterculture; those who put the endless movies into the black; who made the soundtrack to *Blue Hawaii* the best-selling Elvis album of all (over 5 million copies at last count); those who bought reassurance tinged with a memory of excitement and independence. When all this proved too dull and predictable even for Elvis—when he came roaring out in the explosion of vitality and commitment that was his comeback (returning, then, as a King of Rock 'n' Roll who was also a definitive Middle American)—there were plenty from every sort of white rock 'n' roll audience who were glad to leave whatever they had made of the sixties behind and join him in his pageant. Elvis's accommodations, all larger than life, and brilliantly orchestrated on stage to preserve the thrills that were once discovered in his blues, make a very glamorous home for our own retreats.

The country sides, the later music that derived from them, the shining acceptance of the great stage show, give us the contradictions that have kept pace with rock 'n' roll from the beginning (contradictions that are, of course, much bigger than the music): the desire of the rebel to conform; the wish for quiet despite allegiance to an ideology of noise; the need for rest after excitement; the retreat that replaces ambition, be that ambition personal, cultural, or political. But this aesthetic—of rest, of quiet, of retreat—so convincing in those first country records, grows easily into a riskless aesthetic of smooth-it-away. This is really the last word of our mainstream; its last, most seductive trap: the illusion that the American dream has fulfilled itself, that utopia is complete in an America that replaces emotion with sentiment and novelty with expectation. Elvis contained this aesthetic within himself—Tocqueville's bad dream, the aesthetics of playing it safe. When he is ready to play it safe, that aesthetic contains him, just as it usually contains most of us. Breaking loose and starting over cost more every time, and in the America that Elvis has come to symbolize so powerfully, in an America that only wants to applaud, to say Yes and mean it, the risks are hard to find.

MYSTERY TRAIN

It was the last record Elvis made at Sun; to me, it tells the best tale of all.

Junior Parker and Sam Phillips wrote "Mystery Train" together in 1953; the original, a slow, dark blues released under the name of Little Junior's Blue Flames, was exquisite. An odd, chopping beat carried the threat of the title; a sax brought out the inevitable train sound with an unusually ominous flair. And Parker sang halfway from the grave, chasing his lover through the gloom, giving just the slightest suggestion that she had been kidnapped by a ghost. There was a feeling of being in the wrong place at the wrong time, a hint of a curse.

This was the blues realism of Robert Johnson: one of those tunes that says, this is the way the world is, and there's nothing you or anyone can do about it.

> *Train I riiide,*
> *Sixteen*
> *Coaches long*
> *Train I riiide,*
> *Sixteen*
> *Coaches long*
> *Well, that long black train*
> *Carry my baby and gone*

They may ride the same train—somehow, it runs away from itself.

To understand the strangeness of those lines, we have to go back to the place where Parker and Phillips found them: back to the Carter Family's "Worried Man Blues" of some twenty years before. It was a folk song, passed back and forth between the races, that in truth was older than anyone's memory.

"Worried Man" is the story of a man who lays down to sleep by a river and wakes up in chains. The Carters don't tell you if the man is black or white; if he killed someone, stole a horse, or did anything at all, and the man doesn't know either. You would have to go a long way to match that as an image of the devil in the dream, or as the plain symbol of a land whose profound optimism insures that disaster must be incomprehensible.

There is no protest in the song, no revolt, only an absolute, almost supernatural loneliness: a bewilderment that is all the more terrifying because it is so self-effacing and matter-of-fact. The emotion is there in the steady roll of the beat, in the resignation of Mother Maybelle's guitar, and in A. P. Carter's squeaky, toneless singing: the sound of a man who has told his story more times than he can remember, and who hopes that one more telling will finally let him rest. He rides a train to nowhere.

> *The train I ride is sixteen coaches long*
> *The train I ride is sixteen coaches long*
> *The girl I love is on that train and gone* *

Like the rest of the song, it makes no sense; it simply defines the singer's world, and there is no way out, save for the death the man promises will someday save him from his song.

Even without these details—the mystery behind their train song—and even with a tacked-on happy ending that gives the singer back his girl, Parker and Phillips recreated this mood, or submitted to it. So, when Parker sings that his baby will come home, that the train will surely bring her back, you don't really believe him. He sounds as if he has already lost more than anyone can return.

The Carter Family was completely real to Elvis; the white gospel culture they represented was implicitly *his* in a way that no other culture, be it Hollywood or the blues, could ever quite be. This was his inheritance and his birthright; the blues and the movies were something he made real for himself. On the earlier Sun records, Elvis had left home with the blues and come back on the flipside; "Mystery Train" gave him a blues that was rooted in his own community, and the context was not so open.

✳ EE #7. I had a dream one night, 4/25/73. In the dream, I am looking into a carny peep-show machine, wherein tiny shots of Elvis, Scotty Moore, and Bill Black, circa 1954, flicker in and out of view. Naked, they are rehearsing their live act, kicking their legs in tandem like the Rockettes. Slowly, the camera moves in on Elvis's penis. It is an accurate dream: I look to see if Elvis is circumcised, and of course he is not. In close-up his member fills the screen. A message has been carved on his penis in block letters. "ELVIS LIVE AT THE INTERNATIONAL HOTEL LAS VEGAS," it reads.

There was the purely musical side; most of the material
Elvis had used at Sun was weak or undeveloped in its original form, giving him plenty of freedom to exploit possibilities
others had missed. With "Mystery Train," both originals
were brilliant. They took the train as far as it could go—in
one direction—and the hard meaning Junior Parker and the
Carter Family gave to the song was also part of Elvis's inheritance. If that meaning was forcefully obscure, that uncertainty was the song's point: the uselessness of action, the
helplessness of a man who cannot understand his world, let
alone master it. The singer was to enter this world, suffer it,
make that world real, and thus redeem it. Elvis had his job
cut out for him if he was to make the song his own.

One more time, he found an opening and made it
through. His attack on "Mystery Train" is as strong as Sly
Stone's transformation of "Que Sera, Sera" from a little
hymn to the benevolence of fate into a massive ode to dread.
If the two performances go in different directions, maybe
that tells us how far we have come; tells us that rock 'n' roll
had to begin with an honest refusal of doubt and fatalism,
and grow, along with its audience, to the point where it
would have to absorb such things to survive.

Inspired by the feeling of going up against the old meaning of the tune, or determined to beat out Junior Parker, the
black man, or simply thrilled by the music, Elvis sings this
song with shock: he rebels against it. There is so much fire in
his singing, so much personality and soul, that he changes
the meaning of the song without smoothing it over. There is
a tremendous violence to the record: "Train I ride," Elvis
sings, but he sounds as if he's going to run it down. "It took
my baby," Parker had moaned (riding us back to the days
when a black locomotive was the symbol of a force no one
could resist, of fate on wheels), "It's gone do it again."
"Well," Elvis declares, "it took my baby—BUT IT NEVER
WILL AGAIN—no, not again." His rhythm guitar seizes
the music, forcing the changes; Scotty Moore, as he always
did, lives up to Elvis's passion. Moore gives us one hard solo,
which seems to hang the song between what it has always

been and what Elvis is making of it, and then Elvis is back, and he turns the train around. As he speeds off into the night with the girl he has stolen off that mystery train, he cuts loose one more time. "Woo, woo—WOOOO!" he shouts, full of delight; he laughs out loud; and he's gone.

Elvis escaped the guilt of the blues—the guilt that is at the heart of the world the blues and country music give us— because he was able to replace the sense that men and women were trapped by fate and by their sins with a complex of emotions that was equally strong and distinctive. As he sang, Elvis changed the personae his songs originally offered his listeners. When the persona was one of anger, or delight, he outdistanced it. He didn't have to tell us that the blues is about displacement, about not being at home, about a brooding fear the music was meant to ease, but not resist. And if at its deepest the blues is hellfire music, worth the trouble of the black preachers who have damned it, that Elvis escaped this truth and still made his music ring true was precisely his genius.

FINALE

These days, Elvis is always singing. In his stage-show documentary, *Elvis on Tour*, we see him singing to himself, in limousines, backstage, running, walking, standing still, as his servant fits his cape to his shoulders, as he waits for his cue. He sings gospel music, mostly; in his private musical world, there is no distance at all from his deepest roots. Just as that personal culture of the Sun records was long ago blown up into something too big for Elvis to keep as his own, so the shared culture of country religion is now his private space within the greater America of which he has become a part.

And on stage? Well, there are those moments when Elvis Presley breaks through the public world he has made for himself, and only a fool or a liar would deny their power. Something entirely his, driven by two decades of history and myth, all live-in-person, is transformed into an energy that is ecstatic—that is, to use the word in its old sense, illuminating. The overstated grandeur is suddenly authentic, and Elvis brings a thrill different from and far beyond anything else in our culture; like an old Phil Spector record, he matches, for an instant, the bigness, the intensity, and the unpredictability of America itself.

It might be that time when he sings "How Great Thou Art" with all the faith of a backwoods Jonathan Edwards; it might be at the very end of the night, when he closes his show with "Can't Help Falling in Love," and his song takes on a glow that might make you feel his capacity for affection is all but superhuman. Whatever it is, it will be music that excludes no one, and still passes on something valuable to everyone who is there. It is as if the America that Elvis throws away for most of his performance can be given life again at will.

At his best Elvis not only embodies but personalizes so much of what is good about this place: a delight in sex that is sometimes simple, sometimes complex, but always open; a love of roots and a respect for the past; a rejection of the past and a demand for novelty; the kind of racial harmony that for Elvis, a white man, means a profound affinity with the most subtle nuances of black culture combined with an equally profound understanding of his own whiteness; a burning desire to get rich, and to have fun; a natural affection for big cars, flashy clothes, for the symbols of status that give pleasure both as symbols, and on their own terms. Elvis has long since become one of those symbols himself.

Elvis has survived the contradictions of his career, perhaps because there is so much room and so much mystery in Herman Melville's most telling comment on this country: "The Declaration of Independence makes a difference." Elvis takes his strength from the liberating arrogance, pride, and the claim to be unique that grow out of a rich and commonplace understanding of what "democracy" and "equality" are all about: No man is better than I am. He takes his strength as well from the humility, the piety, and the open, self-effacing good humor that spring from the same source: I am better than no man. And so Elvis Presley's career defines success in a democracy that can perhaps recognize itself best in its popular culture: no limits, success so grand and complete it is nearly impossible for him to perceive anything more worth striving for. But there is a horror to this utopia— and one might think that the great moments Elvis still finds are his refusal of all that he can have without struggling. Elvis proves then that the myth of supremacy for which his audience will settle cannot contain him; he is, these moments show, far greater than that.

So perhaps that old rhythm of the Sun records does play itself out, even now. Along with Robert Johnson, Elvis is the grandest figure in the story I have tried to tell, because he has gone to the greatest extremes: he has given us an America that is dead, and an unmatched version of an America that is full of life.

All in all, there is only one remaining moment I want to see; one epiphany that would somehow bring his story home. Elvis would take the stage, as he always has; the roar of the audience would surround him, as it always will. After a time, he would begin a song by Bob Dylan. Singing slowly, Elvis would give it everything he has. "I must have been mad," he would cry, "I didn't know what I had—Until I threw it all away."

And then, with love in his heart, he would laugh.

EPILOGUE

ITINERANT SINGER REVEALS NAME ON TAIL OF SHIRT
'Disgusting,' Witnesses Claim

REPORT HUGE STONES BLOCK ALL ROADS

MAN WITH BLACK WHIP SEEN AGAIN IN CEMETERY—
ONLY COMES OUT AT NIGHT
Gravediggers Threaten Walkout

ALTERCATION OVER STETSON HAT ENDS IN DEATH

AFRICANS EAGER TO 'SEE THE USA' ASSERTS TRAVEL AGENT—
'BIG BUCKS IN NEW TOURIST MARKET'

MAN FOUND IN CHAINS HELD, DENIES ALL WRONGDOING
'Only Wanted Nap,' Claims Prisoner

FIANCEE DISAPPEARS ON TRAIN, REPORTS ASTONISHED PASSENGER—
'Old Story,' Says Stationmaster

MAN AND WOMAN ESCAPE TRAIN WRECK UNHARMED
'Line Hasn't Run For Thirty Years,' Maintains Rail Exec

Walt Whitman once wrote that he didn't want an art that could decide presidential elections; he wanted an art to make them irrelevant. He was interested in an artist's ability to determine the feel of American experience; to become a part of the instinctive response of the people to events; to affect the quality and the costs of daily life. Whitman cared less that he would be remembered (though he certainly cared about that) than that his beliefs in the promises of American life would be lived out by other Americans—those of his time, and those far beyond his time. He thought that his work might affect whether or not his country would grow, and die, and start over again; whether his country would, at the margins of change, maintain a soul and a vitality that could be recognized, loved, and feared far more easily than it could be defined.

I think few artists have come closer to these dreams than those whose stories make up this book. Harmonica Frank, known to no one; Elvis, known to all; and the others: each catch an America that has shape within an America that is seamless—and that, most likely, is the best one can really hope for.

But Whitman, like Elvis or the Beatles or any true pop original, wanted it all, a grand battle between art and politics pitched right here. "Did you too," he wrote in *Democratic Vistas*, "suppose democracy was only for elections, for politics, for a party name?" Whitman thought limits were undemocratic. As good democrats, we fight it out within the borders of his ambition.

NOTES AND DISCOGRAPHIES

This section, organized by chapter, deals with the records, books, and articles discussed in the main text of the book, along with others that seem relevant. I have included information on the year of release and *Billboard* chart positions of records whenever that was to the point. In many cases, I wouldn't have had that information without Joel Whitburn's Record Research compilation books, especially *Top Pop Records 1955–72*, *Top LP's 1945–72*, and *Top Rhythm & Blues Records 1949–71* (all but the first, since replaced by *Top Pop Records & Singles 1955–78*, which is less useful, are available from Record Research, P.O. Box 82, Menomonee Falls, Wisconsin, 53051).

There is also a good deal of other material: a summary of recent research into Robert Johnson's life; a long discussion of rare and unreleased material by the Band; the truth about Stagger Lee (such as I have been able to put it together); and, in the Elvis section, the transcript of a furious argument between Sam Phillips and Jerry Lee Lewis—circa 1957—as to whether or not rock 'n' roll really is the devil's music. Jerry Lee takes a strictly orthodox position; Phillips falls back on Anne Hutchinson's doctrine of the Inner Light, and carries the day.

HARMONICA FRANK

Frank Floyd was born without a given name (he chose "Frank" for himself as a teenager); he got his first regular job in the late '20s, with the Cole Brothers Carnival, and for the next two decades trekked through the country, spending most of his time in the South with such legendary outfits as Happy Phillipson's Medicine Show and the Dr. Hood Medicine Show. In 1951, after nearly thirty years of living off his music and his wits, he cut his first records with Sam Phillips. Of the many numbers put down, seven tunes were released (the rest were erased: tape was expensive). They were once very hard to come by, and I want to thank Greg Shaw for providing the bootlegged tapes that sparked my interest in the first place.

All of those 1951 sides, plus a dazzling 1958 single, "Rock a Little Baby," that Frank issued on his own F&L label (a forgotten Larry Kennon took the B-side with "Monkey Love"), are included on *The Great Original Recordings of Harmonica Frank* (Puritan 3003).* Along with the album come pictures of Frank in 1930 (a ringer for any engraving of Huck Finn), the late '40s (in cowboy regalia), and 1972—one of the latter photos showing how Frank plays two harmonicas simultaneously, one with his mouth, the other with his nose.

Frank's music does not lend itself to classification. He told blues collector Steve LaVere: "I spent a lot of time listening to the darkies in days gone by singing in the cottonfield down South, and I picked up their songs and speech. That is the reason people think

---

* This album, and virtually all early rock, blues, folk, country, and foreign reissue LPs mentioned in the Discography, can be obtained by mail from Down Home Music Co., 10341 San Pablo Ave., El Cerrito, Calif., 94530 (phone: 415/525-1494). Bootleg LPs and hard-to-find books can often be ordered through ads in collectors' magazines; the most easily available is *Goldmine*.

I am a colored man, but I really am white." That seems to matter. "I never played with no blacks," Frank wrote me in response to a query, "but I was a fan of Blind Lemon Jefferson, Lonnie Johnson, and Fats Domino." And, he might have mentioned, a contemporary of all three.

Frank learned many styles so he could play for many audiences—which by the 1970s included college students at folk festivals across the country. His music can be heard in the context of early rock on *The Best of Sun Rockabilly, Vol. 1* (Charly 30123, UK), an unmatched collection of Sun rarities. His masterpiece, "Goin' Away Walkin'," can be heard in the context of Memphis blues on *Memphis and the Delta: The 1950s* (Blues Classics 15), as can his lovely "She Done Moved" on *Genesis, Vol. 2—Memphis to Chicago* (Chess 6641/125, UK), a monumental four-record reissue that contains many of the sides by Memphis R&B singers Sam Phillips leased to Chess. "Train Whistle Boogie," written by Frank but recorded by Charles Dean & the Rondells on the Benton label out of Dyersberg, Tennessee, can be found on *Rare Rock-a-billy, Vol. 2* (Collector 1020, Holland), or on *Ten Years—Collector Records* (White Label 8816, Holland). No version of the song recorded by Frank himself has been released.

Following his rediscovery by Steve LaVere, Frank cut a new album, but *Harmonica Frank Floyd* (Adelphi 1023) was a severe disappointment; virtually every cut lacked flair and spirit. In 1974, however, Frank recorded a magnificent LP, *Blues that Made the Rooster Dance* (Barrelhouse 05), that fully equalled his Sun sides. The man was close to seventy; he sounded thirty. Tunes included the Mississippi Shieks' "Sittin' on Top of the World," a fine tribute to Jimmie Rodgers, "Ring Tail Tom Cat Rag" (featuring some of Frank's many animal imitations), "Shanghai Rooster Breakdown," and "Shampoo (The Whorehouse Special)," a blues that was not merely dirty, but filthy—you've got to hear it to believe it. If this record proves to have been the final note of Frank's career, he will have gone out in style.

Frank Floyd has asked me to mention that of all those who have reissued his music, only Chris Strachwitz, who runs the Blues Classics label, has ever paid him any money for it.

ROBERT JOHNSON

Before Columbia Records began its release of Johnson's songs in 1961, his tunes traveled by rare 78 rpm originals, an occasional foreign blues bootleg, cover versions, tapes passing from hand to hand. Some of his most important compositions—"If I Had Possession Over Judgment Day," for one—had never been heard on record at all.

The sixteen tracks of *Robert Johnson: King of the Delta Blues Singers* (Columbia 1654) offer virtually all of Johnson's greatest songs: "Crossroads Blues," "Terraplane Blues" (his only real hit: Johnny Otis heard it on the radio in Berkeley in 1936), "Come on in My Kitchen," "Walking Blues," "Rambling on My Mind," "Me and the Devil Blues," "Hellhound on My Trail," "Stones in My Passway." There has not been a better album in the history of the recording industry.

Sales throughout the 1960s probably did not exceed fifteen thousand copies, but only a handful of albums released in that decade were so influential. Cream's version of "Crossroads" and the Rolling Stones' "Love in Vain" (Johnson's original was still officially unreleased when the Stones' cover appeared in 1969) prompted *King of the Delta Blues Singers, Vol. II* (Columbia C 30034). It collected the remainder of Johnson's compositions, and included "Love in Vain," "Stop Breakin' Down Blues," "Phonograph Blues," "I Believe I'll Dust My Broom," "Sweet Home Chicago" (by then a South Side standard), and others, plus some alternate takes, and was graced by Tom Wilson's remarkably evocative sleeve paintings of Johnson's first recording session. *Delta Blues* (Roots 339, Austria), a various-artists anthology, collects eight further alternate takes—"Come on in My Kitchen," "Love in Vain," and an important variant of "Crossroads Blues" among them.

In 1975 Columbia announced the imminent release of *The Complete Robert Johnson*, a three-record set, but legal conflicts put the project on the shelf—where it seems likely to remain. The occasion for the new album was the discovery of the facts about Johnson, along with the discovery of the Grail of the blues: photographs of the man himself. Six years later, not one has seen the light of day.

Mack McCormick, an American music scholar associated with the Smithsonian Institute, had, after years of searching, tracked down Johnson's sisters in Baltimore; his work led to a full reconstruction of Johnson's life, including the details of his murder. But another researcher, it seems, was following McCormick's trail; at any rate, the two men came up with much of the same material, obtained releases from Johnson's heirs that cancelled each other out, and provoked a struggle over copyrights and invasion of privacy that may never be settled.

Much of the information itself, however, has surfaced—and though McCormick's own *Biography of a Phantom*, structured as a detective story, has yet to appear, three other works are available. Robert Palmer's *Deep Blues* (New York: Viking, 1981) includes a good summary of McCormick's findings; Peter Guralnick's fully realized long essay, "Searching for Robert Johnson" (*Living Blues* magazine, Autumn, 1981), combines biography with a close musical analysis, and focuses on the sense of mystery that has always surrounded Johnson—and that has survived its own formal solution; and Alan Greenberg's *Love in Vain* (Garden City: Doubleday Anchor, 1982) is a blazingly readable screenplay for an as-yet-unproduced film that I recommend without reservation (a lengthy appendix fixes all references and clarifies the departure of the text from known facts).

This is not the place to reconstruct Johnson's life, but a few details demand inclusion. Almost every great early bluesman had a shadowy "teacher" who provided instruction both in technique and in the black arts, and Johnson, it seems, was no different: after being chased off as an incompetent by the ruling Delta bluesmen, Johnson returned to Hazelhurst, Mississippi, the site of his early childhood, and (to quote Palmer), came under "the tutelage of a musician named Ike Zinneman, who was from Alabama and claimed to have learned to play while visiting graveyards at midnight." Zinneman never recorded, so one can only speculate about the sound he made—but Johnson returned from Hazelhurst as a titan. Startlingly, Johnson attracted international attention in his lifetime: an item from a 1937 issue of *Melody Maker*, the U.K. music weekly, referred to him as "the star" of Hot Springs (while bemoaning the lack of protest material in his recordings!). Late in his brief life, Johnson seems to have formed a band, drums included; there are even reports that he was using an electric pickup on his guitar. This by itself would not have made him unique (Howlin' Wolf was playing an electric guitar in Mississippi about the same time), but the special rhythmic structures of Johnson's songs suggest that his band would have been making music recognizable as rock 'n' roll—full-blown, not protean rock 'n' roll—at least by 1938, the year Johnson was murdered.

Poisoned during a Mississippi juke joint show by a jealous husband (McCormick, having identified the still-living killer, reported him to the local police; they were not interested), Johnson lingered for several days before passing away on a date that now marks the death of Elvis Presley: August 16. Reputedly, Johnson used what strength he had left to set down a final testament: "I pray that my Redeemer will come and take me from the grave." Well, maybe; in the words of "I've Been a Moonshiner," an ancient, authorless Appalachian ballad, "Give me grub when I'm hungry/And whiskey when I'm dry/Pretty women when I'm lonesome/Religion when I die."

Research has also established that Johnson's recordings covered only a tiny part of his repertoire. As a street singer, Johnson no less than Harmonica Frank had to be ready to sing anything, and he did: Jimmie Rodgers blue yodels, Bing Crosby favorites, current hits, show tunes, novelties, spirituals, "the dozens," scatology. Versions of "Take a Little Walk with Me" and "Little Boy Blue," two songs apparently composed but never recorded by Johnson, can be found on *Otis Spann Is the Blues* (Barnaby 30246), 1961 recordings with vocals and guitar by Robert Jr. Lockwood, Johnson's stepson. Both performances are lovely, but too evenly executed; they lack the fire Johnny Shines brought to another unrecorded Johnson tune, "Tell Me Mama" (on Shines's *Sitting on Top of the World*, Biograph 12044). So of course the mystery only grows; it's in the music; no amount of factual information can enclose it; and all that has been learned simply deepens one's sense of what can never be heard.

There will be more to say about Bobby Bland in the Band discography, but I should mention that "Lead Me On," quoted at the beginning of the Johnson chapter, comes from Bland's finest album, *Two Steps from the Blues* (Duke 74). The cover shows Bobby posed in front of a blue building, which does indeed have two steps. Songs include "I Pity the Fool," "St. James Infirmary," and the ghostly "I'll Take Care of You," which opens with these lines: "I know you've been hurt, by somebody else/I can tell by the way you carry yourself." Bobby Bland and Robert Johnson would have had a lot to say to each other.

JOHNSON AND ROCK 'N' ROLL

In recent years, as Johnson's music has been recorded by more and more rock 'n' roll groups, someone calling himself "Woody Payne" has taken to putting his name on Johnson's songs ("Love in Vain" on the Rolling Stones' *Let It Bleed*, for example). "Payne" is not the first to do so and he won't be the last, but the case merely illustrates how wasteful some find it that valuable material is in the public domain. At any rate, I offer a rock 'n' roll top five of Johnson's tunes: the greatest hits of, as he is usually known, P.D.

1. The Rolling Stones, "Stop Breaking Down," from *Exile on Main Street* (Rolling Stones 0996), 1972. This was the fifth straight LP on which the Stones included a classic country blues, but the first album on which they approached country blues as rock 'n' roll—perhaps because in sound and spirit the rest of the album approached rock 'n' roll as country blues. *Exile* was a nice tour of morgues, courthouses, sinking ships, claustrophobic rooms, deserted highways; the whole album was a breakdown, one long night of fear. Johnson's hottest bragging song gave the Stones a chance to blow the fear away. With Mick squeaking his harp, calling for chorus after chorus, this stands as one of the Stones' best.

2. Taj Mahal, "The Celebrated Walking Blues," from *Taj Mahal* (Columbia 9579), 1967. Still *his* best. Not completely Johnson—Taj re-creates the lyric with bits and pieces from Willie Brown's "Future Blues" ("Minutes seem like hours/Hours seem . . . just like days"), Muddy Waters's variant, and other sources. Taj's first guitar strokes are straight from "Stones in My Passway," but he doesn't take the song all that seriously; his "Walking Blues," like

Johnson's, is one cosmic joke life is playing on him, but no one can say he doesn't get it.

3. Eric Clapton, "Ramblin'," from *John Mayall's Bluesbreakers Featuring Eric Clapton* (London 492), 1965. The liner notes to the first Cream album described Clapton as "formerly a rustic"; this early, modest, peaceful, absolutely convincing performance is what was meant.

4. Cream, "Crossroads," from *Wheels of Fire* (Atco 2–7000), 1968. Though the album title is description enough, this is the only cut that lives up to the title.

5. The Rolling Stones, "Love in Vain," from *Get Yer Ya-Yas Out* (London 5), 1970. The studio version from *Let It Bleed* is stiff; on stage, Mick Taylor's guitar and Charlie Watts's drums said whatever it might have been that Mick Jagger left out. (Author's credit went to "Traditional"—you remember him—this time around.)

JOHNSON AND POSTWAR BLUES

Johnson's impact as a stylist cut all across the board, but within the Delta–to–Chicago tradition, Muddy Waters, Robert Jr. Lockwood, Elmore James, and Johnny Shines have been his principal inheritors. Waters's original Mississippi recordings, cut in 1941–42 for the Library of Congress (see *Down on Stovall's Plantation*, Testament 2210) were uncertain imitations; by 1948, with "I Feel Like Going Home" (see *Genesis, Vol. 1*, Chess 5541 047, UK) and 1950, with the extraordinary "Rollin' Stone" (see *Sail On*, Chess 1539), Waters had taken what he wanted from Johnson and made it his own. The spidery lines of his guitar playing are unparalleled for their tension; his singing is hard, unassuming, and terrifying.

As Peter Guralnick has written, Elmore James took Johnson's "Dust My Broom" and made a career out of it. Waters reached for the distant margin of Johnson's music; James went for his sound, his volume, and his flash. A near-contemporary of Johnson, and later the idol of the Rolling Stones, the Yardbirds, and the like, James did not record until 1952, when he emerged with a wild, trebly electric guitar style and a slashing vocal attack that traded subtlety for excitement. Of the many James LPs, my choice would be *The Best of Elmore James* (Sue 918, UK), which collects powerful versions of "Dust My Broom," "Stranger Blues," "The Sky Is Crying," and the stunning "Done Somebody Wrong"—all free of the horns and clumsy rhythm sections that marred much of James's work in the years just before his death in 1963.

Johnny Shines often traveled with Johnson in the '30s. Shines moved to Chicago in 1941, but recorded only occasionally until the blues revival of the mid-1960s; with James dead and Muddy Waters committed to the Chicago band style, Shines remains the one true master of Johnson's music. In his best moments, Shines doesn't simply add to Johnson's story, he tells his own. There is a horror in his "Tom Green's Farm" (see *The Johnny Shines Band*, Testament 2212) that fully equals anything Johnson ever conjured up, and which also speaks a different language. Shines finds evil in the white man's rule while Johnson found it in himself no less than in the world, but it is Shines's ambiguous acceptance of the horror— I mean the peculiar strength he assumes when he speaks *for* it— that makes the song so disquieting.

Shines's first recordings, made in 1946, can be found on the anthology *Chicago Blues: The Beginning* (Testament 2207); his searing "Joliet Blues," cut in 1950, which Chess left unissued until almost twenty years later, is on the anthology *Drop Down Mama* (Chess 411); the anthology *On the Road Again* (Muskadine 100) collects "Brutal Hearted Woman" and "Evening Sun," both from 1953 and both first-class. Shines's six numbers on *Chicago/The Blues/Today*, *Vol. 3* (Vanguard 79218), from 1966, amounted to his "rediscovery," but his best work was still to come. Of the numerous LPs Shines has put out in the last fifteen years, strongest are *Johnny Shines* (Blue Horizon 4607; in the U.K., titled *Last Night's Dream*, Blue Horizon 7–63212, and worth ordering for the astonishing cover photo of a woman who has awakened to find that her hair has turned into a nest of snakes), and *Too Wet to Plow* (Blue Labor 110). This set, cut in 1975, is the record Shines was born to make: all acoustic, unutterably controlled and passionate singing, timeless songs. It's hard to find, and worth any search.

A NOTE ON MISSISSIPPI COUNTRY BLUES

The Mississippi blues was worked out about 1900 in and around Dockery Farms; first recorded in the '20s and '30s, it makes up an aesthetic world that is complete in itself. Sam Charters has written that only a black man, living in the Delta in the '30s, could possibly understand what Son House meant when he sang, "My black mama's face shines like the sun," but to say that the world of the country blues is complete is not to say that it is exclusive. There is a uniquely American language in the shared body of riffs and lyrics that change in meaning from singer to singer: an attempt to deal with a landscape and a way of life that, as a language, escapes the limits of both. There is something very old about this music, a distance that has little to do with dates, or with the words "archaic" or "primitive". The music is old in the way that some of Faulkner's characters, black and white, seem to have been old before they were born.

There are far too many good country blues collections to list here. My favorite is *Really! The Country Blues* (Origin Jazz Library 2), which brings together perhaps the supreme performances of Skip James ("Devil Got My Woman"), Garfield Akers ("Cottonfield Blues"), Tommy Johnson ("Maggie Campbell Blues"), and Son House ("My Black Mama"). Other Origin releases, especially *The Mississippi Blues 1927–1940* (Origin Jazz Library 5), *Country Blues Encores* (OJL 8), and *The Mississippi Blues: Transition* (OJL 17) are hardly less rich. The shift from acoustic to electric music can be heard at its most dramatic in Robert Jr. Lockwood's 1941 recording of "Little Boy Blue" (see *Mississippi Blues in the '40s*, RCA RA–5708, Japan).

Charlie Patton, a rough, fierce singer who may have had as much influence on Captain Beefheart as he had on Howlin' Wolf, was the originator of the music if anyone was; *Charlie Patton: Founder of the Delta Blues* (Yazoo 1020) contains twenty-eight of his sides. Skip James was the most individualistic of the Mississippi singers (and guitarists, and pianists), along with Johnson the most consciously an artist, and arguably the very greatest. *Skip James: King of the Delta Blues Singers* (Biograph 12029)—too bad James and Johnson can't have a battle of the bands—collects ten of James's performances from the late '20s and early '30s. The records James made after his rediscovery in the '60s, especially *Devil Got My Woman* (Vanguard 29237), capture him shortly before his death, and at the height of his powers.

Tommy Johnson made only a handful of records in 1928 and 1930, but played around Jackson until his death in the 1950s. His songs are among the most beautiful and influential in the blues, and his slurred, fading moans are a secret language in and of themselves. *The Famous 1928 Tommy Johnson—Ishman Bracey Session* (Roots 330, Austria) is the most complete, but the bulk of Johnson's work is scattered through the OJL anthologies and the excellent *Jackson Blues 1928–1938* (Yazoo 1007).

Paul Oliver's superbly illustrated *The Story of the Blues* (Baltimore: Penguin, 1972) traces the music from Africa to Chuck Berry; Peter Guralnick's *Feel Like Going Home* (New York: Vintage, 1981, second edition) combines an excellent short history with wonderful portraits of Skip James, Johnny Shines, Muddy Waters, and Howlin' Wolf; Guralnick's *Nighthawk Blues* (New York: Seaview Books, 1980) is a fine novel about the strange process by which forgotten black men were "rediscovered" in the '60s by white admirers they could hardly have imagined existed; *The Blues Line: A Collection of Lyrics from Leadbelly to Muddy Waters*, compiled by Eric Sackheim and illustrated by Jonathan Shahn (New York: Shirmer/Macmillan, 1975), is a triumph of scholarship and design; Robert Palmer's previously mentioned *Deep Blues* makes the development of the country blues as clear as it will likely ever be. And finally, Stanley Booth's "Even the Birds Were Blue" (see *The Rolling Stone Rock 'n' Roll Reader*, ed. Ben Fong-Torres, New York: Bantam, 1974), from which I drew in the Robert Johnson chapter, stands as a moving, depressing account of black bluesmen suffering the good intentions of their white fans, and as the finest example of neo–Raymond Chandler prose I've ever come across. It's a piece that anyone who cares about the complexities of race and American music ought to read.

THE BAND

Music from Big Pink (Capitol 2955) came out late in the summer of 1968, and while it never rose higher than #30 on the charts, it stayed on the charts for nearly a year, and a lot of people thought it was number one anyway. Al Kooper called the Band's debut an event, and in youthful communities around the country it was that and more. The day after the record first hit the stores you could hear people on the street singing the chorus of "The Weight"; before long, the music had become part of the fabric of daily life.

The leitmotif of the record, I think, was obligation: a kind of secret theme, at the heart of both words and music. What do men and women owe to each other? How do they keep faith? How far can that faith be pushed before it breaks? Those are problems community and friendship share. Such questions rose naturally in men who were preparing to present their partnership to the public, and who, after all those years together, had to find out what the essence of their particular group identity was.

Certainly "Long Black Veil," the only song on the album written neither by the Band nor Bob Dylan, takes obligation as far as it can go. A murder has been committed; a man is singled out from the crowd as the culprit, but he will not confess his alibi, because he's "been in the arms of [his] best friend's wife." She keeps silent as well. The singer owes something to his lover, and something to his friend; the woman won't injure her husband by revealing the secret, and she keeps faith with her lover as he goes to the gallows—by allowing him to die with his friendship intact, and then by haunting his grave. The song took the shape of an ancient Kentucky murder ballad on the order of "Omie Wise" or "Pretty Polly"; in fact, it was written in 1959 by Danny Dill and Marijohn Wilkin, and was a country hit for Lefty Frizzell that same year. It was "an instant folk song," Dill told country music historian Dorothy Horstman—inspired by "The Lady in Black" who appeared every year at the grave of Rudolf Valentino, by Red Foley's "God Walks These Hills with Me," and by an old news item. "There was a Catholic priest killed in New Jersey many years ago," said Dill, "under a town hall light [a key image in "Long Black Veil"]. There were no less than fifty witnesses. They never found a motive. They never found the man."

Shortly before making *Big Pink*, the Band, having brought Levon Helm back to the fold, put down several tunes intended for that first album. "Ferdinand the Impostor" and "Little Birds" (the latter, an old folk ditty that featured Levon on mandolin, was performed often on the Band's first tours) have yet to surface; "Ruben Remus," the lovely "Katie's Been Gone," "Ain't No More Cane" (a Texas chain gang song that ranks with the Band's best recorded work), "Orange Juice Blues (Blues for Breakfast)," "Bessie Smith," "Don't Ya Tell Henry," "Long Distance Operator," and "Yazoo Street Scandal" were finally released in 1975 on *The Basement Tapes* (Columbia C2 33682). "Yazoo" is one of the Band's finest rockers: good-humored menace out of Bo Diddley's (and the Hawks') "Who Do You Love," with Levon shouting out with his unique mixture of comic horror and helpless delight. The off-the-wall characters ("The Cotton King," "The Widow," "Breezy," "Sweet William," "Liza"—or is it "Elijah"?) and Biblical imagery ("I just started a flood, for forty days and forty nights") that would later sail through *Big Pink* spur the tale of a man seduced by the town's mystery woman—apparently at the urging of his girlfriend. What's he to make of that? "She rocked me kinda slow, and kinda easy," is all he can tell us.

The Band (Capitol 132), #9 in the fall of 1969, was the group's most popular album, as it deserved to be. The sound was clean and immediate; in every way, the record was easier to understand than *Big Pink*. The single, "Up on Cripple Creek" (in American folklore, Cripple Creek is like the Big Rock Candy Mountain, a place where all fears vanish beyond memory), even got some airplay, though the Band never had much impact on AM radio. The closest they came, in fact, was via Joan Baez's hapless attempt at "The Night They Drove Old Dixie Down" (#9 in 1971), in which she turned Robert E. Lee, in the Band's version the general, into a boat.

Stage Fright (Capitol 425), out in the summer of 1970, climbed a bit higher on the charts than *The Band* (#5), but it was not truly as popular, probably because as a collection of songs rather than a complete world, it depicted so accurately the uncertainty and fragmentation that were its subject. A certain vibrancy was missing; the music was too worked out, too careful. "The Rumor," potentially the most compelling of the tunes, was at the same time overarranged and unfinished. "*Stage Fright* needs one cut to really shake things up," Dave Marsh wrote; "The Shape I'm In" came close, but it wasn't the one. "Baby Don't You Do It (Don't Break My Heart)," recorded as a studio tryout in Bearsville, planned as a single but left unissued, was.

This was hard rock beyond the reach of any band you'd care to name, including, as far as official releases went, the Band itself. On stage they sometimes risked going out of control to make music that can't be reached any other way; on record, never. Here, with a 1964 Marvin Gaye tune they had worked into their act some time before (along with the Four Tops' "Loving You Is Sweeter than Ever," which Rick Danko sang), the Band acknowledged their enormous debt to Motown (mostly the Temptations in the vocals, James Jamerson in Danko's bass, and perhaps the essential Motown aesthetic of control and craftsmanship in the music as a whole); on this one song, the Band outdid Motown as well. They made most rock 'n' roll sound fragile.

What the Band did with Gaye's performance was what white groups usually do with black material: they held to the original arrangement, amplified the beat, turned up the volume, and yelled. They delighted in the technology of two or three electric guitars, an electric organ, super-miked drums. They didn't worry about "worrying" a line into an elusive rendering of "soul"; they simply sang as hard as they could.

They hit everything hard. Robertson is all over the music; Levon sounds as if he has four hands. Danko's bass works like fuel injection on a Corvette. Hudson lets loose a mighty screech that stays constant throughout the number, while Manuel hangs onto the edges of the noise, hitting one key on his piano over and over again. "My biggest mistake was loving you too much"—blam blam—"and letting you know—"

Gaye's "Baby Don't You Do It" (on his *Super Hits*, Tamla S300) is perfectly adequate. It's thin, careful, much like "Ain't that Peculiar," to which it was the follow-up: genre music, a play on the expectations of an audience that had already proven it would buy a similar sound. Motown's strategy of change was always incremental. The Band's version is every man at extremes. Gaye sings against a polite female chorus, and you get the idea his girl won't really do it—break his heart—because, after all, her sisters are right there pleading alongside of him. The Band enlist their full arsenal of voices, each man coming in at his own pace to declaim, "Oh, baby, don't do it, don't break my heart, PLEASE, don't do it," marching across the battlefield of broken dreams like an army of men ready to give it all for love. They wail on until they reach that point where the song ought to end, and suddenly Robbie seizes the music and drives straight out of the song. His pals catch up, cut him off, and slam the tune to a close. There were moments like this in the Band's concerts, but there were never enough of them.

Cahoots (Capitol 651), #21 in late 1971, was literal where the other records had been tantalizing, strained where they had rocked. There was a flatness in the music: good ideas forced through a banal, didactic mesh. The idea of "cahoots" was the soul of the group, but nothing on the LP captured it, except perhaps the original cover photo. Robbie had chosen an Irving Penn portrait of two Peruvian children (see *Photographing Children*, New York: Time–Life Books, 1971), brother and sister, dressed in grown-ups' work clothes and posing formally for the photographer. They weren't cute. The way they looked and held their small bodies told you they would stick to each other forever—that, as long as their bond held, they were ready for whatever life had in store for them. It was a photograph of very strange beauty, and Capitol vetoed it as the cover of *Cahoots* because someone thought the little girl looked pregnant.

Rock of Ages (Capitol 11042), a two-record set recorded in New York City mainly on New Year's Eve, 1971, and released in the fall of 1972, hit #6, and it remains one of the best live albums of that decade. The sound was deep and full, the Band was blazing, and the hornmen—New York City jazzmen on a busman's holiday with the strong, witty charts of Allen Toussaint, the premier rock 'n' roll producer of New Orleans—added a crucial new dimension to mostly familiar material.

On almost every song, the Band and their horn section outran the original, studio versions. The Band and the horns fought over "Chest Fever"; it took on a strident urgency as the hornmen slapped back at Levon's furious drumming near the end. "Rag Mama Rag" was perhaps the album's triumph: Rick Danko's opening slices on his fiddle just before the song kicked off were inexplicably spooky, and Howard Johnson's furious tuba solo ranks with anything King Curtis ever played with the Coasters.

Toussaint dug deeply into New Orleans tradition for his charts—into Dixieland, blues, '50s and early '60s rock. There had always been a lot of New Orleans in the Band, especially the wild piano and general hilarity of Huey "Piano" Smith, and Toussaint brought this to the surface. My favorite touch was the riff he used to open the encore, "(I Don't Want To) Hang Up My Rock and Roll Shoes," which runs like this: "Dat DAH (boomp boomp)/Dat DAH (boomp boomp)." The pattern teases the memory, because it turns out to be one of those timeless fragments that can pop up anywhere, like an ancient blues line in a Top 40 hit, for a moment seemingly tying all of American music together. This riff linked the Band to the first bars of Shirley and Lee's 1956 Crescent City classic, "Let the Good Times Roll"; to the pre-jazz funeral marches of the 1890s; and to the music of a half-forgotten New Orleans blues singer named Rabbit Brown, who probably got more feeling out of the notes than anyone else when he used them to open his 1928 "James Alley Blues." "I seen better days," he sang, "but I'm puttin' up with these."

Rock of Ages also documented Garth Hudson's crazy piano on "The Weight"; his long organ fantasia, which originally grew out of the fanfare that begins "Chest Fever" (here pretentiously titled "The Genetic Method," but nevertheless a tour through 19th-century popular music, from stovepipes to bandboxes to merry-go-rounds, with a pause for "Auld Lang Syne"); a staggering "Don't Do It"; and a tune written years earlier but never released, "Get Up Jake." This last—about a man so lazy the whole town shows up to watch him get out of bed—was in some ways the best of all. "Me and Jake worked out on the river, on a ferry called the *Baltimore*," it began: one of those commonplace evocations of a hazy frontier that the Band had made their signature. It's a very modest song, and perfect. Garth never played more prettily.

Moondog Matinee (Capitol 11214) came out late in 1973. The title was a tip of the hat to Alan Freed's original 1951 Cleveland rock 'n' roll radio show, to which all of the future Band members had listened at the time; the finely detailed sleeve pictured the Band haunting a Toronto dive that had once known them as the Hawks. Made up of rock classics they had often played in those days, the album sold poorly, topping out at #28, even though it coincided with the Band's 1974 tour with Bob Dylan, likely the most publicized outing in rock history.

Flop or not, *Moondog Matinee* contained some of the Band's best music, and "Third Man Theme" might have been the hit single they never had. (The single that was released, a remake of Clarence "Frogman" Henry's "Ain't Got No Home," held a surprise; on the flipside the *Rock of Ages* live version of "Get Up Jake" was listed, but pressed instead was the original studio take of the song, dating from the sessions for *The Band*—see Capitol 45–3758.) "Share Your Love" far outclassed Bobby "Blue" Bland's original; Manuel had more to give the song, and Garth's knack of making his Lowrey organ sound like a complete string section added great warmth. "Mystery Train" was almost completely retooled by Robertson; he kept the first verse, added two of his own, and made up the chords from scratch. After a ha'nt-ridden false start, the Band crept into the standard and took it over, the music dark and funny; when Robbie's new lines emerged, one would have thought they'd been in the song since it was first sung, fifty years or twice as long ago. Levon cried,

> *Come down to the station meet my baby at the gate*
> *Ask the station master if the train's running late*
> *He said, If you're a-waitin' on that old 44*
> *I hate to tell ya son that train don't stop here anymore*

"I tried to get to that old Robert Johnson–Arthur Crudup mood," Robbie said. Well, he did; those were the best lyrics he'd written since *The Band*.

Northern Lights—Southern Cross (Capitol ST–11440) appeared in 1975; as the Band's first album of new material since 1971, it proved disappointingly modest, reaching only #26 on the charts, but it was also a record of very deep feeling. The action took place between the lines; if *Moondog Matinee* was Manuel's album, this one, despite the fact that Robbie wrote all the songs, was Garth Hudson's. He played with deceptive anonymity; his music worked as a presence, tapestries hung on the back walls. No nuance escaped him—no shade of emotion, no matter how elusive, seemed beyond him. The set's "big" piece, "Acadian Driftwood," the story of French Canadians forced to emigrate to Louisiana, where they became Cajuns, aimed for the level of *The Band*, and missed.

The next year saw the release of *The Best of the Band* (Capitol ST–11553), which included one previously unissued cut, the pleasant but inconsequential "Twilight." Late in the year came a new single, "Georgia on My Mind" (Capitol 45 P–4361), nicely sung by Manuel and meant as the Band's endorsement of Jimmy Carter for the presidency. The flip, appropriately enough, was "The Night They Drove Old Dixie Down." The disc missed the charts, but Jimmy was said to have been pleased.

Shortly thereafter, on Thanksgiving night, the Band formally ended their years on the road with "The Last Waltz," a long, star-laden concert at Winterland in San Francisco, where they had made their on-stage debut some seven and a half years before. On hand were Paul Butterfield, Ronnie Hawkins, Muddy Waters, Dr. John, Van Morrison, Joni Mitchell, Neil Young, Neil Diamond, Eric Clapton, and Bob Dylan, plus a *Rock of Ages*-style horn section. Robbie promised the farewell did not mean the Band was breaking up—"The Band will never break up," he said, "it's too late to break up"—but for all practical purposes that, as of five years later, is what it has meant. Robbie went into movie work, producing and starring in *Carny*; Rick Danko made a desultory solo album and undertook a few even more desultory tours; Levon Helm took a memorable turn as Loretta Lynn's father in *Coal Miner's Daughter*, made a fine solo LP, *American Son* (MCA 5102), in 1980, and followed it in 1981 with a string of uproarious club dates. Little was heard from Garth Hudson, and nothing at all from Richard Manuel.

It was a year and a half after Thanksgiving, 1976, before the film and album of "The Last Waltz" appeared; in between came *Islands* (Capitol SO–11602), the Band's weakest and weakest-selling album (#64). It was notable for the Band's first certifiable clinker since *Cahoots* ("Ain't That a Lotta Love"), and for two gems: "Knockin' Lost John," a tune about the Great Depression (vocal by Robertson), and "Livin' in a Dream," a lovely Levon Helm reverie based on, of all things, "Row Row Row Your Boat."

The Last Waltz, directed by Martin Scorsese, was released in the late spring of 1978; it was an immediate hit, and reviewed almost unanimously (and correctly) as the finest rock 'n' roll concert movie yet made. The strongest moments came with Muddy Waters' performance of "Mannish Boy": for seven minutes, the camera kept Waters in tight focus, his face lit by a single ghostly spot (all other lights had failed), and he held the screen like no singer ever had. The album, a three-record set (*The Last Waltz*, Warner Bros. 3 WS 3146), was not nearly as popular as the film (though it reached #16), and lacked the rough, passionate clatter of the in-theater soundtrack. Highlights were a fierce "Who Do You Love," sung by Ronnie Hawkins and powered by Garth Hudson; "Mystery Train" (the Junior Parker/Elvis Presley version), featuring a hurricane vocal by Levon Helm and the strongest harp work of Paul Butterfield's career; "The Night They Drove Old Dixie Down," which, it seemed, Levon sang with the anger he'd always meant to give the song; a stunning "Caravan" by Van Morrison; and the two takes of "Baby Let Me Follow You Down" with which Bob Dylan both opened and closed his set.

The last side of the package was made up of studio material; most impressive was a new recording of "The Weight," with lead vocals shared by Levon, Danko, and black rhythm 'n' gospel singers Pop Staples and his daughter Mavis Staples. Exactly what Elvis had always aimed for with "An American Trilogy," the performance quite intentionally took in the whole of the country: blacks and whites, men and women, northerners and southerners, old and young. It was also a dirge, dark and pietistically apocalyptic. It ended the Band's story right where it had begun.

RONNIE HAWKINS & THE HAWKS

Born in Huntsville, Arkansas, in 1935, Ronnie Hawkins assembled his first group of Hawks in 1952, while a student at the University of Arkansas; they did not, however, play rock 'n' roll or

R&B, but country. In 1957, Hawkins may have auditioned for Sun Records in Memphis; at any rate, nothing came of it. Later that year, after six months in the Army, Hawkins joined with former Conway Twitty guitarist Jimmy Ray "Luke" Paulman to form a new band. A year later, following Twitty's advice, they were in Canada, working the Golden Rail in Hamilton, Ontario.

As leader of the Ron Hawkins Quartet, Hawkins made his first recording in 1958, in a Toronto garage: "Hey Bo Diddley"/"Love Me Like You Can," which was issued on the tiny Canadian independent, Quality. The Quartet included Levon Helm, then fifteen, on drums, Will "Pop" Jones on piano, and Jimmy Ray Paulman on guitar. The disc went nowhere commercially, but someone must have heard it, because in the spring of 1959 it brought Hawkins his first break.

Working with the Fury label and producer Bobby Robinson, longtime one-man-band Wilbert Harrison redid an old Jerry Leiber–Mike Stoller tune, "K.C. Loving," changing the title to "Kansas City." The record took off like a shot, but various problems prevented Robinson from keeping the disc in the stores; the record hung between a goldmine and oblivion as people all over the country tried to find the hit they were hearing on the radio. Quick to take advantage, label after label rushed out cover versions (the best, and most successful, being Little Richard's). One producer on the case was the legendary George Goldner; he put Hawkins into the studio post-haste. Credited to Rockin' Ronald and the Rebels, Hawkins' "Kansas City" (End 45–1043) stands as perhaps the least-known of all attempts to steal Wilbert Harrison's thunder (when all was said and done, it was he and no one else who took "Kansas City" to the top of the charts), but that was not the end of the story. End was under the umbrella of Roulette, run by Morris Levy, famous for his connections with Alan Freed and other parties; he signed Hawkins to a long-term contract. Still working out of Toronto, Hawkins and the Hawks—now adding James Evans on bass—cut *Ronnie Hawkins* (Roulette 25078) in 1959, and, with Fred Carter, Jr., replacing Paulman, *Mr. Dynamo* (Roulette 25102) the following year.

The Hawks were by this time a rough combination of early Drifters and rockabilly, bent on speed and flash; the endless rehearsals on which Hawkins insisted put them well beyond most journeyman backup bands of the time. Paulman and Carter sounded like Carl Perkins, Jones like Jerry Lee Lewis, and Levon sounded like himself. He was faster than most rock drummers, and he used a much heavier beat; at his best, he dominated the music, which for a drummer was unheard of. The Hawks played brash and dirty; Hawkins sang like a lunatic when he could pull it off, which put him square into the company of the heroic Southern rockers he longed to emulate.

Ronnie Hawkins contained two chart entries: "Mary Lou," a remake of Young Jessie's 1955 R&B ballad (revived again in 1976 by Bob Seger on *Night Moves*), and "Forty Days," a remake of Chuck Berry's "Thirty Days." They topped out at #26 and #45, respectively, with "Mary Lou" also going top ten on the R&B charts. Also memorable was "Odessa," a tribute to the Hawks' favorite hooker (who likely reappeared as "Bessie" in the Band's "Up on Cripple Creek"). *Mr. Dynamo* was highlighted by the very spooky "Southern Love," Hawkins's most distinctive number from this period, and by "Hey Boba Lu," Robbie Robertson's first song to be recorded—and also, I think, his first recording as a guitarist, though he was not credited, having joined Hawkins as roadie and occasional bass player at this point. He was soon very much more involved, appearing with Hawkins at one of Alan Freed's last Brooklyn Paramount shows ("How old are you, kid?" Freed, then under assault by bluenose district attorneys and federal prosecutors, asked Robertson. "You wanna get me in trouble on a child-labor rap, too?"), scouting songs in New York from the likes of Doc Pomus and Mort Shuman, and generally learning the music business from the inside.

Not long after, Robbie took over as lead guitarist, and Manuel, Danko, and Hudson (over much parental opposition) were recruited in turn over the next year or so. The Hawks began to play blues, and two of the albums they treasured most were by Howlin' Wolf. *Moanin' in the Moonlight* (Chess 1434; reissued as *Evil*, Chess 1540) collected Wolf's early sides, and featured Willie Johnson's fiery guitar on "How Many More Years" (cut by Sam Phillips in Memphis in 1951), along with "Smokestack Lightning," "I Asked for Water" (Wolf's remake of Tommy Johnson's 1928 "Cool Drink of Water Blues"), and other classics. *Howlin' Wolf* (Chess 1469, with the famous rocking chair jacket) was all Chicago, and guitarist Hubert Sumlin's record as much as Wolf's; he contributed a crazed solo on "Wang-Dang-Doodle" (the model for Robbie's solo on the Hawks' "Who Do You Love"), plus stunning efforts on "Down in the Bottom," "Spoonful" (a Charley Patton standard), "You'll Be Mine," and "Going Down Slow." This music, which was to have such an impact on the Rolling Stones and the Yardbirds, was at once rougher and more sophisticated than the rockers and ballads the Hawks were used to: it had drive *and* nuance.

Just as important as Wolf to the Hawks was an album split between Junior Parker and Bobby "Blue" Bland: *Blues Consolidated* (Duke 72), which collected '50s recordings by the two men. Both had started out in the late '40s in Memphis, singing with the Beale Streeters, a seminal group that also included Johnny Ace on piano (see *Blues for Mr Crump*, Polydor 2383 257, UK). Recording in Memphis for Sam Phillips (among others), and later for Duke in Houston, the three, as soloists, were to define a whole new form of rhythm and blues by stressing a kind of tragic sentimentality expressed through delicate, carefully arranged and written blues ballads. *Blues Consolidated* showcased Bland's first big hit, "Farther Up the Road," and his incredible "It's My Life, Baby." This last was a much more exciting performance than "Farther Up the Road," which may have been why the Hawks didn't attempt it. They passed Bland with their version of "Farther," but there was no way on earth they were going to catch him, or his guitar player, on "It's My Life, Baby."

At first one of many Roy Brown imitators, Bland found his style and began a string of superb recordings that still continues; kin to Charlie Rich, whose songs he has covered, he remains the most sensitive and original blues singer of the last twenty-five years. The deceptively quiet, despairing moods of his most distinctive tunes shaped Richard Manuel's singing in particular, not merely in terms of phrasing, but in terms of sensibility. See, for Bland, *Two Steps from the Blues* (Duke 74), *The Best of Bobby "Blue" Bland* (Duke 84), and *Best of, Vol. 2* (Duke 86); for Junior Parker, *The Best of Junior Parker* (Duke 83); for Johnny Ace, *Memorial Album* (Duke 71).

While the Hawks were listening to Bland and Wolf—and to early Motown, a lot of gospel music (especially the Staple Singers), the New Orleans rock of Ernie K-Doe and Irma Thomas, and everything else—they and Hawkins slogged on together. During the folk boom Hawkins grew so desperate he even recorded "The Ballad of Caryl Chessman" (who knows, maybe he thought it'd get him a spot on "Hootenanny"). He cut two more albums with the Hawks, both in 1963: *The Best of Ronnie Hawkins* (Canadian Roulette 252250), which featured "Who Do You Love," and *Mojo Man* (Canadian Roulette 25390), which contained Levon and the Hawks' remarkable versions of "Farther Up the Road" and Muddy Waters's "She's 19" (mistitled as "Have a Party"). On his own numbers, Hawkins sounded very tired.

"Who Do You Love," "Forty Days," "Mary Lou," "Odessa," "Bo Diddley," and others less memorable are available on *Rockin' Ronnie Hawkins* (Pye NSLP 28238, UK). Steaming, little-known versions of "Little Red Rooster" and Fats Domino's "Going to the River" (both featuring Helm, Robertson, Danko, Manuel, and Hudson, and both dating probably from 1963) can be heard on *Transfusion* (Union Pacific 044, UK), an excellent anthology of early rock rarities.

Hawkins gained new fame after the success of the Band, and went on to make two smooth, expert albums—*Ronnie Hawkins* (Cotillion 9019) and *The Hawk* (Cotillion 9038)—and even brushed the singles charts again with a fine "Down in the Alley," #75 in 1975. Among many half-hearted, small-label efforts that followed, there was one definitive, drooling mess-around, *Rock and Roll Resurrection* (Monument 31330), that finally told his story as it was meant to be told: "Willie and the Hand Job," more or less. Now pushing fifty, Hawkins still performs in his own club in Toronto, cuts records, cultivates his legend, embroiders his tall tales, hopes for one more hit—and in his own way remains as unregenerate as Jerry Lee Lewis.

On their own from 1963 through 1965, drifting from border to border, the Hawks made three singles: "Leave Me Alone" (a toughened-up rewrite of Chuck Berry's "Almost Grown")/"Uh-Uh-Uh" as the Canadian Squires (Ware 45–6002), and, as Levon and the Hawks, "Go Go Liza Jane"/"He Don't Love You" (Atco 45–6625) and "The Stones I Throw (Will Free All Men)"/"He Don't Love You" (Atco 45–6383). All the ambition, a bit of the sound, and none of the poetry of *Music from Big Pink* and *The Band* are present in "The Stones I Throw": "Something makes me want to stand up and do what's right . . . and take my brother's hand," Richard Manuel sang. "I will show them by the stones that I throw." Anything this explicit would have sunk *Big Pink*; that was a drama of morals, not moralism, and the difference is everything.

In 1965, Robbie and Rick Danko worked with John Hammond, Jr., on the sessions that later came out on Hammond's *I Can Tell* (Atlantic 8152). Anyone with the stamina to sit through Hammond's ludicrous blackface vocals can hear what Robbie considers some of his best blues playing: all rough edges, jagged bits of metal ripping through the spare rhythm section.

WITH BOB DYLAN

Stories about how the Hawks hooked up with Bob Dylan abound: through John Hammond, Jr.; through Mary Martin, a Canadian working in the music business in New York; through pure serendipity. However it happened, Robbie and Levon, with Harvey Brooks on bass and Al Kooper on organ, backed Bob Dylan at his chaotic 1965 Forest Hills concert—the first to follow the infamous Newport Folk Festival performance at which Dylan, backed by members of the Paul Butterfield Blues Band, scandalized much of the audience by singing his "poetry" with "commercial" electric accompaniment, thus demonstrating he had sold out to the almighty dollar. ("Cocksucker!" shouted one offended fan at Forest Hills. "Aw, it's not that bad," replied Dylan.) As for Levon and Robbie, to whom rock 'n' roll was as "commercial" as living off peanut butter, and nevertheless the staff of life, the response could only have seemed absurd.

Dylan's tours with the Hawks began that fall. Levon left the group, and was replaced by Bobby Gregg, who was himself replaced in the winter by Mickey Jones, then Trini Lopez's drummer, and later Kenny Rogers's. Boos and catcalls from disillusioned folkies followed the troupe all the way to the West Coast—

where, for a change, crowds fidgeted during the first half of the shows, when Dylan appeared alone with acoustic guitar, and welcomed the electric noise with standing ovations. The boos were to return with a vengeance in 1966, when Dylan kept the tour going through Australia, Europe, and the United Kingdom.

In December, 1965, Dylan and the Hawks went into the studio to cut singles. The first to be released was "Can *You* Please Crawl Out Your Window?" (Columbia 4–43477). It was a wild, carnival version of the song Dylan had earlier recorded (and accidentally released, and then pulled) with the group he'd used on *Highway 61 Revisited*. I don't think he and the band ever sounded as if they were having more fun. "You gotta lotta *nerve* to say you are my friend," Dylan croaked, parodying "Positively Fourth Street," a hit some months earlier, "if you won't crawl out your window!"

"Crawl Out" missed the Top 40; next up was "One of Us Must Know (Sooner or Later)" (Columbia 4–4341), which didn't make the charts at all. The record was frenzied, yet stately; Richard Manuel never played with more soul, and Robbie closed out the tune with a few stinging notes worth more than all the solos Dylan's songs had no room for. The tune appeared on Dylan's *Blonde on Blonde* (Columbia C2S 841), released in June, 1966, cut mostly with Nashville sidemen, though Robbie also played guitar on "Obviously Five Believers."

Several other numbers from that singles session remain officially unreleased, though most have been bootlegged. "I Wanna Be Your Lover" is a straight rocker, with chains of images that go nowhere in particular; "Number One" is the instrumental track to lyrics that were never written. Close to "One of Us Must Know," it stands on its own, mostly because of the power of Garth Hudson's straining organ. There are two different versions of "Seems Like a Freeze-Out" (the original title for "Visions of Johanna"), which Dylan and the Hawks were performing on stage at the time. One take moves on a loose, startlingly syncopated rhythm; the piece is riveting, but the beat doesn't give Dylan the groove he needs to find the rhythm in the lyrics. The other take is gorgeous— perhaps too gorgeous for the doomy, fated mood Dylan is trying to build. Garth's organ seems instantly to lift the song about

twenty feet off the ground; with Manuel's piano on one side and
Robbie's inobtrusive guitar on the other, the music swirls, round
and round, until Dylan ends it with a long, low moan. And there
is "She's Your Lover Now," also in two versions, both rough: one
with Dylan alone on piano, singing tentatively, the other with the
Hawks. A guitar chord cutting in here, a piano rumble there, Dylan's bitterest lyrics and an unforgiving vocal make it a terrifying
performance. "You just sit around and ask for ashtrays," Dylan
sings. "Can't you reach?"

Many of the concerts Dylan and the Hawks played in 1965
and '66 were recorded. Officially, only one number has ever been
released: "Just Like Tom Thumb's Blues," the flipside of "I Want
You" (Columbia 4–43683), taped in Liverpool in 1966. The Hawks
outran themselves, as did Dylan—this was pure hoodoo. When
Dylan sang his lines about Angel, "who just arrived here from the
coast/Who looked so fine at first/But left looking just like a ghost,"
Garth's organ made it clear Angel got off lucky.

"He didn't know anything about *music*," Robbie says of the
Hawks' partnership with Dylan. "He was all folk songs, Big Bill,
and we were Jerry Lee. So it'd be, 'Down the streets the dogs are
barking—WHAM!' A huge noise. And Bob would say, 'Hey,
that's great. Do it again that way.' We had no help; everyone who
wasn't telling him the combination was wrong for him was telling
us it was wrong for us."

What Dylan didn't know about music was how to work with
a group. The marriage of his instincts, his hipster savvy, and his
unmatched feel for the mysteries of American song to the Hawks'
training and flair took them both to places they never could have
reached alone. The music they made in the mid-'60s was hard,
hard rock, surrealistic dandy's blues, with moments of extreme
gentleness and wild humor. On stage, they *moved:* Dylan and Robertson charged across the stage, stopping dead to play head to head;
Rick Danko rocked back and forth on his heels, dipping and weav-
ing as if, in Ralph J. Gleason's memorable line on their San Francisco show, he could swing Coit Tower. They reveled in provoca-
tion. In Paris, to face a crowd of French students who idolized Bob
Dylan as the definitive anti-American ("Il est un *Vietnik*," said a
student in Godard's then-current *Masculin-Feminin*), Dylan wangled

an enormous Stars-and-Stripes, hung it up behind the amps, and almost caused a riot. They reveled in melodrama. To open a number, Dylan, Robertson, and Danko would turn from the audience toward drummer Mickey Jones, who would raise his sticks high, hold the pose, and then suddenly bring the sticks down with a crash as the three guitarists leaped into the air, kicking off the song as they hit the ground.

Out of this period came one album and two movies (omitting the Band's appearance in *You Are What You Eat*, a hippie film Pauline Kael described as "The kind of movie about youth one might expect Spiro Agnew or George Wallace to make"). The album, a bootleg, is *The Royal Albert Hall Concert 1966* (Royal Albert Hall AH–LP–3A, UK—with numerous copies in its wake). It features eight songs—an entire electric half of a Dylan–Hawks concert—beginning with the otherwise-unreleased "Tell Me Mama," and ending with a mean fencing match between Dylan and the audience ("Judas!" screams an outraged folkie) that leads into, and is resolved by, "Like a Rolling Stone." "Tell Me Mama" has some fine lines ("Your cemetery hips . . . your graveyard lips"); more to the point, it is one of the most exciting pieces of rock 'n' roll ever made. The musicians' timing—the way Robbie's careening solo falls perfectly into Mickey Jones' thump, the way Danko's bass flips into a cymbal smash—is unlike anything I've ever heard. "If I told you what our music is really about we'd probably all get arrested," Dylan said to an interviewer in 1965. Listening to "Ballad of a Thin Man," to the shocking blues chord Robbie uses to open it, to Dylan's fury, or to the otherworldly tentacles of Garth Hudson's organ work, that boast seems altogether sensible.

D. A. Pennebaker, who had filmed Dylan in London the previous year for the *cinéma vérité* documentary *Don't Look Back*, shot the 1966 tour as well: mostly in the U.K., with some footage from Europe. With Howard Alk, Dylan edited bits and pieces into "Eat the Document," intended for TV but turned down by the networks, and screened only occasionally since. It's not much of a movie: there is a lot of travel footage, endless shots of crowds gathering outside the Albert Hall, much hotel-room composing and playing between Dylan and Robbie Robertson, and the fundamental text seems to be a variation on the theme of the betrayed fan

("Rubbish," says one English student after another of Dylan's electric music). The many songs included are only touched on—a verse here, a chorus there.

Far more successful was Pennebaker's own version, *Something is Happening*, which he was never permitted to release, and which remains unfinished. There are a score of unforgettable moments: Dylan and a very thin, scarred-looking Johnny Cash harmonizing on "I Still Miss Someone," going on and on as Dylan tries to find the melody on the piano, the duet finally succeeding in glorious camaraderie, and then Cash leaving the room as Dylan begins to pick out a ballad on the piano and the film, without warning, takes a turn into the darkest night; Dylan singing "Like a Rolling Stone" on stage, shouting into the mike through cupped hands; a cut from street hassles right into the middle of "Ballad of a Thin Man," the shift coming just as the song's chords change from narrative to threat.

This is the great undocumented period of Dylan's work, and of the Band's. The concert recordings ought to be released, and Pennebaker's film ought to be seen.

In July, 1966, just after the release of *Blonde on Blonde*, Dylan's tours with the Hawks came to an end when he was injured in a motorcycle accident near his home in Woodstock. Dylan, Robertson, Danko, Manuel, and Hudson—the former Hawks now sometimes calling themselves the Crackers—regrouped in the Catskills, worked on "Eat the Document," and began rehearsing and writing songs. In 1967 they made the Basement Tape, so named because it was cut in the basement of the Crackers' house in West Saugerties. Never intended for release (the new tunes were officially publishing demos, and sent off to various artists—the Byrds, Manfred Mann, Peter, Paul & Mary, etc.—who immediately began recording them), but soon bootlegged all over the world, the music the combo made was of greater emotional depth and subtlety than any either Dylan or the Hawks had recorded, and it was also more of a collaboration.

Most of the material was finally issued in 1975 on *The Basement Tapes* (Columbia C2 33682), a two-record set that included sixteen of Dylan's performances, plus eight numbers by the Band (with Levon Helm now back in the fold), cut shortly after the sessions with Dylan. Of Dylan's songs, "I Shall Be Released," "Sign on the Cross," "Quinn the Eskimo," the hilarious "Get Your Rocks Off," and the chillingly beautiful "I'm Not There (I'm Gone)," plus many alternate takes, remain available only on bootlegs. The sessions, lasting through the summer of 1967, were loose and experimental: Danko and Manuel often sang back-up to Dylan's leads, yet on hand, Robbie sometimes played drums. eter, funkier, and funnier than that Dylan and de on stage; just right for songs divided about confessional and the bawdy house, and which on from the fated ballads of the Blue Ridge and standards like "Froggy Went A-Courtin'." This is be music as satisfying and complex as anything or The Band (see my notes to The Basement Tapes) but that Dylan went on to John Wesley Harding / Music from Big Pink is not hard to understand. line on The Basement Tapes: "If there are tests, ed, and what you're hearing are the results."

1968, Dylan and the Band showed up for the morial concert in New York; the album that recorded, and most of the performances were the Band ripped out a lean, ragged rockabilly; e Dam" they came across (see A Tribute to mbia 31171). Their show at the Isle of Wight mmer of 1969 did not fare as well; the record- produced, with the Band shoved far into the an's muddled, unsure singing forced up front. as killed, but four numbers were spliced into in 1970 (Columbia C2X 30050). Most of the egs that appeared were better, because they formance sounded like to the audience—occa-sionally distracted, often tight and funny. On such evidence, the highlight was "Highway 61 Revisited," with Garth leading the Band around supercharged twists and turns while Dylan, Levon,

Robertson, Manuel, and Danko screamed "OUT ON HIGHWAY SIXTY-ONE!" like Mexican tour guides hustling customers for the best whorehouse in Tijuana.

Late in 1973, preparing for a joint nationwide comeback tour, Dylan and the Band cut *Planet Waves* (Asylum 1003), mostly first takes of songs the Band had not heard before they walked into the studio. The six came up with a loose, scrawny sound—"stray-cat music," Bob Christgau called it—nothing like past music they had made together or solo, and nowhere near so good, either. The joys-and-sorrows-of-family-life tunes that dominated the album tended to the slick ("Wedding Song," which Dylan recorded alone, was an exception), but the tour that followed made *Planet Waves* beside the point.

Before the Flood (Asylum 201), a two-record set recorded almost entirely on February 14, 1974, in Los Angeles on the last night of the tour, collected the guts of the performance Dylan and the Band offered the country (scores of bootlegs collected the rest of it). It was proof that the best music of both had endured and changed along with the men who made it.

Separately, neither Dylan nor the Band did anything astounding; the Band's eight numbers on *Before the Flood* ("Après moi, le déluge"? Now, really!) included an old, never-before-performed number called "Endless Highway" (the song, however, was no more imaginative than its title), and in general their music was a lot more raucous than on *Rock of Ages*: "Up on Cripple Creek" was a drunken brawl. Together, Dylan and the Band cut loose with a noise that made the Rolling Stones' live show sound polite, and yet within the storm was an emotional complexity that often went beyond Dylan's lyrics. Roaring with fury and wit, riding Levon's enormous beat, and fusing all parts into a collective momentum, this was rock 'n' roll at its limits.

With Dylan there to take the heat, that side of the Band that was scared of the crowd, that sought shelter in craftsmanship and arrangements, disappeared, and was replaced by the chaos and intensity of those old Howlin' Wolf records. With the Band around him, Dylan broke through the strictures of casualness and ease that had weakened his albums after *John Wesley Harding*. He was forced to use most of what he had just to keep up, and so he became that stray cat, howling at the moon.

The music, as I heard it in concert, was hard and angry, with Levon (sometimes Richard Manuel joined him on a second set of drums) at the center. On record, the textures in the sound were primary, with Garth Hudson the star: shifting the rhythms, darting in and out of every song like a phantom horn section, sometimes wrestling the tunes away from the other five and tossing them back like lit firecrackers. The music broke open with a freedom few other records have even hinted at: the earlier, studio versions of "Highway 61 Revisited" and "All Along the Watchtower" were momentarily blown away as Dylan and the Band charged through the songs as if they had little idea what route they were traveling, let alone where they were headed, playing with the good-humored, nervy conviction that the trip would return in surprises whatever it cost in uncertainty.

The music was made in a particularly American spirit: loud, crude, and uncivilized. It was an old-fashioned, back-country, big-city attack on all things genteel, an up-to-date version of Walt Whitman's YAWP.

SLY STONE

Ben Fong-Torres' "Everybody Is a Star: The Travels of Sylvester Stewart" (see *The Rolling Stone Rock 'n' Roll Reader*, ed. Ben Fong-Torres, New York: Bantam, 1974), a history of Sly & the Family Stone through 1970, is one of the finest rock profiles I have ever read, and I relied on it for much biographical information, not to mention inspiration. Thanks, Ben.

Fong-Torres notes that Sly Stone's first record was "On the Battlefield for My Lord," cut with his siblings under the name of the Stewart Four. Sly played drums and guitar. He was five.

Early in his teens, Sly began his apprenticeship with local Vallejo, California, bands such as the Viscanes (a doo-wop group that may or may not have recorded "Yellow Moon") and Joey Piazza and the Continentals, a racially mixed soul-and-stomp outfit whose repertoire would have been familiar to anyone who attended a high school dance in the late '50s or early '60s. Under his given name, Sly made "Long Time Away"/"Help Me with My Heart" (G&P 45-901) in 1960 or 1961.

In 1964, Sly was working in what passed for the record business in San Francisco, and co-authored Bobby Freeman's "C'mon and Swim" (a dance popularized by a North Beach topless club) with Tom Donahue. It was a hit, but Sly's own "I Just Learned How to Swim"/"Scat Swim," out in 1964 (Autumn 45-3), and his "Buttermilk, Parts 1 & 2," from 1965 (Autumn 45-14), were not. An album of Sly's demo tapes from this period, released long after he became famous, is almost unlistenably bland.

By this time, however, Sly had taken over as house producer for Donahue's Autumn and North Beach labels. His efforts are collected on *San Francisco Roots* (Vault 119), where lie the hits and nonhits of the Beau Brummels, the Mojo Men, the Vejtables, the Tikis, and the Great Society (Grace Slick's first band). Legend has it that Sly drove the Great Society through more than two hundred takes of "Free Advice," the flipside of the strong, original version of "Somebody to Love"; from the evidence of the record it certainly wasn't worth it, but then, maybe Sly just didn't like hippies.

Sly and the Family Stone (Sly, guitar, organ, other instruments; Rosie Stone, piano; Freddie Stone, guitar; Larry Graham, bass; Jerry Martini, sax; Cynthia Robinson, trumpet; Gregg Errico, drums) first released a single, "I Ain't Got Nobody"/"I Can't Turn You Loose" in 1966, on the local Loadstone label (45-3951). Their first album, *A Whole New Thing* (Epic 30333), appeared in 1967. It missed the charts, and while 1968's *Dance to the Music* (Epic 26371) did little better (#142), the single of the same name—which really was a whole new thing—made the pop top ten. *Life* (Epic 26397), also released in 1968, flopped (#195), but the band broke through with "Everyday People," a completely unclassifiable kind of rock 'n' roll and a number one single in early 1969.

The follow-up album, *Stand!* (Epic 26456), which appeared in mid-1969, permanently changed black popular music. It rose to #13 on the charts, sold over two million copies, and stayed on the charts for two solid years. From it came the songs that made the Family's name: "Stand!," "I Want to Take You Higher," and "Sex Machine." Live versions of "I Want to Take You Higher" and

"Dance to the Music" confirmed the Family's ability to set a crowd on fire—or, some said, to rouse a mob to quasi-fascist ecstasies (see *Woodstock*, Cotillion 3–500).

Next up were "Hot Fun in the Summertime," #2 in 1969, and "Thank You falettinme be mice elf agin"/"Everybody Is a Star," number one in 1970. Sly announced the band's next album, *The Incredible and Unpredictable Sly and the Family Stone*. Unpredictably, it did not materialize; for the reasons why not, and for an unmatched portrait of the personal and professional troubles behind *Riot*, see Timothy Crouse's "Sly Stone: The Struggle for His Soul" (in *What's That Sound?*, ed. Ben Fong-Torres, Garden City: Doubleday Anchor, 1976, or in *Reporting: The Rolling Stone Style*, ed. Paul Scanlon, Garden City: Doubleday Anchor, 1977). To fill the long dry spell between releases, Epic assembled *Greatest Hits* (Epic 30325) in late 1970, and it reached #2, eventually selling over three million copies. A collection of singles and crowd-pleasers, it remains an essential album.

There's a riot goin' on (Epic 30986) reached back to the Robins's (later Coasters) 1955 hit, "Riot in Cell Block #9," for its title ("Scarface Jones said, 'It's too late to quit/Pass the dynamite, 'cause, uh, the fuse is lit,' " wrote Jerry Leiber and Mike Stoller. "There's a riot goin' on." See *The Coasters—The Early Years*, Atco 371). It shared the present with George Jackson's *Soledad Brother* (New York: Bantam, 1970), a book that, while now almost as discredited as its author, certainly had its effect on my ideas about Staggerlee and Sly Stone. (The great study of Jackson, the breakup of the Black Panther Party, and the collapse of radical left politics in the U.S. is Jo Durden–Smith's *Who Killed George Jackson?*, New York: Knopf, 1976. Completely ignored on publication by both the left and mainstream reviewers, it provides no comfort for anyone—and no excuses.) *There's a riot goin' on* was an immediate number one when it was released late in 1971, as was the first single taken from it, "Family Affair." Whether Sly's many white listeners were more open to his difficult new music than his white critics is a question chart positions will not answer; by this time, the black record-buying public was big enough to put a disc over the top all by itself.

Fresh (Epic 32134), complete with Richard Avedon portrait

(the curse of rock—the Band's *Cahoots* had one, too), arrived in 1973, and promptly settled into the Top Ten (#7); its single, "If You Want Me to Stay," topped out at #12. *Fresh* documented conflicts within the group: Rusty Allen replaced Larry Graham on bass (Graham went on to a successful career as a purveyor of bland funk), and Andy Newmark briefly replaced Gregg Errico on drums. Added also were Pat Rizzo on sax and Little Sister (a female vocal trio headed by Sly's sister Vanetta) on backing vocals. Rumors of Doris Day accompanying Sly on "Que Sera, Sera" did not pan out.

In 1974 Sly and Kathy Silva celebrated their marriage (they were later divorced) and the birth of their son with a sold-out wedding at Madison Square Garden—the subject of a full-scale *New Yorker* report. Arriving about the same time was a new album, *Small Talk* (Epic 32930), which documented, by way of further personnel changes and failed music, the disintegration of Sly's "family." The album peaked at #15, a good deal higher than it deserved to go.

From there the road was downhill. In 1975 came *High on You* (Epic 33835), a pointless set that reached #45; *High Energy* (Epic 33462), from the same year, a repackaging of tracks from early LPs, did not make the charts at all. By 1976 Sly was beholden to Parliament–Funkadelic (a band whose leader, George Clinton, told anyone who would listen he was simply building on the inventions of Sly and James Brown) for a spot as opening act; he had to leave the tour after only a few gigs. There were no bookings; *Jet* magazine reported Sly was broke and in hiding. He did produce the optimistically titled *Heard Ya Missed Me, Well I'm Back* (Epic X 698), complete with on-the-jacket apologies from writer Al Aronowitz, an endorsement from producer Kenny Gamble, and a happy-face, one-man-band picture of Sly, but the album did not live up to its title—nor make the charts. The last cut on the LP was "Family Again"; it convinced no one.

In 1979, as the disco craze was fading, Epic released an album of old Sly hits remixed disco-style. (After all, hadn't Sly anticipated the entire movement? But who remembered?) Later that year, Sly "& the Family Stone" (a few original band members returned, for the moment) issued *Back on the Right Track* (Warner

Bros. BSK 3303). Though it was a more than decent album, the "Hey, I'm *fine*, don't believe the rumors, I'm *O.K.!*" titles had begun to drag, and the record had no impact at all. In 1981, Sly worked with George Clinton on Funkadelic's excellent *The Electric Spanking of War Babies* (Warner Bros. BSK 3482), and also collaborated with Clinton in getting arrested for drug possession (charges were later dropped). *Anthology* (Epic E237071), a two-record collection of Sly and the Family Stone hits, appeared about the same time. Sly may still return to surprise everyone; it is more likely that his career is over. One fact remains: in the decade since the release of *There's a riot goin' on*, nothing short of the Sex Pistols' singles has touched it.

STAGGER LEE

"Stack O'Lee" or "Stagolee" was one of several turn-of-the-century ballads about semilegendary characters (they were real, but their legends were more so): figures like Tom Dula (Dooley), John Henry, Casey Jones, Railroad Bill, Frankie and Albert (later Johnnie). Endless variants were popular among both whites and blacks; they were first recorded in the '20s by such songsters as John Hurt, Furry Lewis, Frank Hutchinson, Leadbelly, and many others (see *Anthology of American Folk Music, Vol. 1, Ballads*, ed. Harry Smith, Folkways 2951). These ballads form a special genre; characters sometimes jump from song to song. Furry Lewis put Alice Fry (source of the trouble between Frankie and Albert) into his "Kassie Jones"; in Tom T. Hall's recent "More About John Henry," which draws on folk sources, John Henry meets up with Stackerlee, kills him, and throws his body into a river.

Yet while folklorists have tracked down Frankie and Albert, Railroad Bill, and Casey Jones, and have come close to agreeing on the "real" John Henry, Stagger Lee remains a mystery. Almost all versions of the song share certain details: Stagolee fights Billy over Stack's Stetson hat (in a version collected by John Lomax, Billy *spits* in it); Billy begs Stackerlee not to kill him because he has a wife and children to support; Stack-o-Lee invariably kills him anyway. Beyond that, the story, and Stacker Lee's fate, were up to the singer.

Alan Lomax seems to have been the first to print the song; it was given to him by one Ella Scott Fisher, in 1910, as an account of a murder that had taken place in Memphis about ten years earlier. At the time, Memphis had the highest murder rate in the world; the daily carnage among blacks was so high that on Saturday nights meat wagons were regularly stationed at the end of Beale Street. It seemed odd to me that a single incident, no matter how colorful, would be considered so memorable; that thought, plus the confusion in early versions of the song as to whether Stagger Lee was black or white, made me wonder if a strange reversal might not be hidden in the ambiguities of the tune. Perhaps, I speculated, a white man—Stacker Lee—killed a black man—Billy Lyons. Stagolee was no doubt never even charged, let alone hung. So blacks might have fought back through myth, first exacting justice in song, and then, wishing for a freedom and mastery they could never possess, identifying with their oppressor, subsuming his image into their culture, taking his name, and sending him out to terrorize the world as one of their own. Reversals of this sort are what myth is all about—Frankie, celebrated in almost every variant of her ballad for shooting her unfaithful lover, in fact died by *his* hand—but proof that the true Staggerlee was white would constitute almost as deep a subversion of cultural identity as Freud's claim that Moses was an Egyptian, and I had to find out.

I asked my friend Pat Thomas, a Nashville journalist, to go to Memphis and try to dig out the truth. The truth seems to be that there were two Stagger Lees: one black, and one white.

Samuel Stacker Lee was born on May 5, 1847; he died on April 3, 1890. According to Paul Coppock, a Memphis newspaper writer, Stacker Lee was the brother (others say the son) of James Lee, Sr., who founded the Lee Steamship Line, which ruled the Mississippi from Cincinnati to New Orleans after the Civil War. Lee himself was born in 1808 and died in 1889; to my mind that makes him an unlikely brother of Samuel Stacker Lee, but hardly an impossible one.

"Father of the river packet service," James Lee began his career as a river man in 1833, on the Cumberland. He was close to Jefferson Davis and Nathan Bedford Forrest, later a Confederate hero; in 1863, at the age of sixteen, Stacker Lee went off to fight at

Forrest's side, black manservant in tow. According to Shields McIlwaine's *Memphis Down in Dixie* (New York: Dutton, 1948), which was researched by William McCaskill, Stacker Lee came out of the war ready for bear: a hell-raiser, gambler, rounder, all-round tough guy and ladies' man, known up and down the river once James Lee gave him a boat of his own. James Lee liked the boy, McCaskill told Pat Thomas; the rest of the Lee family, developing a few pretensions to gentility, spurned him—perhaps because his women were mulatto as often as they were white. And though Stacker Lee did have at least one legitimate son—Samuel Stacker Lee, Jr., whom Memphians lost track of when he "moved west"— the second Stacker Lee seems likely to have been Samuel Stacker Lee's son by a mulatto mistress: to put it mildly, his father's son in almost every way.

That, at least, is what many older black residents of Memphis believe today. Stacker Lee, Pat Thomas was told by Thomas Pinkston ("the last man alive to have played with W. C. Handy"), was a roustabout, a waterfront gambler, a legend in his own time; when someone threw a seven, it was called a "Stagolee roll." A very early version of the song places Stagger Lee "in the Bend"—the Tennessee penetentiary—but that was a common ending to ballads of the time. In *Memphis Down in Dixie*, McIlwaine identifies Stagger Lee as a small, dark man with a bad eye, who worked on the Anchor Steamship Line, but there is no documentation; Pinkston remembers hearing his elders speak of Stack-o-Lee as tall, good-looking, and mean.

A date of 1900 seems distinctly too late as an historical date for Stacker Lee's encounter with "Billy"; the late Furry Lewis, who was singing the song well before he recorded it in the '20s, recalled nothing of any specific incident. Lawrence W. Levine notes in *Black Culture and Black Consciousness* (New York: Oxford, 1977) that "Charles Haffer of Coahoma County, Mississippi, remembered first singing of Stagolee's exploits in 1895, while Will Starks, also a resident of the Mississippi Delta, initially heard the Stagolee saga in 1897 from a man who had learned it in the labor camps near St. Louis." No one recalls anything very clearly about a Billy Lyons— though, McCaskill told Thomas, Billy Lyons might be a recasting of Sam de Lyon, or Sandy Lyons, a Memphis cop who was famous for killing five men in one night. And that might turn my imagined reversal on its head. If the Stagger Lee ballad truly incorporated de Lyon, it would mean that, in the fantasy of the song, a black man, Stagolee, killed a white sheriff.

What happened to Staggerlee, Pat Thomas asked Pinkston. "He just disintegrated; old Joe Turner took him up . . . he took 'em all up." By that, Pinkston meant to prison in Nashville; Sheriff Joe Turner was infamous for running black prisoners, or sometimes just blacks rounded up off the streets, from Memphis to Nashville, where the state sold their labor to white planters. "They tell me Joe Turner come to town, brought one thousand links of chain," Leadbelly sang in "Joe Turner." "Gonna have a nigger for every link." But Thomas's search of prison records, birth records, death certificates, and burial records turned up nothing.

In 1902, twelve years after the first, white Stacker Lee was buried (not, for what it's worth, in the Lee family plot), James Lee, Jr., put a boat called the *Stacker Lee* on the river. It was the crack boat of the Lee Line, 223 feet long, built at a cost of $75,000, the most famous boat on the Mississippi, known not only as "Stack O'Lee" but also as "Stack O'Dollars." In 1916, it dragged a landing and went down; the Lee line itself was soon to be put out of business by land transport. James Lee, Jr., was the last river man in the family, and he died in 1905; he left well over a million dollars, and the members of his family fought over the money until the estate was finally settled, thirty years after his death. Blacks took possession of another descendant of the Lee family a long time ago, but the fight over his legacy is a fight over meaning, not money, and no settlement is in sight.

A telling example: in 1977, in Washington, D.C., a man named Mike Malone was fired as arts director of the Western High School for the Performing Arts. Relying on his ties with the virtually all-black student body, he responded with a street play called "The Life and Times of Stagolee" (the play was originally meant to be staged in a nightclub—but shortly before it was to open, the owner was shot to death and the club closed). The Washington *Star* tells the tale: "Malone's adaptation of the Stagolee ballad is [a] somewhat allegorical view of the problems at Western. . . . To Malone, Stagolee 'represents that part of each of us that strives to be free to live our lives as we wish.' And more than that, said one teacher who worked closely with the production, Stagolee represents Malone himself, who fought unsuccessfully to lift the school for the arts out of the institutional constraints of the school system.

"The symbolism comes out strongest when Stagolee, who has 'shot poor Billy dead' over a gambling argument, is called before the Lord to answer for his sins. The teacher pointed out that the Lord took on the image of Superintendent Vincent E. Reed, who dismissed Malone. The Lord's chief advisor in the play consults a female St. Peter, who was said to represent Superintendent Dorothy L. Johnson, who bumped heads with Malone throughout the Western controversy. In the play, the Lord tells Stagolee: 'You have been disruptive and insubordinate and you ain't got no respect for nothing. So we gone have to get rid of you because if there's one thing we cannot have, it's disorder.' But down on earth, Stagolee's mentor, the Voodoo Woman, complains that the powers that be don't understand Stagolee, because they have 'stopped up their ears and closed their minds,' a charge Malone's supporters have often leveled at school authorities.

"Whether or not the audience understood the allegorical connections, they clearly enjoyed the play, despite the poor acoustics and faulty sound system. The audience was made up mostly of residents and regulars of the 14th and T Street area—children, teenagers on bikes, winos and prostitutes. Some T Street residents had box seats at their bedroom windows and front stoops. Some stood on milk crates or trash cans to watch the action.

"Assistant D.C. Police Chief Tilman O'Bryant, one of the Street Theatre's strongest supporters, said he attends the opening performance every year. 'It takes the kids out of the ghetto, develops their talent, and then brings it back to the ghetto,' he said. 'Who else has nerve enough to bring something into the ghetto? They're all scared to come down here.'"

As usual, Billy got lost in the shuffle—unless, through Chief O'Bryant, he had the last word.

Frank Hutchinson, who was white, cut one of the earliest recorded versions of "Stackalee" in 1927; remarkably, its details (not merely the inevitable Stetson hat, but the barking bulldog, the fight in the alley) seem to reappear more clearly in Lloyd Price's 1958 pop hit than in any of the many versions put down in the intervening years. Hutchinson makes a good joke out of the story: "God bless your children, I'll take care of your wife," Stack says after Billy makes his plea; "They taken [Billy] to the cemetery," Hutchinson sings, "they failed to bring him back." But as the song ends, we find Stack in jail—haunted by the phantoms of Billy that crawl around his bed (see *Anthology of American Folk Music, Vol. 1, Ballads*, ed. Harry Smith, Folkways 2951).

Mississippi John Hurt's "Stack O'Lee Blues," made in 1929 and featuring an irresistibly pretty guitar intro, is one of the loveliest of his many recordings (see *The Mississippi Blues, No. 3: Transition, 1926–1937*, Origin Jazz Library 17; also included on *The Story of the Blues*, Columbia 30008, but with very inferior sound quality). The most influential postwar version, before that of Lloyd Price, was by the New Orleans singer Archibald; his "Stack-A-Lee, Parts 1 & 2" was a top ten R&B hit in 1950 (Imperial 5068, now unavailable). Archibald offers the complete scenario of Stagger Lee's fight with the devil, and here we find Stack not hounded by Billy's ghost but chasing the poor fool down to Hell, where Billy suffers still further tortures. Dr. John covered Archibald on his tribute-to-New Orleans album, *Gumbo*, in 1972 (Atco 7006), retaining the words and adding the classic guitar solo from Guitar Slim's "The Things That I Used to Do," plus a horn intro that can break your heart. It is said Dr. John can sing "Stagger Lee" for half an hour without repeating a lyric.

Lloyd Price, also from New Orleans, put the tale on jukeboxes and car radios all across the country in 1958. "Stagger Lee" was his first and only number one hit; he had topped the R&B charts in 1952 with his lovely "Lawdy Miss Clawdy." Judging strictly by lyrics, Price's version takes the prize, if only for his completely original introduction: four lines that, with the perfection of a haiku, set the scene with extraordinary tension and grace.

> *The night was clear*
> *And the moon was yellow*
> *And the leaves . . . came . . . tumbling*
> *Down.*

Price's record was hard rock, driven by a wailing sax, and in retrospect his manic enthusiasm seems to be what many earlier versions lacked. However, an interesting thing happened. As "Stagger Lee" was rising up the charts, Dick Clark booked Price onto "American Bandstand"—and then realized he could not possibly take the responsibility of exposing his millions of young viewers to a song that celebrated gambling and murder. So, true to form, he had Price change the lyrics. Immediately, Price's label pulled the original record, had Price record the "Bandstand" version, and the result was a story wherein Stack and Billy "argue," not gamble, about a girl, not money and a hat. Stagger Lee and Billy go home, suffer remorse for all the mean things they've said to each other, and then *apologize*. "Stagger Lee and Billy were no more sore," Price concluded. Paradoxically, Price sounded even more impassioned on this version than he had in the first place, and his band outdid itself. Though Price (or Dick Clark) had succeeded in turning the great tradition not just on its head but inside out, the tradition, as might have been expected, won in the end: today, when the radio calls up Price's hit, it is only the once-banned version that is played. The reformed Stagger Lee must be sought out on a 45 (ABC–Paramount 45–9972); you can hear the bullet go through Billy and break the bartender's glass on *Lloyd Price's 16 Greatest Hits* (ABC 763).

Wilbert Harrison's 1970 version, which follows Price's story line, is unique among modern treatments for its cautionary tone: "That'll teach ya 'bout gamblin'," Harrison warns (see his *Let's Work Together*, Sue 8801). The Isley Brothers may have added to the subtradition of Billy's "sickly" wife when in 1963 they cut a raging stomp (withering guitar fire courtesy of a young Jimi Hendrix) that, swears Dave Marsh, has Billy trying to talk Stack out of the inevitable by hinting, "I got four little children and a very *shapely* wife." I confess I don't hear it, but I do like the idea, and it's a great record anyway (see *The Famous Isley Brothers Twisting and Shouting*, United Artists 6313).

Because Jamaican rock began in the 1950s partly in response to R&B broadcasts originating in New Orleans, it's no surprise that Stagger Lee made himself felt in early reggae—but in fact he virtually took it over, ruling the symbolism of the new music at least until the late '60s, when he was ousted by Natty Dread and the

Rastafarians (much as Malcolm X finally buried Big Red Little). The years between were spent in a long and frequently hilarious cultural struggle, as Stagolee in the person of the rude boy—the Kingston hooligan who terrorized his own community—claimed his rights, celebrated his prowess, and then fought off the inevitable answer records that called for his rehabilitation (or, failing that, his demise). Literally hundreds of discs told this story; the most striking were the tunes that made up Prince Buster's mid-'6os, anti–rude boy "Judge Dread" trilogy: "Judge Dread," "The Appeal," and "Barrister Pardon"—which were, of course, accompanied by numerous rudie-talks-back answer records (for "Judge Dread" and "Barrister Pardon," see *Prince Buster's Fabulous Greatest Hits*, Fab/Melodisc MS 1, UK). This is a set of three-minute comedic morality plays: a black judge arrives from Ethiopia to clean up the Kingston ghetto, sentences various murderous rude boys to hundreds of years in prison ("*I* am the rude boy now," Judge Dread crows), jails their attorney when he has the temerity to appeal, and then, having reduced all wrongdoers to tears, sets everyone free and steps down from the bench to dance in the courtroom. The final lines, "I am the judge/But I know how to dance," pretty well sum up the ethos of post–rude boy reggae—but Prince Buster was years ahead of his time.

Merging Jamaica's cultural work with the street life of punk-era Great Britain, the Clash used the Stagger Lee–rude boy legend as the underpinning of their epochal *London Calling* (Epic E–2 36328) in 1979. Changing names, faces, and races, the old troublemaker appeared in "Jimmy Jazz," "Rudie Can't Fail," "The Guns of Brixton," and, most powerfully, in the shattering "Death or Glory," which was Stackerlee brought down to earth and made domestic. "Every cheap hood strikes a bargain with the world," Joe Strummer sang, piercing the Stagger Lee aura with a realism it had always deflected, "and ends up making payments on a sofa or a girl/Love 'n' hate tattooed across the knuckles of his hands/The hands that slap his kids around cos they don't understand/How death or glory/Becomes just another story." Fittingly, Stack had surfaced under his own name just a cut earlier, in "Wrong 'em Boyo," originally a Jamaican rock-steady hit by the Rulers. The Clash redid the number with bits of the old ballad itself ("Billy said, 'Hey Stagger!/I'm gonna make my big attack/I'm gonna have to leave my knife/In your back' ") before making the conventional plea for good behavior.

Those seem to me to be the most memorable Stagolees, though I've omitted many of the more famous recordings. A version very close to that offered by Bobby Seale can be found on *Get Your Ass in the Water and Swim Like Me!—Narrative Poetry from Black Oral Tradition* (Rounder 2014), a collection of jailhouse "toasts"—ritualized declamatory insults and stories that in many cases date back to the last century—collected by Bruce Jackson. All of them, not the least "Stackolee," are so obscene they constitute a subversion not only of "decency," but of English itself.

As for the Staggerlee reflection in blues and rock 'n' roll, the records mentioned in the text are: "Crawling Kingsnake," by John Lee Hooker, first recorded in 1949 (available in many versions); "Canned Heat Blues," by Tommy Johnson, 1928 (see *Blues Roots/Mississippi*, RBF 14, or *The Famous 1928 Tommy Johnson–Ishman Bracey Session*, Roots 330, Austria); "Rollin' Stone," by Muddy Waters, 1950 (*Sail On*, Chess 1539); "Brown-Eyed Handsome Man," by Chuck Berry, 1956 (*Chuck Berry's Golden Decade, Vol. 1*, Chess 1514D); "Who Do You Love," by Bo Diddley, 1960 (*Got My Own Bag of Tricks*, Chess 2CH 60005, a superb greatest hits package); "Midnight Mover," by Wilson Pickett, 1968 (*The Best of Wilson Pickett, Vol. 2*, Atlantic 8290); "Midnight Rambler," by the Rolling Stones, 1969 (the studio version on *Let It Bleed* is weak; see the definitive, live performance on *Get Yer Ya-Ya's Out*, London 5); "Back Door Man" and "Going Down Slow," by Howlin' Wolf, 1960 and 1961 (*Howlin' Wolf*, Chess 1469); and "There Is Something on Your Mind," by Bobby Marchan, 1960 (originally released as Fire 45–1022, reissued as a single on Flashback FLB 2).

RECORDS BEFORE AND AFTER 'RIOT'

The tension between black movies and black records that emerged in the late '60s and early '70s brought a realistic necessity to the pop charts—but social comment has not been particularly common in American black music. There have been the rare

Depression blues songs, a few about Korea (brought up to date for Vietnam), not much more. Numerous Coasters records—"Riot in Cell Block #9," "What About Us" ("He's got a car made a' suede/ . . . If we go out on dates we go in a box on roller skates"), "Framed," "Hongry," and the cryptic "Run Red Run" (a monkey, who may represent the Negro, pulls a gun on his master, who may represent the white man)—are notable partly because they were so anomalous; and all were strictly white inventions, or white fantasies about black life, by Jerry Leiber and Mike Stoller ("Run Red Run" and "What About Us," two sides of a 1959 single, are worth seeking out on *Coast Along with the Coasters*, Atco 135).

More typically, black voices have channeled the emotions kicked up by social despair into songs of sexual and romantic tragedy. It took the civil rights movement to make black protest acceptable on the radio, and certainly Sly's "Everyday People" was a turning point, along with Jerry Butler's saddening "Only the Strong Survive," #4 in 1969 (on *The Best of Jerry Butler*, Mercury 61281), and the Temptations' brilliant "Cloud Nine," #6 in 1968, which was the first black record to hit dope head-on—as far as the singer was concerned, with open arms, though the irony of the song was hard to miss (see *The Temptations/Anthology*, Motown M 782A3, a well-organized, extensive career survey, as are all the Motown, Tamla, and Gordy "Anthologies").

Butler's hard look at the world at large and the Tempts' tour of the streets let Paul Kelly into the church to cast out the money-changers; his "Stealing in the Name of the Lord" (Happy Tiger 45-541), #49 in 1970, was a marvelously effective attack on shyster preachers preying on the black community. "Step right up, drop a buck," Kelly chanted over a fast blues guitar. Even more impressive was Swamp Dogg's eccentric *Total Destruction to Your Mind*, 1970 (Canyon 7706), which combined a weird selection of protest songs, among them Joe South's "Redneck," with the year's most elegantly executed soul arrangements. Other seminal discs included Edwin Starr's "War," number one in 1970 (Gordy 45-7101), with its nicely understated chorus: "WAR! What is it good for? ABSOLUTELY NUTHIN'!", and, all from 1971, the Chi-lites' brooding "(For God's Sake) Give More Power to the People," #26 (see *The Chi-Lites' Greatest Hits*, Brunswick 754184); Marvin Gaye's

What's Going On, #6 (Tamla 310), and his historic "Inner City Blues," #9 (see *Marvin Gaye/Anthology*, Motown M782A); Undisputed Truth's "Smiling Faces Sometimes (Tell Lies)," #3 (Gordy 45–7108); and the Staple Singers' occasionally ridiculous ("Put your hand over your mouth when you cough/It'll help your solution") but mostly hard-headed "Respect Yourself," #12 (Stax 45–0104). On most the music was even stronger and more inventive than the politics, which only made the politics more convincing.

If the breakthrough came late in 1971 with *There's a riot goin' on*, the takeover came in 1972 with Curtis Mayfield's soundtrack to *Superfly* (Curtom 8014). With the Impressions and later as a soloist, Mayfield had been exploring a somewhat bland, Martin Luther King-style progressivism for years, complete with open heart, boundless optimism, tortured lyrics, and brotherhood speeches to nightclub audiences; he sang buoyant numbers like "We're a Winner," sticky ones like "Choice of Colors" ("Which one would you choose, my brother?"). With the blasted truths of "Freddie's Dead," #4 in October, and the sardonic yet sympathetic "Superfly," #8 in December, Mayfield found a new voice, and the post-Sly-of-the-'60s music to go with it. His assault was complete when the soundtrack album itself hit the top of the charts.

Along with *Superfly* came the deluge: the O'Jays' "Back Stabbers," #3 (on *Back Stabbers*, Philadelphia International 31712, which also includes "Love Train" and "992 Arguments"); War's "Slipping into Darkness," #16 (United Artists 45–50867; on LP, the complete version can be found only on War's *All Day Music*, United Artists S5546); Stevie Wonder's "Superstition," number one (on *Talking Book*, Tamla 319); Johnny Nash's shimmering "I Can See Clearly Now," number one (Epic 45–10902); the Staple Singers' "I'll Take You There," number one (Stax 45–0125); and the Temptations' terrifying "Papa Was a Rolling Stone," number one (on *Anthology*)—most of them crammed into the last months of 1972.

Contrasting most sharply with the heroes of the new black inner-city Westerns were Al Green and the Chi-Lites: they were vulnerable, open, searching for new ways to define what it meant to be a man. Green's string of hits began in 1970, with "Tired of Being Alone," #11; "Let's Stay Together" was quickly number one in 1971; his likely best, "Look What You've Done for Me," was one of three top ten hits in 1972 (see *Greatest Hits,* Hi 32089). His superb albums from this period, of which *Call Me*, from 1973 (Hi 32077), may be the finest, drew on Hank Williams and Willie Nelson as easily as gospel—but not as deeply. After a violent incident in which a woman killed herself after covering Green with burning grits, Green turned ever more surely toward sanctified music in the late '70s, producing one masterpiece, *The Belle Album* (Hi 3210), in 1977. He now records for the Myrrh label, a subsidiary of Word, Inc., the giant religious media conglomerate that has given us the born-again testimony of, among others, Eldridge Cleaver and Charles Colson. The Chi-Lites' more extreme, and in some ways even more moving music can be best heard on *Greatest Hits* (noted above); it collected "Have You Seen Her," #3 in 1971, "Oh Girl," number one in 1972, plus "A Lonely Man" and "The Coldest Day of My Life."

The chart positions of these post-*Riot* records were, flatly, extraordinary: they represented the most politicized black music in the history of rock 'n' roll, and at the same time the most commercially potent. Never before, and never since, have black voices so dominated American radio. But even as this unique outburst of creativity and commercial success was peaking, a retreat was underway—as if those responsible for the music trusted neither themselves nor their audience.

The Chi-Lites' "We Need Order" (Brunswick 45–55489), which died at #61 in 1972, was joined in anti-Stagger Lee overcompensation by the Four Tops' "Keeper of the Castle," #10 in 1972 (Dunhill 45–4330), which linked *Superfly* streetlife to politics, and damned both: "While you're worryin' about society/The leaves are witherin' on your family tree." This conservatism, or withdrawal from realism, was matched in a completely idiotic way by Brighter Side of Darkness's "Love Jones," #16 early in 1973 (20th Century 45–2002), and more subtly by the Gamble–Huff labels. The contingent social vision of the O'Jays' "Back Stabbers" was undercut by the sentimental social vision of "Love Train," a brotherhood anthem (and a wonderful sound, notwithstanding); when the O'Jays' next few releases flopped, the group returned with *Ship Ahoy* (Philadelphia International 32408), #11 in late 1973, and almost an answer record to Randy Newman's "Sail Away"—because the ship in question was a slave ship. The album was tied to a single, "For the Love of Money," that rather tiredly pegged all evil to filthy lucre, but the killer was the title tune, a ten-minute Middle Passage epic. It was pretentious, overblown, and powerful.

Most black groups, writers, and producers continued to retreat from the work of 1971–72, or trivialized that work with poor self-imitations; their music, like Sly's *Fresh*, though formally well-made, lost much of its feeling. Still scoring in 1973 were Marvin Gaye, who turned to pure sex with the unbelievably erotic "Let's Get It On," number one (see his fine LP of the same name, Tamla 329, certainly the first Motown album to be introduced by a quote from T.S. Eliot), and Stevie Wonder, who continued his mastery of the charts with "Higher Ground" and the deathly "Livin' for the City"—wherein the young hero of *Sounder* leaves his southern home for New York, is set up for a bust by a black "brother," and, years later, emerges from prison trying to remember the dream that first brought him to the city streets he now haunts, his search reduced to an endless circle. The hit single version of the tune stopped with a description of the man's ambitions—you have to go to the album for his fate—but it was to Wonder's credit that the song worked either way (see *Innervisions*, Tamla 326 VI).

Four other records deserve mention; they fell into no ready-made genre, but played in the gap between the imperatives of the new black movies and the music discussed above. First and most important was Diana Ross's much sneered-at soundtrack to *Lady Sings the Blues*, number one in 1972 (Motown 758), a remarkably personal and vital piece of music that served as a backdrop, and a necessary historical anchor, for the other records of the period. It was also perhaps the first time since the careers of Bessie Smith and Billie Holiday herself ended that the Staggerlee story had been revised and publicly acted out by a woman.

The Credibility Gap's comedy album, *A Great Gift Idea* (Warner Bros. 2154), featured a trailer for the ultimate blaxploitation flick: "Black Ivory Productions' *King Pin*, the first movie that has dared to be suggested by the life of the late Dr. Martin Luther King, Jr.—a film of great importance not only to the Afro-American community, but to all Negroes." Opening with an uncanny imitation of Curtis Mayfield's *Superfly* soundtrack ("He's a king, he's a pin"), the piece offered the audience "Denver Deveroll, *eighth-round draft choice* of the New York Jets, who *is* King Pin." "He's got a plan—to stick it to the Man—they call him *'The Doctor'*—and he's got a special treatment—for *whitey!*" Executive producer, "Samuel Hirschorn," of course. Also on the album was a very strange "Evening with Sly Stone," in the form of an educational TV show, where one could find Sly discussing the most arcane points of black culture with William F. Buckley, and then begging off because he has to get to bed by ten so as not to be late for the next day's "recital."

Taj Mahal's music for *Sounder* (Columbia 31944), variations on traditional themes played on traditional instruments, was to me the finest black album of 1972. The movie itself could not have been more different from every other black film on the market: this was a story (based on a white writer's book for children) about sharecropping, family life, oppression, and education. Taj's music and the performances of Cicely Tyson and Paul Winfield spoke for a kind of strength and pride that have everything to do with love between a few people—the mother, father, and children of *Sounder* did not stand simply for their "race," but for themselves. The movie was more painful than the big-city romances that outflanked it; Taj's music had more joy than the records that were hits.

And, finally, there was *Hustler's Convention* (Douglas–United Artists UA–LA 156), by Lightnin' Rod, a former member of the Last Poets: a two-LP version of a story implicit in all of the blaxploitation films. In first-person monologue, with music in the background, Lightnin' Rod recounted the adventures of Sport, a black street kid who reaches the top of the hustler's heap. About halfway through the opus, Lightnin' Rod moved into a detailed account of Sport's climactic poker game. Sport is way ahead (about $100,000 ahead) when an opponent accuses him of cheating; Sport pulls his gun, grabs the pot, and flees. The losers give chase; Sport shoots two dead, but the rest follow—and duck out when the cops arrive. Sport is shot, caught, sent up, and spends twelve years on Sing Sing's death row. "But I kept on coppin' a stay/Till the death penalty was done away/And after a retrial they let me go." It has cost him all that time, Sport says as the record ends, to discover that he has lived exactly as the white man would have wished him to.

No one picked up the movie rights.

RANDY NEWMAN

Randy Newman seems to have taken his first small step toward fame in 1962, when the Fleetwoods recorded his "They Tell Me It's Summer" as the flip of "Lovers by Night, Strangers by Day" (Dolton 45-62). The Fleetwoods vanished from sight almost immediately.

Working as a contract songwriter for Metric Music, a division of Liberty Records, which passed his compositions on to singers on the label and its subsidiaries, Newman turned out formula pop songs, made demos, and released at least one teen-market disc under his own name: "Golden Gridiron Boy"/"Country Boy" (Dot 45-16411), issued in October, 1962. Neither tune was exceptional, though "Golden Gridiron Boy" today has a certain ironic poignancy—since, here, Randy sings in the voice of one who is "too short" to get the girl.

Gene McDaniels cut "Somebody's Waiting" as the flipside of "Spanish Lace" (Liberty 45-55510), also in 1962; Newman considers the number his first "big record" ("Spanish Lace" topped out at #32), probably because it brought him his first measurable royalty check. Other singers who recorded his early songs included Irma Thomas ("While the City Sleeps" on her superb *Wish Someone Would Care*, Imperial 9266), Billy Storm ("Baby Don't Look Down," Loma 45-2001), Frankie Laine ("Take Her," Columbia 45-42884), Little Peggy March ("Leave Me Alone," RCA 45-8357), the O'Jays ("Friday Night," Imperial 45-66197), and Irma Franklin ("Love Is Blind," Epic 45-9610). Mostly, Newman tried to match such Aldon Music Co. writers as Carole King and Gerry Goffin—and hoped for a chance at a Bobby Vee B-side.

Newman's first real notoriety came in 1966, with Judy Collins' recording of "I Think It's Going to Rain Today" on her arty *In My Life* LP. In 1967 there was Van Dyke Parks's fey version of the fabulous "Vine Street," a Hollywood "On Broadway" that Newman never released himself (see Parks's *Song Cycle*, Warner Bros. 1727). 1968 brought Alan Price's *This Price Is Right* (Parrot 71018), which featured five Newman songs, including the perfect sweet sixteen fantasy, "The Biggest Night of Her Life."

Randy Newman Creates Something New Under the Sun (Reprise 6286) also appeared in 1968, decked out with a cover photo that pictured Randy as a throwback to the thrilling days of, say, 1947; Reprise later substituted a shot of Randy with longer hair, but it didn't do much good so far as sales were concerned. Overproduced, occasionally musically cute, the album lived up to its title anyway. "Love Story," the first cut, was the clincher: here was an American romance, from proposal to the grave, with every warm promise undercut by a darker promise. When the kids are grown, Randy-the-Suitor tells his bride-to-be, "they'll send us away, to a little home"—and that's all part of the dream, or the deal. Also included were "So Long Dad" ("Love Story" sung from the point of view of Dad's grownup son: "Drop by anytime," he assures his father. "Just be sure and call before you do"), "Living Without You" (marvelously redone in 1972 on *Manfred Mann's Earth Band*, Polydor 5015), "Davy the Fat Boy," and "The Beehive State," a weird little masterpiece about the forgotten territory between L.A. and New York. At some grand all-American convention, the delegate from Utah rises. "We gotta tell this country about Utah," he says with all his courage, "because nobody seems to know."

12 Songs (Reprise 6373), released in 1970, was a far better record; Randy's piano and voice were up front, and the orchestration was stripped down and muted. If *Something New* was a showbiz fantasia, *12 Songs* leaned on the blues and New Orleans piano rock. Newman's imagination went wild within his tight little structures, producing "Let's Burn Down the Cornfield" ("And I'll make love to you, while it's burning," Newman added), "Suzanne," "Lucinda" (the victim of the beach-cleaning machine), "Yellow Moon," "Old Kentucky Home," "Underneath the Harlem Moon," and a few other works of genius. Three Dog Night got a number one hit out of a Stepin Fetchity version of "Mama Told Me Not to Come" later in 1970.

Randy Newman Live (Reprise 6459) was Newman's first chart entry, fading away at #191 in 1971. Despite "Lonely at the Top," it's not a good record; the sound and feeling are thin, and little of Newman's wonderful stage personality comes across. "Tickle Me" and "Maybe I'm Doing It Wrong," neither much more than one-line jokes, were thankfully left off other albums.

Sail Away (Reprise 2064) was issued in 1972, and rose to #163 on the charts. It collected "Lonely at the Top," "Burn On," "Political Science," and "Memo to My Son," a song about fatherhood that insisted on "When the going gets tough, the tough get going" as an absolute non sequitur. The album closed—and felt as if it were closing down the world—with "God's Song (That's Why I Love Mankind)."

"Sail Away" was recorded by many singers; Linda Ronstadt accomplished the dumbest version, while Salvation was responsible for altering the "little wog" reference to "little child." Newman's ironies were compounded geometrically when the tune was cut by veteran black songsters Sonny Terry and Brownie McGhee: they sang "Sail Away" as the lament of two ex-slaves reminiscing about the good old days before the Yankees came and ruined their happy home, and it was not for the tender-hearted. (See *Sonny & Brownie*, A&M 4397, an album that promoted some ironies of its own when it showcased archetypal British bluesman John Mayall on "White Boy Lost in the Blues.")

In 1974 Newman unveiled a project he'd been threatening for years: *Good Old Boys* (Reprise 2193), a picture of the American South that spanned half a century. The ethos Newman aimed for was one of fierce pride undercut by terrible guilts, of guilt driven off by pride—or, when that failed, whiskey. Included were love songs, work songs, a tune by Huey Long ("Every Man a King," done as the sing-along the Kingfish had written it to be—though he probably hadn't had a couple of the Eagles in mind—and not as the weird piece of soul music Newman alone could have made it), and a few strange adventures involving whites disguised as blacks, rural degeneration, exhibitionism, and the like.

The album's one moment of triumph was "Louisiana 1927." A beautiful Stephen Foster–like string intro—close to something out of Walt Disney's *The Song of the South*—kicked it off, and then those familiar piano notes from "Sail Away" drifted in, guiding a first line that in its simplicity and mystery—"Art," to quote Kathleen

Cleaver, "that conceals art"—is as pure an American language as anyone will ever hear. To begin a song about a flood, Newman simply sang: "What has happened down here, is the wind have changed." And then, as one of the people that happened to, he tried to tell you what it meant. It was, the song struggled to say, no accident: the country, or luck, or nature, or God, was taking revenge on the South. The great Mississippi flood of 1927 inspired dozens of songs—Blind Lemon Jefferson's "Rising High Water Blues," Bessie Smith's "Muddy Water (A Mississippi Moan)," and Vernon Dalhart's "The Mississippi Flood" among them—but Newman's is the best, because it has the strongest sense of place. (How Pete Daniel missed mentioning "Louisiana 1927" in his fine *Deep'n As It Come: The 1927 Mississippi Flood*, New York: Oxford, 1977, is beyond me: he missed nothing else.)

Good Old Boys was not a complete success, perhaps because Newman's ambitions were a good deal grander than his will to put them into practice. Many of the songs on this concept album are part of the concept only by fiat, and the orchestration is sometimes out of control, as if to hide the real action—or the lack of it. Still, the concept helped sell the record, which did well for a Newman set, reaching #36 in the U.S., and even winning Randy a gold record—in Holland. "I think they like me there because they think I hate America," Randy said. "How depressing."

In 1977 Newman got his hit: the notorious "Short People," which, climbing all the way to number one on some charts, pulled the accompanying *Little Criminals* (Warner Bros. BSK 3079) to #9, high enough to achieve all-American gold-record status. The single, which remains Randy's sole dent in *Billboard*'s Hot 100, could have been taken as a slap at the irrationality of prejudice; many saw it as a pleasurable indulgence in the very same thing. Rock 'n' roller Graham Parker and novelist John Irving, both certified short people, told me how impressed they were that "a short person like Randy Newman had the nerve to write a song like that"; both were notably unhappy to learn of Randy's excessive height. Addressing the controversy ("Short People" was actually "banned in Boston"), critic Dave Marsh, who was once known as "the teenage dwarf," formulated the doctrine that no one was "short" who was taller than he; he also coined the word "sizist" which was immediately put into use by organizations representing people with the appropriate physical deformity.

Little Criminals was, *Randy Newman Live* aside, Newman's poorest LP. With such tunes as "Jolly Coppers on Parade," "In Germany Before the War" (an equation of fascism and sexual perversion no more convincing than Alberto Moravia's in *The Conformist*), and "Sigmund Freud's Impersonation of Albert Einstein in America" (a tune meant for the soundtrack to the film of *Ragtime*), the music was pallid, and Newman's ironies seemed more than anything a fey substitute for a commitment to his material. Backing vocals by the Eagles didn't just sound smooth; they were highlights.

Born Again (Warner Bros. HS 3346), released in 1979, was a rebound—significantly going no higher than #41 on the charts. The album jacket pictured Randy in Kiss-style makeup, with dollar signs painted over his eyes. "It's Money that I Love" was a number Fats Domino would have appreciated, if not sung. "I don't love Jesus, he never done a thing for me," Randy proclaimed. "Short People" had clearly made Randy suspicious of his audience, and of himself—not, perhaps, an ideal position for a popular artist, but the only position Newman can work from. And if nothing else on *Born Again* quite matched "Money," at least "The Story of a Rock and Roll Band," "Half a Man" (an unfashionable expression of homophobia), and "Pretty Boy" (an unfashionable assault on, depending how one heard it, John Travolta or Bruce Springsteen) kept up the pace. The disc ended in a tailspin with "Pants," yet another kinky sex number, and there were easy-target tunes throughout—but there was hope. With Ronald Reagan as president, Newman's task is clear; the only question is whether he's willing to work at it. Myself, I'm looking forward to a song about a right-to-lifer who has an abortion.

Newman's only other recorded vocal work is a cut on the soundtrack to the 1970 film *Performance:* a dynamic, near-hysterical rocker about premature ejaculation called (after an old King Solomon Hill blues) "Gone Dead Train" (see *Performance*, Warner Bros. 2554). Of songs Newman has written for others but not recorded himself, Dusty Springfield's lovely "Just One Smile," and her "I

Don't Want to Hear It Anymore" (both on the great *Dusty in Memphis*, Atlantic 8214) are likely the best.

I want to thank Susan Lydon for the help she gave me on the Newman chapter; I had the benefit of her conversations with Randy, and I have taken some quotes and much biographical information from her excellent profile, "Randy Newman—Out of Cole Porter, Hoagy Carmichael, Bob Dylan, Groucho Marx, Mark Twain, and Randy Newman" (*The New York Times Magazine*, November 5, 1972). We had a good time trading ideas one night at the Palace Theater in San Francisco, as Randy played God up on stage and the audience gave him the cheers he deserved.

CAMEOS: RAYMOND CHANDLER, NATHANAEL WEST, THE BEACH BOYS, & OTHERS

All of my quotes from Chandler come from *Raymond Chandler Speaking* (Boston: Houghton Mifflin, 1977), a collection of letters, articles, and fiction fragments. Chandler's mysteries, especially *The Big Sleep* (1939) and *Farewell, My Lovely* (1940), have greatly influenced my picture of Los Angeles, as have Ross MacDonald's detective stories, notably *The Way Some People Die* (1951) and *The Chill* (1964). Chandler's books are in various Ballantine editions; MacDonald's are published by Bantam. I think Nathanael West's *Day of the Locust* (1939), though quite inferior to Chandler's best, belongs to the same "There's nothing wrong with Southern California that a rise in the ocean level wouldn't cure" (MacDonald) genre—though each of these writers would expect to go under along with everybody else (see *Miss Lonelyhearts/Day of the Locust*, New York: New Directions, 1962).

The other side of the California story ("There's nothing wrong with surfing conditions a rise in the ocean level wouldn't cure") is best told by Jan & Dean and the Beach Boys. The former's immortal "Surf City," number one in 1963, and cowritten by Beach Boy Brian Wilson, can be found on *Jan & Dean Anthology Album* (United Artists 9961), a crazed two-record set that comes with a concordance that matches the duo's discs with the car and girl friend each singer had at the time any given 45 was released. The Beach Boys' wondrous mid-'60s work is best heard on *The Best of the Beach Boys, Vol. 2* (Capitol 2706), which includes "409," "Let Him Run Wild," the touching what-if-summer-doesn't-last-forever anthem "When I Grow Up to Be a Man," "California Girls," and the group's finest, "I Get Around." Also worth seeking out from this period are *Beach Boys' Party* (Capitol 2364), to which Dean of Jan & was luckily invited, and the marvelous *Wild Honey* (Capitol 2859). If at all possible, avoid the *Endless Summer* and *Spirit of America* reissue albums, which present lifeless stereo versions of songs that were never meant to be heard in anything but pure punchy mono. If the original LPs are hard to find, try the oldies bin in the singles section of your local good record store.

The Beach Boys wanted more out of life than cars and surf could give them; their vision had always been a passive one, and like many they went from easy questions to easy answers. When they recorded a song by an aspiring singer/songwriter named Charles Manson—pal of Beach Boys drummer Dennis Wilson, and a shaman who combined in equal parts the displaced lumpen proletariat West found crusted beneath Hollywood and the high-rent Dr. Feelgoods Chandler hated above all others—the Beach Boys were truly faced with the challenge of growing up: a challenge they failed to meet. *The Family* (New York: Dutton, 1971), Ed Sanders's classic investigation of Manson loose in postsurf Hollywood, lays out the facts of the Southern California synthesis of sun and horror, just as Randy Newman's songs capture its soul.

Unlike so many Los Angeles groups that come from somewhere else, the Beach Boys were never fakes. Empty, tired, and desperate as they may have been throughout the '70s, they still dealt with, or acted out, life as some people actually lived it. The Beach Boys celebrated California hedonism, looked for its limits, experienced its failures. Their pleasures, as opposed to those claimed by such latter-day inheritors as the Eagles, have always radiated affection—because those pleasures were rooted in friendship, or a memory of it.

THE KINKS

The Kinks, now pressing on to their twentieth year, will likely be remembered as one of the oddest of rock 'n' roll bands, and as one of the best. For crude, brutal hard rock, their early singles outclassed those of the Beatles and the Rolling Stones, probably because the resentment and rage such music communicates was exactly what Kinks leader Ray Davies felt: he really doesn't like it here. Davies is genuinely at home only in his fantasies of a simpler time, when class lines were clear, when everyone knew everyone else's place, when, presumably, there would have been a place even for Davies. His search for a phantom paradise has taken him as deeply into the throes of nostalgia as anyone in pop music—thus the dull pleas for the preservation of village greens, and thus the power to make records as disturbing and haunting as "The Way Love Used to Be" and "I'm Not Like Everybody Else."

Those last are the highlights of *The Great Lost Kinks Album* (Warner Bros. 0598). The initial 1964–66 smashes (the hard rockers, like "You Really Got Me," and the first attempts at social satire, like "A Well Respected Man") are on *The Kinks' Greatest Hits* (Reprise 6217). Davies's sharpest work came in 1967, with *Face to Face* (Reprise 6228), which included "Sunny Afternoon," and in 1968, with *Something Else* (Reprise), which sings to a close with the band's masterpiece, "Waterloo Sunset."

These last records sold hardly at all, but *Arthur (Or, the Decline and Fall of the British Empire)* (Reprise 6366), released in 1969, and *Lola Versus Powerman and the Moneygoround* (Reprise 6423), from 1970, brought the Kinks new fans even as Davies's songs grew more heavy-handed. The great "Lola" is best heard on *The Kink Kronikles* (Reprise 6454), a collection of album cuts, nonhits, and unreleased tunes.

Ever campy, struggling, and hopefully trendy—with "Superman" and a hapless attack on punk—the Kinks roll on. By the end of the '70s their very "survival" was cause for praise, but save for the occasional wonderful surprise like "Celluloid Heroes" or "20th Century Man," they roll downhill. Randy Newman is smarter than Ray Davies, but whether his career will have a better ending remains to be seen.

ELVIS PRESLEY

ELVIS: AN INTRODUCTION

In 1974 RCA issued *Elvis: A Legendary Performer, Vol. 1* (RCA CPL 1–0341), a single album that illustrates, historically and aesthetically, virtually every side of the man's music. As an outline of my concerns, I could hardly have made a more useful selection myself.

Legendary Performer begins at Sun, with "That's All Right (Mama)," Elvis's first single, followed by "I Love You Because," the sentimental country-tune-with-narration that was in fact his very first officially logged professional recording—though Sam Phillips never released it, and this complete version was never previously released by RCA. Then immediately to "Heartbreak Hotel," altogether unlike the Sun discs (and a concession to the "cool jazz" sound popular at the time, if the truth be told), number one on pop, country, and R&B charts early in 1956. A snatch of interview from that time: a reporter asks Elvis if his success is due to luck or talent, and Elvis, naturally, answers Luck. Without a pause we are into "Don't Be Cruel," also a 1956 three-chart number one, and it gives the lie to Elvis's modesty (if not his guile): no one has ever sung with such confidence.

We hear "Love Me Tender," the title song from Elvis's first movie; we hear "(There'll Be) Peace in the Valley (For Me)," from 1957, Elvis's first, and perhaps best, gospel record.* Then to "(Now and Then There's) A Fool Such As I," from 1958, where

---

*A country hit in 1951 for Red Foley, this remarkable song was written by the Rev. Thomas A. Dorsey, a man who might have understood the contradictions of Elvis's music: in the 1920s, as the bluesman Georgia Tom, he scandalized pious black families throughout the South with his suggestive lyrics. Born in 1899 and still living as I write in 1981, he became "the father of modern gospel" by combining blues and jazz modes with sanctified themes; drawing on the spiritual "We Shall Walk through the Valley in Peace," Dorsey composed "Peace in the Valley" while riding on a train in 1939, thinking about the war that had just begun in Europe, and measuring his fears against the suddenly comforting valley he found himself passing through. For his blues, see *Georgia Tom Dorsey, 1928–1932: Come on Mama Do that Dance* (Yazoo 1041), and *Georgia Tom and Friends, 1928/31* (Mercury 6332 991, France); for his gospel, *Precious Lord: New Recordings of the Great Gospel Songs of Thomas A. Dorsey* (Columbia CG 32151); and for an inspired essay (on Dorsey, Elvis, and much more), Tom Smucker's "Precious Lord," in *Stranded,* ed. Greil Marcus (New York: Knopf, 1979).

Elvis distances himself from his style with outrageous parody; then to "Tonight's All Right for Love," a ghastly number from the 1960 film *G.I. Blues*, where we find that the parody has become the style.

Scattered through the album are three songs, cut live with a small combo and an audience, from the television comeback performance of 1968: a joking "Are You Lonesome To-night?"; a staggering "Love Me," with Elvis wavering between parody and passion until passion finally wins; and "Tryin' to Get to You," a song Elvis first recorded in 1955. Thirteen years later he sings it as a message to his audience: his way of telling anyone who cared to know how hard it was for him to find his way back, and what the trip was worth. His singing makes his early classics seem immature, unfocused, almost empty. They were not, of course, but this music—all glamour, fury, and drama—is not like anything else in rock 'n' roll.

Legendary Performer ends, as it should, with "Can't Help Falling in Love," from the *Blue Hawaii* soundtrack of 1961—the song that became the theme of Elvis-in-the-'70s, at least until the end, when it was replaced by "My Way." Here, it sounds like a hymn.

On this album, Elvis's long career makes sense, it has shape. One can hear the artist grow, the god fail, the King return, the man endure. As a version of American possibility and American limits, it is fully the equal of Robert Johnson's *King of the Delta Blues Singers*. Given hindsight, a version of "Hellhound on My Trail" is all the set is missing.

With *Legendary Performer* as a map, we can turn to Elvis's music in detail.

THE SUN SIDES, 1953–55

Original Sun discs by Elvis now go for well over $100 each; RCA reissued all five singles immediately upon signing Elvis in late 1955, and reissues of *those* 45s are still available (and, because of the drop in sound quality whenever these sides have been transferred to LP, are well worth ordering). All of the Sun material that has so far come to light—with the exception of certain alternate takes noted below, and a 1954 version of "Harbor Lights," which turned up in 1976 on *Legendary Performer, Vol. 2* (RCA CPL 1-1349)—is collected on *The Sun Sessions* (RCA APM 1-1675).

Elvis's initial recordings were made in June, 1953, at the Memphis Recording Service, a cut-your-own-disc operation ("$3 one side, $4 two sides") Sam Phillips had set up to supplement the uncertain income of the prerock Sun label. Although according to legend Elvis showed up to make a birthday record for his mother, I side with Hans Langbroek, author of a Dutch booklet called *The Hillbilly Cat*, who suggests that since Gladys Presley's birthday fell in April, Elvis really made the record for himself, hoping someone would notice him. Whatever his motive, Elvis put down two standards: the Ink Spots' "My Happiness," and "That's When Your Heartaches Begin," a country weeper he had been singing since childhood. A few months later he was back, to record "A Casual Love" and "I'll Never Stand in Your Way." Though the performances (none of which has ever been released) were reportedly ordinary, Marion Keisker, Phillips's co-manager at Sun, heard something special in Elvis's voice, taped some of his singing, and pushed her boss to give the boy an audition.

Not long after—in late 1953 or early 1954—Elvis had his chance. A demo acetate of a song called "Without You" had arrived in the mail at Sun; Sam Phillips liked the song, but he was even more taken with the black singer's voice. Phillips tried to locate the man, to make a finished record, but the Nashville publisher who had sent the demo had no idea of the singer's identity; he was just someone hanging around the office. "Why not try the boy with the sideburns?" Marion Keisker said.

Elvis was called back to Sun; Phillips played him the demo. The performance has never been released or bootlegged; only one copy exists, and no tapes are in circulation. To listen to the disc today is ghostly; it is to be transported to the very instant before the beginning of the present age. The lost singer's voice is full of pain and full of acceptance; it glides along the stately lines of the song, reaching for solace, falling short, reaching once more. It's pure Sisyphus—and, as Camus said of Sisyphus, one must imagine this singer happy.

One can hear the gospel tones of Johnny Bragg of the Prisonaires, Sonny Til of the Orioles, Bill Kenny of the Inkspots. But most of all, one hears—Elvis. And yet as soon as one identifies what, it seems, Elvis must have taken from the demo, that element vanishes. Then it creeps back. What could Elvis have heard?

All afternoon long, Elvis tried to sing "Without You." He couldn't do it; take after take ended in a shambles. He couldn't match the singer who has never been discovered. Finally, Elvis turned away from the mike and pounded his fists against the wall. "I hate him!" he shouted. "I hate him!"

Phillips was intrigued. He brought Elvis together with guitarist Scotty Moore and Bill Black;* they spent months rehearsing, trying to work out a distinctive sound. On July 6, 1954, they got results. Elvis's Sun singles followed in this order:

"That's All Right (Mama)" b/w "Blue Moon of Kentucky," released July 19, 1954 (Sun 209, RCA 447–0601). Original version of "That's All Right" by Mississippi blues singer Arthur "Big Boy" Crudup, 1946 (see *Arthur Crudup: Father of Rock and Roll*, RCA V–573; also included are Crudup's originals of "So Glad You're Mine" and "My Baby Left Me," which Elvis recorded soon after leaving Sun for RCA). Original version of "Blue Moon of Kentucky" by bluegrass singer Bill Monroe, 1946 (see *Bill Monroe's 16 Greatest Hits*, Columbia 1065). Elvis's slow, early version of the song, with studio dialogue between Elvis, Scotty Moore, and Sam Phillips, can be found on *Good Rocking Tonight* (Bopcat 100, Holland), an essential bootleg that has itself been bootlegged countless times, or on *The Rockin' Rebel* (Golden Archives 250), also a bootleg.

"Good Rockin' Tonight" b/w "I Don't Care if the Sun Don't Shine," released September 25, 1954 (Sun 210, RCA 447–0602). Original versions of "Good Rockin' Tonight" by urban jump blues singers Roy Brown (who wrote it), 1947, and Wynonie Harris (who had the hit), 1948 (for Brown's version, see *Good Rocking Tonight*, Route 66 KIX–6, UK; for Harris's, see *Good Rockin' Blues*, King 1086). "I Don't Care if the Sun Don't Shine" previously re-

---

*Elvis's first two singles featured only "Scotty and Bill" (as the labels read), but later Sun recordings often included drums (on the "country" sides more frequently than on the "rhythm" sides, interestingly enough). The drummer was not, as has long been assumed, D. J. Fontana, Elvis's first on-stage drummer, but one Johnny Bomero—who seems to have vanished into oblivion, where he is no doubt trading tales of what might have been with Jimmy Nicol, who replaced an ailing Ringo when the Beatles toured Australia in 1964.

corded by various singers, including Georgia Gibbs in 1951; alternate takes on the *Good Rocking Tonight* bootleg. Rhythm (hands slapped on cardboard box to simulate bongo drums) by Sun singer Billy Cunningham.

"Milkcow Blues Boogie" b/w "You're a Heartbreaker," released January 8, 1955 (Sun 215, RCA 447–0603). Original versions of "Milkcow" by Georgia country blues singer Kokomo Arnold, 1934 (as "Milk Cow Blues"; see *Kokomo Arnold/Peetie Wheatstraw*, Blues Classics 4), and by the Western swing orchestra Bob Wills and His Texas Playboys, 1946 (as "Brain Cloudy Blues"; see *The Bob Wills Anthology*, Columbia 32416). "You're a Heartbreaker" first recorded by Elvis.

"Baby Let's Play House" b/w "I'm Left, You're Right, She's Gone," released April 1, 1955 (Sun 217, RCA 447–0604). Original versions of "Baby Let's Play House" by country singer Eddy Arnold, 1951 (as "I Want to Play House with You"; see *All-Time Favorites*, RCA 1223), and by R&B singer Arthur Gunter, 1955 (see *Black & Blues*, Excello 8017). Buddy Holly's first clumsy attempts to turn himself into Elvis can be heard in his version of the tune (which owes as much to Arnold as to Elvis), cut in late 1955 as "I Wanna Play House with You" (see *Holly in the Hills*, Coral 757463, or *The Complete Buddy Holly*, MCA 6–80.000). "I'm Left, You're Right, She's Gone" first recorded by Elvis; the slow, torchy alternate version Sam Phillips made available only to DJs, as "My Baby Is Gone," is on the *Good Rocking Tonight* bootleg. "Baby Let's Play House" was the first Elvis record to make the national charts, reaching #10 on *Billboard*'s country rankings.

"Mystery Train" b/w "I Forgot to Remember to Forget," released August, 1955 (Sun 223, RCA 447–6000). Original versions of "Mystery Train" by the Carter Family, 1930 (as "Worried Man Blues"; see *The Famous Carter Family*, Harmony 11332), and by Little Junior's Blue Flames (blues singer Junior Parker), 1953 (see the broadly programmed anthology *Catalyst*, Charly 30101, UK; *The Legendary Sun Performers: Junior Parker and Billy Love*, Charly 30135, UK; or the highly recommended EP, *Junior Parker*, Charly CEP 104, UK). "I Forgot to Remember to Forget," cowritten by Charlie Feathers and first recorded by Elvis, was a number one country hit.

The following Sun recordings (included on *The Sun Sessions*), were sold, along with Elvis's contract, to RCA Victor in 1955, and released on Elvis's first album in 1956: "I Love You Because," "I'll Never Let You Go (Little Darlin')," "Just Because," and "Blue Moon" (recorded in 1954), and "Tryin' to Get to You" (recorded in 1955). The original version of "Tryin' to Get to You" is interesting as one of the first rockabilly recordings made outside of Memphis: it was cut in 1955 in Clovis, New Mexico, by the Teen Kings—lead singer, Roy Orbison—and produced by Norman Petty, who later guided Buddy Holly and the Crickets to fame (sharing composing credits was Shelby Singleton, who was to buy the Sun label from Sam Phillips in 1969). Released on Jew-el, the Clovis recording (Orbison later redid the tune and its flipside, "Ooby Dooby," for Sun) can be found on *Memphis Rocks the Country* (Redita 106, Holland), a collection of sides featuring Sam Phillips's first attempts to teach rock 'n' roll to country singers like Malcolm Yelvington and Hardrock Gunter.

A number of Sun cuts still remain in the vaults: most often mentioned are versions of various country hits, including Bill Monroe's "Uncle Pen," Red Foley's "Tennessee Saturday Night," Roy Acuff's "Night Train to Memphis"; there are perhaps a dozen others, plus alternate takes. One Sun recording not advertised as such is a cover of bluesman Lonnie Johnson's 1947 ballad "Tomorrow Night," which RCA dressed up with additional accompaniment and released in 1965 on *Elvis for Everyone* (RCA 3450). Those seeking more music from this period should search out *Elvis, Scotty and Bill: The First Year* (Very Wonderful Golden Editions/Virgin King–1, UK), an official release which includes live recordings made in Houston at Eagle's Hall in March, 1955. Elvis is quite audible, his band less so ("I'd like to shake around here for ya all night," Elvis drawls, "but we're booked into Alcatraz tomorrow—got a long drive ahead of us"). *The Rockin' Rebel, Vol. II* (Golden Archives 300), a bootleg, collects the Eagle's Hall numbers along with radio checks of Louisiana Hayride appearances from the summer of 1954, December, 1954 (a cover of Lavern Baker's "Tweedlee Dee"), and December, 1956; save for the last date, the sound is excellent and the performances classic.

On December 4, 1956, Elvis, already a national hero/

Antichrist, returned to the Sun studios in Memphis (by then known as "the chicken shack with the Cadillacs out back") and sat in with Carl Perkins and Jerry Lee Lewis for an informal country sing of gospel and rock. Phillips recorded the session, which became famous as "The Million Dollar Quartets" (Johnny Cash, who was thought to have completed the "quartet," appeared in group photos taken that day, but didn't sing), and release of the music was announced several times following Elvis's death. No release was forthcoming, though, because of conflicts between Shelby Singleton, by then owner of rights to Lewis's and Perkins's contributions, and RCA, which, by virtue of its original deal with Sam Phillips, owned rights to Elvis's performance. But late in 1980 a very official-looking (but not very well-pressed) bootleg appeared: *The Million Dollar Quartet* (One Million Dollars 001, UK) —and, at least in Great Britain, a release under the same title followed six months later (Sun/Charly 1006). Rumors of several hours of material notwithstanding, the album runs only about thirty minutes; there are seventeen songs and snatches of songs, including "Little Cabin on the Hill," "Keeper of the Key," "Just a Little Talk with Jesus," "Walk that Lonesome Valley," "Peace in the Valley," "Down by the Riverside," "Farther Along," and a hilarious and stirring version of Pat Boone's then just-released "Don't Forbid Me." "Hey, have you heard Pat Boone's new record?" Elvis says, to much derogatory laughter all around. "It was written for *me*. It stayed around my house for ages, never did see it—*junk!*" The singing, when it has time to get going, is free, impassioned, and ironic; Carl Perkins and Elvis provide punchy rockabilly guitar.

THE TRIUMPH, 1956–59

Elvis's first recording for RCA, "Heartbreak Hotel" b/w "I Was the One," coincided with his first national television appearances (Elvis had previously been rejected by "Arthur Godfrey's Talent Scouts," in the mid-'50s America's principal showcase for unknown talent), and the exposure did much to divide the country into friends and enemies. The U.S.A. initially saw Elvis on Tommy and Jimmy Dorsey's "Stage Show" (six appearances in the first three months of 1956); these performances can be found on

The Elvis Presley Dorsey Shows (Golden Archives 100), a well-made bootleg that includes "Blue Suede Shoes," "Tutti Frutti," Joe Turner's "Flip, Flop and Fly," "Baby Let's Play House," Clyde McPhatter & the Drifters' "Money Honey," and others. In June, 1956, Elvis made his second appearance on "The Milton Berle Show"; for "Hound Dog," "I Want You, I Need You, I Love You," and a hilarious interchange with Debra Paget, later Elvis's co-star in *Love Me Tender*, see *The Rockin' Rebel* (Golden Archives 250).

It was about this time that Ed Sullivan, then king of American television, declared that "Elvis will never appear on my show." However, since Elvis turned up on "The Steve Allen Show" on July 1, opposite Sullivan's presentation of skits based on John Huston's film version of *Moby Dick*, and, not unlike Melville's monster, sank Sullivan in the ratings, "never" meant only a few months—probably about as long as it took to negotiate Elvis's unprecedented $50,000 fee. *From the Waist Up* (Golden Archives 150), again a bootleg, collects Elvis's performances on "The Ed Sullivan Show" (three appearances between September 8, 1956 and January 6, 1957). These were the shows that put Elvis over as a national figure: according to Neal and Janet Gregory's meticulous *When Elvis Died* (Washington, D.C.: Communications Press, 1980; New York: Washington Square Press, 1981), 82.6 percent of the American population watched the first program. (This figure is completely unbelievable—it is not altogether certain that on September 8, 1956, 82.6 percent of the American population even knew Eisenhower was president—but what the hell.) Songs on the three shows included "Don't Be Cruel," "Peace in the Valley," "Love Me," "Too Much," "Love Me Tender," and an amazing "Ready Teddy." It was only on the 1957 show, incidentally, that Elvis was telecast "from the waist up"; the previous shows displayed him in—as the vaguely pornographic phrase generally used has it—"full body shot."

An excellent alternative to these hard-to-find bootlegs is the two-LP soundtrack to Malcolm Leo and Andrew Solt's 1981 film *This Is Elvis* (RCA CPL 2–4031), an unusually well-programmed retrospective that includes performances from the Dorsey, Berle, and Sullivan programs: sound quality is excellent. An even better (if more expensive) alternative is video. Most of Elvis's early TV appearances, many of his movies, the 1968 comeback TV special (with hours of small-combo, big-band, and production-number outtakes), and the later TV specials, are now available on licensed video cassettes, and can be ordered through video magazines. Sound and picture quality on the early material is often poor; the later material is first-rate. And *Elvis in Concert in 1968* (All Star Video Corp.)—ninety uncut minutes from the '68 Special, with Elvis jamming with his little rockabilly combo and then outrunning the big studio rock band—is beyond human ken.

This Is Elvis itself, crammed with period footage, makes it clear why Elvis's early TV performances caused so much trouble: Elvis, clearly perceiving the limits of what America had learned to accept as shared culture, purposefully set out to shatter them. He is erotic in a manner so outrageous memory cannot contain it, and were he to appear on TV today, for the first time, the spectacle would be no less shocking. "My God," I said to myself, as I watched him move a quarter of a century after the fact. "They let *that* on *television?*"

Some months earlier, Elvis had appeared at the New Frontier Hotel in Las Vegas (it seems Judith Campbell Exner wasn't all JFK picked up in Vegas), third-billed (as "The Atomic-Powered Singer") below the Freddy Martin Orchestra and comedian Shecky Green; his show from May 6, 1956, was released by RCA in 1980 as part of the label's gargantuan and mostly very poor eight-LP set of "rarities," *Elvis Aron Presley* (RCA CPL 8–3699). The music on the four New Frontier cuts is good (though D. J. Fontana plunges into nightclub schlock with horrifying enthusiasm); Elvis does his best to mock the setting, the audience, his music, and himself.

The best account of Elvis facing his real audience is Gordon Bowker's "Rock!" (*Seattle* magazine, February, 1970), which places several teenagers at Elvis's 1957 Seattle concert, and then catches up with them twelve years later. Bowker's concluding words cannot be topped, and they sum up the moment:

"The rosy glow had gone from the cap of Mount Rainier, and the infield was bright with the best night-baseball lights in the minor leagues. The noise from the 15,000 people was immense. Finally the crowd grew quiet.

" 'I alluz like to begin mah concerts with the national anthem,'

the King said, into the mike. 'Will y'all please rise?' Boyd Graf-
myre and Willie Leopold and Ted Shreffler and Dennis Lunder
and Merrilee Gunst [who, as Merrilee Rush, would score a top
ten hit in 1968 with the shining "Angel of the Morning"] and Tom
Hullet and Pat O'Day who had driven over from Yakima with his
wife to celebrate his second wedding anniversary and the other
15,000 people all stood up. Also on his feet was Jimi Hendrix, then
a Seattle schoolboy.

"Elvis picked up his guitar, twitched once more, took a breath,
and groaned: 'You ain't nothing but a hound dog. . . .'

"The crowd was stunned. Then it erupted into a frenzy that
dwarfed the one a few minutes earlier. The grandstands seethed
back and forth like a huge sea anemone. Not even Elvis could be
heard above the roar."

On TV, on stage, and on his early RCA recordings, Elvis was
backed by Scotty Moore, Bill Black, D. J. Fontana, and (usually)
the Jordanaires on vocals. In the studio, saxophonist Shorty Long,
pianist Floyd Cramer, guitarist Chet Atkins, and others were
brought in as well. Though Atkins was nominally in charge, in
essence Elvis served as his own producer.

His first album, *Elvis Presley* (RCA 1254), number one in 1956,
was, as noted above, made up of Sun leftovers (save for "Tryin' to
Get to You," the sides were distinctly inferior to those Sam Phillips had chosen for release), and covers of recent rock 'n' roll hits.
His second LP, *Elvis* (RCA 1382), also number one in 1956, was
quite mild (this was the "folksinger" album)—as if Elvis were in
retreat from the furor he'd kicked up. But neither album contained
his hits of the time, most of which are found on *Elvis' Golden Records*
(RCA 1707), #3 in 1958, a superbly annotated LP that includes
"Hound Dog," "Don't Be Cruel," "Jailhouse Rock," "All Shook
Up," "Treat Me Nice," and "Anyway You Want Me." This is one
of the basic—one can say founding—rock 'n' roll records. (Mono
originals or mono reissues—the latter available in UK versions—
should be sought out; the fake stereo used on reissues with "LSP
(e)" notation, which utilize not bass/treble separation but a time
delay between left and right channels, verges on the unlistenable.)

Elvis' Christmas Album, number one in 1957, has been reissued
in mono (RCA/Camden 2428); the original version, a double-jack-

eted artifact complete with picture booklet, now goes for at least $200. Along with the predictable standards, Elvis added an R&B-styled recasting of country singer Ernest Tubb's "Blue Christmas," a version of "White Christmas" based on Clyde McPhatter & the Drifters' weird 1954 rendering, plus Jerry Leiber and Mike Stoller's wonderful "Santa Claus Is Back in Town," which gave the Big E the chance to leer, "Santa Claus is coming in a big black Cadillac!" It was, in Charles Perry's phrase, like finding a hamburger in a medicine cabinet.

50,000,000 Elvis Fans Can't Be Wrong—Elvis' Gold Records, Vol. 2 (RCA 2075—with the famous gold lamé suit on the cover), #31 in 1960, handled chart entries from 1957 through 1959. It was during this period, as my friend Langdon Winner once put it, that Elvis "sold out to girls," by which he meant that Elvis had stopped threatening and had begun pleading. Already, on this album, the music was somewhat hackneyed, and even the parodies ("Wear My Ring Around Your Neck") sound like clichés. The highlight was a comparatively minor hit, "One Night."

By this time, Elvis was devoting himself almost strictly to the movies; soundtracks to *Loving You* and *King Creole* offered dubious rock and ineffectual ballads. Elvis's best movie, *Jailhouse Rock*, also contained his best movie music, partly because Leiber and Stoller were writing the songs, which can be found on *Jailhouse Rock* (RCA 31,126, South Africa): the fabulous "(You're So Square) Baby I Don't Care," "Young and Beautiful," "Treat Me Nice," "I Want to Be Free," and the still-fresh title tune (also included are Sun numbers and early RCA hits). Elvis left for the Army still on top.

DECLINE AND FALL, 1960–67

Elvis returned in 1960, and immediately made *Elvis Is Back* (RCA 2231), #2 in that year; though the album, Elvis's first stereo LP, is uneven, every minute of it screams release, freedom, and relief. And what better way to affirm that rules and regulations were behind him than to cut loose with the blues? The sound Elvis and his band got on this record is amazing: nothing like the country blues of the Sun singles, but full-blown Chicago menace, driven by Presley's own super-miked acoustic guitar, brilliant playing by

Scotty Moore, and demonic sax work from Boots Randolph. Elvis's singing wasn't sexy, it was pornographic. "Dirty, Dirty Feeling" and "Such a Night" were standouts, but the killer was "Reconsider Baby," which Lowell Fulson had first recorded in 1954. Fulson meant the song as a plea; Elvis, pushing the band hard, sang the tune as a slow, measured threat.

With that burst of life out of the way, Elvis settled down to work. He made two, sometimes three movies a year, plus full soundtracks for each. He was more successful than ever—"It's Now or Never" (1960) sold nine million copies; the *Blue Hawaii* soundtrack sold five million straight off—and had less impact than ever. Like a contract player in a B-movie factory—which, in a way, he was—he did his job. There were echoes of genius, humor, and excitement in his singles, but they were only echoes. *Elvis' Golden Records, Vol. 3* (RCA 2765) collected hits from 1960 through 1963, but there was a soullessness in the music (even "Little Sister," which stands out as a tough blues, is ultimately slick) that he escaped only with the lovely "Fame and Fortune," and with a remake of Chuck Willis's "I Feel So Bad," a wild, frenzied piece that in fact owed more to Boots Randolph's sax than to Elvis's fine vocal, and which was a cut left over from the sessions for *Elvis Is Back*.

One must look long and hard through *Elvis for Everyone*, and soundtracks like *Roustabout*, *Girl Happy*, *Paradise Hawaiian Style*, and the like, for even a glimmer of style and feeling. One such moment comes on *Spinout* (RCA 3702), 1966, with Elvis's version of Bob Dylan's "Tomorrow Is a Long Time." ("Are there any particular artists that you like to see do your songs?" Jann Wenner asked Bob Dylan in 1969. "Yeah, Elvis Presley," Dylan replied. "He recorded a song of mine. That's the one recording I treasure the most.") Invariably during this period, Elvis's best music was gospel. *His Hand in Mine* (RCA 2328), #13 in 1961, was straightforward and convincing; *How Great Thou Art* (RCA 3758), #18 in 1967, which included a really profound version of "Crying in the Chapel" (actually recorded in 1960, but inexplicably left unreleased until it was put out as a 45 in 1965), was enough to make you convert. But there was little more. When *Elvis' Gold Records, Vol. 4* (RCA 3921), #38 in 1968, appeared, it contained not a single interesting track.

But late in 1967, Elvis began to stir. In short order he cut "Big

Boss Man" (RCA 45–9341), "Guitar Man" (RCA 45–9425), and "U.S. Male" (RCA 45–9465). They weren't big hits—"U.S. Male," the most successful, reached #28 in 1968—but they made people wonder if something wasn't about to change. Something was.

THE COMEBACK, 1968–69

Thanks to producer Steve Binder, Elvis reappeared on December 3, 1968, before a national TV audience and saved his career. *Elvis TV Special* opened with "Trouble" and closed with "If I Can Dream," a stunning ballad; in between were the pretaped live performances that proved Elvis really was the King.

There were, in fact, two sorts of live performances taped for the show: those done with a large studio orchestra ("Jailhouse Rock," "Heartbreak Hotel," and others), and those done informally, without rehearsal, with a small audience, as Scotty Moore, D. J. Fontana, a couple of Elvis's pals, and the man himself sat in a circle and casually made history. ("Casually" is perhaps not strong enough a word; while Scotty Moore played a real guitar, Fontana kept time banging his sticks on a guitar case.) Except on a few numbers, among them "That's All Right" (still officially unreleased, but screened in the expanded version of the 1968 special NBC aired shortly after Elvis's death), Elvis took over on lead guitar, and he did so with the same rough, violent emotion he put into his singing.

The transcript of this music—two complete invitation-only concerts held in a studio auditorium on June 27, 1968—can be found on *The Burbank Sessions, Vol. 1* (Audifon 62768), a two-LP, two-hour, thirty-eight-take set that is disguised as an official release from West Germany but is in fact an American bootleg, dubbed straight from RCA master tapes. There are many tries at the same song here—Elvis attacks his tunes, struggles with them, backs away, roars forward, grabs hold, and then shakes a number until he's taken every bit of it for himself. The music is full of humor, full of delight, full of blood—with Elvis's buddies shouting for another chorus or Elvis forcing one. Compared to this—quite likely the very greatest rock 'n' roll ever recorded—the Million Dollar Quartets are nothing. Even the handful of these performances that have surfaced officially make up a body of work that is clearly equal to the Sun sides and, in some ways, much superior: the feeling is more raw, more dangerous. The Sun sides leave you satisfied; these leave you both satisfied and on the edge. As Elvis said— hoisting his mike stand like a harpoon, thrusting it out over the audience, and, perhaps, remembering a TV show of some twelve years before—"Moby Dick!"

Elvis TV Special (RCA 4088) reached #8; it was the first top ten Presley LP in three years. It includes, of the Elvis–Moore– Fontana cuts, "Lawdy Miss Clawdy," "Baby What You Want Me to Do," "Blue Christmas," and the heart-stopping "One Night" (Smiley Lewis's original 1955 version can be heard on *Shame, Shame, Shame,* Liberty 83308, UK). "Tiger Man," an old Rufus Thomas Sun number, appears on the throwaway album, *Elvis Sings Flaming Star and Others* (RCA/Singer 279). As previously mentioned, *Legendary Performer, Vol. 1* contains "Love Me," "Are You Lonesome Tonight?" and "Tryin' to Get to You"; *Legendary Performer, Vol. 2* (RCA CPL 1–1349) harbors "Blue Hawaii," an instrumental version of "Baby What You Want Me to Do" built around Elvis's furious guitar playing, and "Blue Suede Shoes." Avoid *The '68 Comeback* (Memphis King 101), an unlistenable bootleg made up entirely of backing tracks and production numbers NBC wisely cut from the TV special, and also *The Burbank Sessions, Vol. 2* (Audifon 62968), messy big-band rock numbers—including "Hound Dog" with, of all things, a flute.

"If I Can Dream" the single from the TV special, reached #12 on the charts; in May of 1969 came *From Elvis in Memphis* (RCA 4155)—Elvis's first nonmovie soundtrack, nongospel, nonrandom, non–greatest-hits studio album since *Elvis Is Back*—which reached #13. There were no weak spots. "Long Black Limousine" and "I'll Hold You in My Heart (Till I Can Hold You in My Arms)" were powerful, mature performances, but perhaps best was "Any Day Now," a Burt Bacharach composition that Elvis sang with a naked emotion—a naked piety, really—that cannot be heard in any of his other recordings.

"Suspicious Minds" (RCA 45–9764) was number one in the fall of 1969; it was Elvis's first chart-topper in seven years. Along with it came *From Memphis to Vegas/From Vegas to Memphis* (RCA

6020), a two-record set. One disc was made up of decent but unexciting studio material left over from the *From Elvis in Memphis* sessions; the other was the first of many, many, many live albums—this one drawn from the first comeback shows in Las Vegas—that in the '70s would serve the same function as had the soundtrack albums of the '60s: blind product. This was, though, a good live album; the seven-minute "Suspicious Minds" was astonishing.

THE APOTHEOSIS, 1970–77

His comeback assured, Elvis settled into a public state of grace; his only sin, in Bob Dylan's words, was his lifelessness. Elvis played New York City for the first time in 1972; reviews were ecstatic (hard-bitten rock critics went mad for El's version of "Bridge Over Troubled Waters," best heard on *That's the Way It Is*, RCA 4445), and *Elvis as Recorded at Madison Square Garden* (RCA 4776) was in the stores a week after the concerts. Twenty songs, including "American Trilogy," were crammed onto the single LP, but clearly, one had to be there. A good part of the magic must have come from the crowd, and they took most of it home with them. Elvis reversed field later that year with "Burning Love," an aching 45 that fought past records by Chuck Berry and Rick Nelson on its way to number one ("The most exciting single Elvis has made since 'All Shook Up,'" wrote Bob Christgau in *Newsday*, adding: "Not only that, it's dirty. Who else could make 'It's coming closer, the flames are now licking my body' sound like an assignation with James Brown's backup band?"). Some said "Burning Love" reached the top only because of a brief revival of interest in the '50s, but they couldn't have been listening. "Burning Love" was a very rare kind of record: a natural, unstoppable hit, on the order of "I Heard It through the Grapevine," "You're So Vain," or "Don't Be Cruel." Typically, RCA made it available on a budget LP called *Burning Love and Hits from His Movies, Vol. 2*. Get the single instead (RCA 45–0769).

His rocker's dues paid up again, the King floated on with various gruesome ballads, and, in 1973, launched another live opus, *Aloha from Hawaii via Satellite* (RCA 6089). This double album, issued to commemorate a planetwide TV special, featured a map of the world emblazoned with "WE LOVE ELVIS" in twenty-nine languages, if my count is accurate. There was one song for each tongue, more or less, though all were in English. *Aloha* was Elvis's first number one LP in nine years—the last, appropriately enough, had been *Roustabout*.

And they kept coming, album after album, the sloppy, mindless releases all too accurately reflecting the drugged and helpless off-stage life of the man himself. Occasionally the songs changed, but not often. Elvis gained and lost and gained weight; saw his wife leave him for a karate instructor; bought Cadillacs for, it seemed, anyone who would take one; and made the papers when, as began to happen regularly, he checked into a hospital for "rest." One was left to pore through the records for hidden gems—proof that, against all odds, the *truth* was still alive—and they were there, mostly revivals of old R&B hits. *Elvis,* issued in 1973 (RCA APL 1–0283), contained a beautiful version of Ivory Joe Hunter's "I Will Be True"; 1974 brought a stunning "Promised Land" (RCA 45–10074), Elvis's first successful cover of a Chuck Berry song, though the disc oddly rose no higher than #14. It was followed by the bizarre *Having Fun with Elvis on Stage* (RCA CPM 1–0818), which consisted of the King saying "Well . . . welllll . . . *wellllllll*" for thirty-seven minutes. In 1975 there was *Elvis Today* (RCA APL 1–1039), which offered a magnificent reading of Faye Adams's 1953 R&B classic "Shake a Hand," and a priceless version of Billy Swan's "I Can Help," in which Elvis changed a line to say, "Have a laugh on me/I can help." In 1976, on *From Elvis Presley Boulevard, Memphis, Tennessee* (RCA APL 1–1506), there was an apocalyptic attack on Timi Yuro's "Hurt." In 1977, on *Moody Blue* (RCA AFL 1–2428), Elvis sang Johnny Ace's "Pledging My Love," a song that has been associated with death ever since 1955, when Ace shot himself while the song was climbing the charts. The release of Elvis's version as a single was no more fortuitous; it too was headed up the charts the day he died.

Clearly, Elvis—no matter how troubled—retained the power to be as exciting, or as dull, as he chose: that was always the rhythm of his career. In some ways, then, an album that appeared in late 1971, *Elvis Sings the Wonderful World of Christmas* (RCA 4579), was the truest statement of all—for here, in the midst of ten painfully genteel Christmas songs, every one sung with appalling sincerity and humility, one could find Elvis tom-catting his way through six blazing minutes of "Merry Christmas, Baby," a raunchy old Charles Brown blues. And that was what Elvis had to tell us: if his sin was his lifelessness, it was his sinfulness that brought him to life, even if something very much like a sense of sin finally did him in. Twenty-odd years from now, when RCA puts out its Deluxe Golden Anniversary Retrospective Album, that story will still be worth hearing.

ELVIS IN PRINT AND IN THE GRAVE

Elvis has inspired some of the very best rock writing—and, of course, much of the worst. While any number of "I Knew the King" books appeared following Elvis's death on August 16, 1977—and we will get to some of those—Jerry Hopkins's *Elvis* (New York: Simon and Schuster, 1971), supplemented by Hopkins's *Elvis: The Final Years* (New York: St. Martin's, 1980), remains the most useful biography. The book lacks any real point of view, but it's neither sensationalist nor sycophantic, and I certainly couldn't have worked without it. *All About Elvis* (New York: Bantam, 1981), an amazingly complete A-to-Z encyclopedia by Fred L. Worth and Steve D. Tamerius, is generally reliable and entertaining. Far more illuminating, though, are these essays: Stanley Booth's "A Hound Dog, to the Manor Born" (see *The Age of Rock*, ed. Jonathan Eisen, New York: Vintage, 1969), a moving, personal account of Elvis's emergence in Memphis in 1954 contrasted with his '60s limbo; Jon Landau's "In Praise of Elvis Presley" (in Landau's *It's Too Late to Stop Now*, San Francisco: Straight Arrow, 1972), a report on a 1971 Boston concert; Stu Werbin's "Elvis and the A-Bomb" (in *Creem* magazine, March, 1972), a cosmic attempt to place Elvis in a cosmic context, written following the same concert Landau saw; Robert Christgau's "Elvis Presley: Aging Rock" (see Christgau's *Any Old Way You Choose It*, Baltimore: Penguin, 1973), an analysis based on Elvis's comeback shows in Las Vegas in 1969 and his Madison Square Garden concerts in 1972; Nik Cohn's chapter on Elvis in *Rock from the Beginning* (New York: Stein and Day, 1969), or the revised and updated version in (same book, new title) *Awopbopa-*

loobop Alopbamboom (London: Paladin, 1972); and Peter Guralnick's "Elvis Presley," in *The Rolling Stone Illustrated History of Rock & Roll*, ed. Jim Miller (New York: Rolling Stone Press/Random House, 1976 and 1980), which also appears as "Elvis Presley and the American Dream" in Guralnick's *Lost Highway: Journeys and Arrivals of American Musicians* (Boston: Godine, 1980).

Elvis's death, of course, resulted in a frenzy of promotion and hucksterism, much of it licensed by Col. Parker himself—at least until a federal court ruled that Elvis's name and likeness could not be inherited as part of his estate (an appeal to the Supreme Court is underway as I write). Most notable of the official products was "Always Elvis," a wine advertised as "The wine Elvis would have drunk, if he drank wine." Pressing plants ran day and night to keep up with the demand for records; one optimistic collector asked $10,000 for an unidentified "original Elvis 78 on black [as opposed to purple?] plastic." Ads in British tabloids offered video cassettes of the autopsy performed on Elvis's corpse; in the tradition of James Dean, Elvis spoke frequently from the Beyond, usually through the magic of one-shot magazines. Elvis imitators roamed the land, the most interesting being "Orion," a masked singer whom Shelby Singleton promoted as a prophet who could make the blind see and the lame walk, the suggestion being that Elvis had staged his own death (and also changed his name, face, and voice) in order to commune with his followers while escaping the pressures of fame. Scores of cripples and other unfortunates from across the South appeared at Orion's concerts, waiting patiently for the laying on of hands. Appalled, a Seattle filmmaker named John Myhre produced a six-minute movie, *He May Be Dead, But He's Still Elvis*—in which, *Rolling Stone* reported in 1979, "the King's decaying body is exhumed and brought back for one last concert tour (unfortunately, it keeps falling off its stool and collapsing onstage in a heap). The corpse is trotted out for record-store autographing sessions. . . . Finally, slices of flesh are hacked off and sold in 'Piece o' Presley' packages."

More than twenty "tribute" singles were rushed onto the market, including Misty's "Dead on Arrival," Leigh Grady's "Blue Christmas (Without Elvis)," and Billy Joe Burnette's "Welcome Home Elvis," which, sung as it was in the voice of Jesse Garon

Presley, Elvis's stillborn twin brother ("El, I been waitin' forty-two years. . . . Not long ago, Mama joined me here. . . . She's waitin' for ya, Elvis. Yeah, she's right over there. And soon our daddy will take our hand, and we'll be a happy family once again"), defied credence. Only one tune justified the inherent tastelessness of such records: "Back 2 the Base," by the Los Angeles punk band X, which appeared in 1981 on *Wild Gift* (Slash 107). This was a batteringly naturalistic account of a psychotic bus rider railing curses on the King ("Presley's been dead/The body means nothing/Man in the back says Presley sucked dicks/With a picture of Li'l Stevie over his head/I'm in the back with a hole in my throat"); not only was it likely the best song ever written about Elvis (Bill Parsons's "The All-American Boy" is the only real competition), it was, as Tom Carson wrote, "about how culture shapes lives—as indiscriminately as water shapes wood." It was, in other words, the first song about Elvis's place in the American unconscious.

Ten million copies of bad books made their way into print. *Elvis: What Happened?* (New York: Ballantine, 1977), by former longtime Presley bodyguards Red West, Sonny West, and Dave Hebler, with Steve Dunleavy starring as "As Told To," was the first of the scandal-bios, appearing only days before Elvis's multiple-drug overdose; while in places quite obviously inaccurate and overinflated, the book is worth reading. Less so are any number of memoirs by friends, distant relatives, in-laws, a nurse, a gatekeeper, and so on, though occultist Jess Stearns's *The Truth About Elvis* (New York: Jove, 1980)—heralded as "The book that Elvis planned to write!", and written "with" one Larry Geller, "Elvis's spiritual advisor"—deserves mention for its barely-hedged thesis that the man we knew as "Elvis Presley" was in truth none other than . . . yes, the Son of God Himself, back for another look. Albert Goldman's much-ballyhooed *Elvis* (New York: McGraw–Hill, 1981) is a 598-page attempt to discredit Elvis, the culture that produced him, and the culture he helped create. "Like most country boys of his time," Goldman writes of Presley, "he was uncircumcised . . . he saw his beauty disfigured by an ugly hillbilly pecker. . . ." Beyond greed, the sole motivation of the book is its author's contempt for his subject. Paul Lichter's hagiographic, self-promoting publications are also to be avoided.

Out of all this, four books of real value appeared. Albert Wertheimer's *Elvis '56: In the Beginning* (New York: Collier, 1979) is a photo-journal by the only photographer (or, for that matter, reporter) ever given complete access to Elvis: it combines historic, indelible images of Elvis in the studio, on tour, and behind the scenes with a serious, witty memoir (Wertheimer on Col. Parker: "He looked like a football referee from the Panama Canal Zone"). Just as indelible, but also indelibly subversive, is *Private Elvis* (Stuttgart: FEY, 1978, available through Rolling Stone Press), a production by punk artist Diego Cortez that combines a probing text by Duncan Smith with accidentally discovered photos by a cameraman named Rudolf Paulini: photos of Elvis consorting with whores, junkies, actresses, and strippers in a Munich nightclub in 1959. It's Elvis after the manner of Michael Lesy's *Wisconsin Death Trip:* a seamy, erotic smashup of American health with European decay, and a version of the pornographic film Elvis's fans dreamed for twenty years.

Neal and Janice Gregory's previously mentioned *When Elvis Died* is a heroically researched account of the press reaction to and panic over August 16, 1977; along with the inside dope about why CBS decided not to lead with Elvis's death and how President Carter's tribute was almost derailed come scores of wonderful stories—the best of which I can't resist setting down. On the occasion of Elvis's death, the Gregorys report, a Mrs. Joel Hurstfield wrote to the *London Times:* "In 1956, the year when Elvis Presley's extraordinary talent burst upon the world, I started to teach in a large mixed comprehensive school in northwest London. I shall never forget the elderly senior mistress coming into the staff room one morning and saying sternly, 'I must speak to a boy called Elvis Presley because he has carved his name on every desk in the school.' "

And lastly there is *Elvis: Images and Fancies* (Jackson: University Press of Mississippi, 1979), ed. Jac L. Tharpe, an anthology of essays by academics and fans that reveals as much about Presley—as phenomenon, artist, and heartthrob—as any other book I know. Charles Wolfe's "Presley and the Gospel Tradition" breaks new ground; Van K. Brock's "Images of Elvis, the South, and America" provides a needed analysis of Elvis's Pentecostal roots. Strongest of

all is Linda Ray Pratt's "Elvis, or the Ironies of a Southern Identity," which confronts my own book and (though I don't completely
accept her characterization) goes it one better. I wrote, she says,
"that Elvis created a beautiful illusion, a fantasy that shut nothing
out. The opposite was true. The fascination was the reality always
showing through the illusion—the illusion of wealth and the psy-
che of poverty; the illusion of success and the pinch of ridicule; the
illusion of invincibility and the tragedy of frailty; the illusion of
complete control and the reality of inner chaos." One hopes for
more on Presley from Pratt; also to be anticipated is Elizabeth Kaye's
Elvis Your the Only One Who Cared, a study of the King as seen
by his fans: as religious figure, American hero, American martyr.

As for fiction, the only novels of interest about Elvis were
published well before his death and remain almost completely unknown. Harlan Ellison's *Spider Kiss* (New York: Pyramid, 1975),
first issued in 1961 as *Rockabilly*, was the first, and it's still the best.
At once a *roman à clef*, a trash rock novel, a prescient version of
Elvis: What Happened?, and a true look at the sources of American
culture, it chronicles the rise-and-inevitable-fall of a Southern
flash. Characters include a soul-searching flack (the narrator), a
Col. Tom–style manager, and "Stag Preston," né Luther Sellers, a
rockabilly hero who is not only a great big hype but a natural artist
whose genius no evil, including his own, can ever quite snuff. Out
of these materials comes a story that makes sense, and an ending
with some real tragedy in it.

Nik Cohn's *King Death* (New York: Harcourt Brace Jovanov-
ich, 1975) is about the thanatology of pop: the story of how an
English producer makes a professional killer, whom he has first
glimpsed at work in Tupelo, Mississippi, into America's biggest
star—*as* a killer. Almost all novelists who use pop as their subject
exploit the repressed violence, sexual repression, and death wishes
that seem to lie behind the ecstasy of pop thrills; Cohn bypasses
the usual fake apocalyptic ending (in which the star's big concert
closes with an orgy of murder, mayhem, and, more often than not,
cannibalism) by making the underside of the story the story's foun-
dation. Of course, that the killer—"King Death," as he's known to
his fans—is from Tupelo is no accident. The book's dedication
makes it clear that King Death is none other than the risen ghost

of Jesse Garon Presley, Elvis's dead twin: in other words, a version of Elvis himself. Cohn doesn't mean the conceit as a joke, and it doesn't read like one; a lifelong fascination with the King, an attempt to *understand*, is the motive of the book.

Though no Elvis-novels of note have turned up since 1977, the man himself (or anyway his myth) has begun to make his way into fiction: as a motif, as a touchstone. A fictional character's reaction to John F. Kennedy's assassination is conventionally used by novelists both to attach the character to the reader and to locate the character in American life; we can expect that a fictional character's attitude toward Elvis will be used in the same way in the future. It's doubtful that anyone will get more out of the strategy than William Price Fox did with *Dixiana Moon* (New York: Viking, 1981). Set following Elvis's death, the story concerns a young New Yorker and an old-time Southern hustler who join forces to stage the ultimate revival: the Great Monzingo–Arlo Waters Jubilee Crusade and Famous Life of Christ Show, complete with snake-handling fundamentalists and Drano-drinking Pentecostals. One night, driving through the South, the New Yorker picks up an old Sun single on the radio. "Wonder what he was like," he says to his tent-show mentor. "He wasn't like anyone," says the would-have-been Col. Parker. "You start trying to compare Elvis to something and you can forget it. . . . Bo, all you can do with a talent that big and that different is sort of point at it when you see it going by, and maybe listen for the ricochet."

The overwhelming, and continuing, response to Elvis's death—in the four years since, more people have visited Elvis's grave than visited the grave of John F. Kennedy in a similar period—suggests that people felt more than a sense of loss: it suggests they felt a sense of guilt. The best of the obituaries that appeared caught this complex and difficult theme at the outset, and they deserve to last: Dave Marsh's "How Great Thou Art: Elvis in the Promised Land," in *Rolling Stone*'s superbly illustrated special issue (September 22, 1977), and Lester Bangs's "How Long Will We Care?", in the *Village Voice* (August 29, 1977). Bangs talked about the way Elvis, as private and distant a man as could be imagined, had forged a generational solidarity in the '50s, and about the way that solidarity had broken apart in the '70s. He concluded with this paragraph, which may be Elvis's finest epitaph: "If love is truly going out of fashion forever, which I do not believe, then along with our nurtured indifference to each other will be an even more contemptuous indifference to each other's objects of reverence. I thought it was Iggy Stooge, you thought it was Joni Mitchell or whoever else seemed to speak for your own private, entirely circumscribed situation's many pains and few ecstasies. We will continue to fragment in this manner, because solipsism holds all the cards at present; it is a king whose domain engulfs even Elvis's. But I can guarantee you one thing: we will never agree on anything as we agreed on Elvis. So I won't bother saying goodbye to his corpse. I will say goodbye to you."

THE CARTER FAMILY, JIMMIE RODGERS
& HANK WILLIAMS

The Carter Family (A. P., his wife Sarah, and his sister-in-law "Mother" Maybelle Addington) came from the Clinch Mountains in Virginia, near the Tennessee border. Ralph Peer recorded both the Carters and Jimmie Rodgers for the first time in August, 1927; they dominated country record sales and country radio for most of the next decade. Maybelle's guitar and autoharp playing has influenced almost every first-rate white guitarist since that time, not to mention a good many black guitarists; the Carters' songs—traditional folk material, gospel, some blues, and 19th-century sentimental standards—have gone all over the world. Of many albums on the market, *The Famous Carter Family* (Harmony 11332) is probably the best introduction, featuring "My Clinch Mountain Home," "Keep on the Sunny Side," "Can the Circle Be Unbroken," "Wildwood Flower," "Worried Man Blues," and the joyous "Gospel Ship." *The Original and Great Carter Family* (RCA/Camden 586) includes the mystical "Diamonds in the Rough," "Little Moses," and "Wabash Cannonball." Discs that do not say "The Original" usually indicate records made after the Second World War by Maybelle and her daughters, without Sarah and A. P.; they bear little resemblance to the music cut in the '20s and '30s. (See John Atkins's "The Carter Family," in *Stars of Country Music*, ed. Bill C. Malone and Judith McCulloh, Urbana: University of Illinois, 1975.)

Jimmie Rodgers was one of the most important and creative singers in American history. Born in Meridian, Mississippi, in 1897, he spent a good part of his youth on the railroad, listening to black minstrels and work gangs; when tuberculosis forced him to quit the rails in 1925, he turned to music. By the time he began to record in 1927 he had mastered a unique blues style: the "blue yodel" that Howlin' Wolf claimed taught him how to howl. Rodgers's most striking album is *My Rough and Rowdy Ways* (RCA 2112), which collects "Blue Yodel No. 1 (T for Texas)," Rodgers's first real hit, "Blue Yodel No. 9" (backing by Louis Armstrong and Earl Hines), and "Long Tall Mama Blues." The superb *Never No Mo' Blues* (RCA 1232) includes the great "California Blues," Rodgers's ironic tribute to the dispossessed Okies and Arkies who sang the song all the way to the coast. He died in 1933; the most complete biography is Nolan Porterfield's *Jimmie Rodgers: The Life and Times of America's Blue Yodeler* (Urbana: University of Illinois, 1979).

Hank Williams was born in 1923; he left home to sing in 1937, and first recorded in 1946. He was the first country singer whose music reached into every corner of the United States; in terms of music and impact, he might be called the white Ray Charles. His career, dragged down by drinking, drugs, illness, and divorce, was as chaotic as it was successful; by the end, Williams had been expelled from the Grand Ole Opry for his sins. He died on New Year's Day, 1953, only twenty-nine years old, though the coroner didn't believe it; people still pay to see the death car, but they would do better to read Ralph J. Gleason's beautifully elegiac "Hank Williams, Roy Acuff, and Then God!" (in *The Rolling Stone Rock 'n' Roll Reader*, ed. Ben Fong-Torres, New York: Bantam, 1974), or Chet Flippo's disturbing *Your Cheatin' Heart: A Biography of Hank Williams* (New York: Simon and Schuster, 1981). *Hank Williams' Greatest Hits* (MGM 4775) is the basic collection; *Lost Highway and Other Folk Ballads* (MGM 4524) is essential, if only for the title track, the song on which Bob Dylan based "Like a Rolling Stone" and Don McLean based "American Pie." *I'm Blue Inside* (MGM 3926) is almost all blues, and great; *I Saw the Light* (MGM 3926) is the best for spirituals. Avoid the sets that present Hank

Williams, Jr., singing along with tapes of his dead father; morbidity and necrophilia, as logical extensions of rural nostalgia, have always been central to country music—but this is too much.

CAMEOS: FROM CHARLIE RICH TO "LOUIE, LOUIE"

Charlie Rich's "I Feel Like Going Home" was released in 1973 as the flipside of "The Most Beautiful Girl," and again in 1974 on *The Silver Fox* (Epic 33250). This harmless version had nothing to do with the performance I saw Rich dedicate to Richard Nixon; producer Billy Sherrill buried the vocal in choruses and horns, and smoothed away the broken melody and confusing chord changes that gave the music its unsettling power. Rich did record the tune as he meant it to be heard: his piano was the only accompaniment, a strange wedding of Skip James craziness and stately country gospel. The performance, perhaps the most distinctive of Rich's long career, finally saw the light of day on the 1981 anthology *Rockabilly Stars, Vol. 1* (Epic EG37618).

The most formally soulful of all white singers, Rich's late-'50s work for Phillips International (a Sun subsidiary) can be found on *The Best of Charlie Rich* (Trip 8502), or on *Lonely Weekends* (Charly 30004, UK); his superb mid-'60s recordings, cut with producer Jerry Kennedy, are on *Fully Realized* (Mercury 7505), with notes by Peter Guralnick, whose chronicle of Rich's career should be followed with "Lonely Weekends" (in Guralnick's *Feel Like Going Home*, New York: Vintage, 1981, second edition), an account of Rich's commercial failure, and with "Snapshots of Charlie Rich" (in Guralnick's *Lost Highway: Journeys & Arrivals of American Musicians*, Boston: Godine, 1980) an account of his commercial success. *The Best of Charlie Rich* (Epic 31933) contains music Rich cut for Epic before "Behind Closed Doors" made him a star: "Life's Little Ups and Downs," "Sittin' and Thinkin'," "A Woman Left Lonely," "I Take It on Home," and the magnificent "Set Me Free" define how far a country singer whose spirit comes from the blues can go.

Dolly Parton's "My Blue Ridge Mountain Boy" can be heard on *A Real Live Dolly Parton* (RCA 4387), an album that also features "Bloody Bones," a ditty about orphans who burn down their orphanage, or on *The Best of Dolly Parton* (RCA 4449), which isn't.

The Allman Brothers' "Blue Sky" is on *Eat a Peach* (Capricorn 0102); their "Pony Boy" is on *Brothers and Sisters* (Capricorn 0111). William Moore's timeless 1928 celebration, "Old Country Rock," can be found on *Really! The Country Blues* (Origin Jazz Library 2).

As for the saga of "Louie, Louie," the records that tell the story are: "Riot in Cell Block #9," by the Robins (later Coasters), lead vocal by Richard Berry, 1955 (originally on Spark; see *The Coasters—The Early Years*, Atco 371); "The Big Break," by Richard Berry, 1955 (originally on Flair; see *Richard Berry and the Dreamers*, United Superior 7798); "Louie, Louie," by Richard Berry and the Pharaohs, 1956 (originally on Flip; out of print, no reissue); "Louie, Louie," by the Kingsmen, 1963 (originally on Jerden; see *Best of the Kingsmen*, Scepter 18002); "Louie, Louie," by Paul Revere and the Raiders, 1963 (originally on Sande; see *Paul Revere & the Raiders' Greatest Hits*, Columbia 3164); and "Brother Louie," by Stories, 1973 (Kama Sutra 45–577).

The initial recording of this last tune was by the integrated U.K. band Hot Chocolate, 1973 (see *Greatest Hits*, Big Tree 76002); in their version, "Louie" was black and his girlfriend white, while with Stories it was the other way around. The tale continues to evolve (what *can* Richard Berry think of all this?): the latest wrinkle, Bow Wow Wow's wonderful "Louis Quatorze," from 1980, continues the tradition of forgetting "Louie" was originally female, but also gives the song back all the sex anyone ever imagined was in it (see *Your Cassette Pet*, EMI cassette WOW 1, UK). And for those who must hear the *real* lyrics, Iggy and the Stooges sing every last one of them on *Metallic 'KO* (JEM/Skydog 82.854, France), cut at the band's last concert, in 1973, in a hail of beercans and bottles.

SAM PHILLIPS, SUN RECORDS & ROCKABILLY MUSIC

Sam Phillips, for those who haven't guessed, is the secret hero of this book. I don't know if he was the right man in the right place at the right time, or much more than that, and I don't really care. The man's history is in the records he made.

"My greatest contribution," he said in 1978, "was to open up an area of freedom within the artist himself, to help him express what *he* believed his message to be. Talking about egos—these people unfortunately did not *have* an ego. They had a desire—but at the same time to deal with a person that had dreamed, and dreamed, and dreamed, looked, heard, felt, to deal with them again under conditions where they were so afraid of being denied again— it took a pure instinctive quality on the part of any person that got the revealing aspects out of these people . . . I don't care if it was me or somebody else. Because I knew this—to curse these people or to just give the air of, 'Man, I'm better than you,' I'm wasting my time trying to record these people to get out of them what's truly in them. I *knew* this.*

Moonlighting from his jobs as a disc jockey and hotel announcer, Phillips built his studio at 706 Union Avenue in Memphis—it was the town's first permanent recording facility—and in 1950 began recording local blues talent (along with speeches, weddings, and commercials), leasing the results to Chess in Chicago and Modern in Los Angeles. The Sun label was founded in 1952; though it still exists under the auspices of Shelby Singleton, interesting releases had pretty well ceased by the late '50s.

The Charly label was set up in London in the '70s to make the Sun legacy available to the public. Not only were virtually all of the original classics reissued, the likes of Colin Escott and Martin Hawkins unearthed literally hundreds of unknown recordings— many treasures and, not surprisingly, a lot of dross (unfortunately, no one at Charly seems able to distinguish between the two). At present there are well over fifty albums on various labels consisting all or in part of previously released or previously unheard Sun material—and that figure includes only various-artists anthology LPs. There are at least as many albums by single performers. To untangle them in detail would require a small book in itself; only the briefest comments can be made here.

For pre-rock material, recommended are *The Blues Came Down*

---

*From Peter Guralnick's previously mentioned *Lost Highway*. For more on Sun and related topics, see Nick Tosches's *Country* (New York: Delta, 1979), a down-and-dirty account of white America's lust for miscegenation, as represented in its music; Colin Escott and Martin Hawkins's *Sun Records: The Brief History of the Legendary Record Label* (New York: Quick Fox, 1980), a cultish history with an excellent discography and a fine selection of blurry photos; and, for comment on Sun and the blues, Robert Palmer's *Deep Blues* (New York: Viking, 1981).

from Memphis (Charly 30125, UK); *706 Blues* (Redita 111, Holland), which includes Pat Hare's incredible "I'm Gonna Murder My Baby"; *Memphis Blues at Sunshine* (Redita 105, Holland); *Delta Rhythm Kings* (Charly 30103, UK), Ike Turner's early powerhouse sessions, with Bonnie Turner's bizarre "Down in the Congo"; *Sun Blues* (Charly 30114, UK), important recordings including James Cotton's "Cotton Crop Blues"; and especially *Genesis, Vol. 2—Memphis to Chicago* (Chess 6641/125, UK), a four-LP set that includes historic sides by Howlin' Wolf ("Moanin' at Midnight," "How Many More Years"), Jackie Brenston ("Rocket 88," a huge R&B hit in 1951, and one of many "first" rock 'n' roll records), Doctor Ross, and Harmonica Frank. As for LPs collecting the work of individuals from the 1950–54 period, see, for Howlin' Wolf, *The Legendary Sun Performers—Howlin' Wolf* (Charly 30134, UK), which contains the hilarious "C.V. Wine Blues" (Wolf and his band had been hired to make a wine commercial, but they apparently drank up the samples first); *More Real Folk Blues* (Chess 1512); and *Big City Blues* (United 7717). For Harmonica Frank, see *The Great Original Recordings of Harmonica Frank* (Puritan 3003). For Billy the Kid Emerson, a stunning R&B singer with bottomless soul, see the superb *Little Fine Healthy Thing* (Charly 30187, UK). For the Prisonaires, a doo-wop and gospel group of unparalleled delicacy and emotion that Sam Phillips recorded while they were still incarcerated, see *Five Beats Behind Bars* (Charly 30149, UK). Various country collections mostly confirm that Sam Phillips had no aesthetic interest in country music; *Sun Sounds Special—Tennessee Country* (Charly 30149, UK) includes, along with Malcolm Yelvington's excellent protorock (and post-Elvis) "It's Me, Baby," Doug Poindexter's "She Cares for Me No More," a 1954 pre-Elvis release significant only in that Poindexter's band, the Starlight Wranglers, included Scotty Moore and Bill Black.

With Elvis, Sun changed. Blues vanished almost completely; Phillips went for the main chance, which meant white boys who could sing country rock. The aforementioned Malcolm Yelvington—who looked like an accountant attending an office Halloween party in a cowboy costume—was the first to record after Elvis; he is best heard on *Memphis Rocks the Country* (Redita 106, Holland), which collects "Drinkin' Wine Spo-Dee-O-Dee" and "Just Rollin' Along," both from 1954.

When Elvis left Sun in the fall of 1955, dozens of new white singers were beginning to record in Texas, Nashville, Alabama, and other Southern centers; the rest were in Memphis, begging Sam Phillips for auditions. The best were Carl Perkins, Roy Orbison, and Billy Lee Riley, all of whom first recorded in 1955, and Jerry Lee Lewis, who began in 1956.

Perkins made beautiful records for Sam Phillips. "Blue Suede Shoes," "Boppin' the Blues," his gentle re-creation of the Platters' "Only You," the jailhouse rocker "Dixie Fried," and his stomping "Matchbox" (Jerry Lee on piano) can be found on *Carl Perkins—Original Golden Hits* (Sun 111); also recommended are *Rocking Guitarman* (Charly 30003, UK) and *Sun Sound Special—Carl Perkins* (Charly 30152, UK). Perkins cut many more albums for many labels; he never really had another hit, nor matched his first music. Some of the best of his later work is on *Carl Perkins* (Bopcat 207, Holland), which includes soulful early '60s material plus the amazingly fierce "Big Bad Blues," cut with the Nashville Teens in 1964. His "I Wanna Be Black" anthem, "Put Your Cat Clothes On," is on *The Best of Sun Rockabilly, Vol. 1* (Charly 30123, UK), an essential anthology that also collects Sonny Burgess's "We Wanna Boogie," Ray Harris's "Come on Little Mama," Hayden Thompson's "Love My Baby," Jerry Lee Lewis's perfect "Milkshake Mademoiselle," and Warren Smith's unforgettable "Red Cadillac and a Black Mustache."

Roy Orbison, after the one Teen Kings single for Jew-el in New Mexico, cut "Ooby Dooby" and "Go, Go, Go" on Sun; "Peanuts" Wilson's guitar playing on the latter tune formed Buddy Holly's hard-rock style almost completely. "Go, Go, Go," one of the most thrilling rockabilly records ever made, is available on *Don't You Step on My Blue Suede Shoes* (Charly 30119, UK), a fine collection. Most of the rest of Orbison's Sun work, including "Domino," which, though originally unreleased, anticipated virtually all of surf music, is on *Roy Orbison—"The Big O"* (Charly 300008, UK). Orbison went on to many memorable pseudo-operatic hits (see *The All-Time Greatest Hits of Roy Orbison*, Monument 31484); he's still working, and he still wears dark glasses. "I knew his voice was pure gold," Sam Phillips is reputed to have said. "I also knew that if anyone got a look at him he'd be dead inside of a week."

Billy Lee Riley cut "Trouble Bound" for Memphis's Fernwood label, playing all the instruments; he hit a dark, moody tone that only Presley surpassed. Phillips leased the disc and issued it on Sun (see the Dutch bootleg *Good Rocking Tonight* or, if absolutely necessary, *Sun Sound Special—Billy Lee Riley*, Charly 30151, otherwise awful). Riley then recorded two unforgettably scorching sides: "Red Hot" and "Flying Saucers Rock 'n' Roll," the latter being one of the weirdest of early rock records—and early rock records were *weird* (see *The Legendary Sun Performers—Billy Lee Riley*, Charly 30131). Riley drifted into session work and occasional discs under other names; he's still around, looking for that hit.

Jerry Lee Lewis started off playing piano in church, and turned to rock 'n' roll full-time when a preacher canned him for sneaking too much boogie woogie into the hymns. Claiming Al Jolson as a principal inspiration, Lewis recorded far more extensively than any other Sun artist (he didn't leave the label until 1962): blues, country, rock, schmaltz, gospel, coon songs, Stephen Foster, and even a comedy break-in—in the mode of Buchanan and Goodman's "The Flying Saucer"—celebrating the scandal over his marriage to his teenage cousin Myra. The many, many, many Charly reissues (the basic collection is *The Original Jerry Lee Lewis*, Charly 30111, UK) lack the presence and bite of the original Sun recordings or of most other reissues (as do Charly LPs in general); if you can find it, *Rockin' Up a Storm* (Sun/Polydor 6641/162, UK), a two-LP set, is the best bet (the near-title song, "Lovin' Up a Storm," may be Jerry Lee's finest moment). Highly recommended is *Rockin' Rhythm and Blues* (Sun 107), for the insanely salacious "Big Legged Woman" (Charly albums include a song by this title, but it's a cleaned-up version); an even stronger LP is *Ole Time Country Music* (Sun 121). I don't know who made up the title, but it's an historic misnomer: Jerry Lee transforms everything from "Deep Elem Blues" to "You Are My Sunshine" into one long roadhouse stomp.

Jerry Lee never reformed, never slowed down, never quit. He left Sun for the Smash label, and immediately turned out *The Greatest Live Show on Earth* (Smash 67056); many fine country albums; a duet LP with his sister Gail that is raunchier than his legend (*Together*, Smash 67126); and even a supersession with U.K. musicians (*The Session*, Smash 2–803) that featured a version of "Drinkin' Wine Spo-Dee-O-Dee" that cut a swath through most everything else on the radio in 1973. New albums appear yearly; 1980 brought an utterly personal "Over the Rainbow," of all things. If the day ever comes when rock 'n' roll is just a memory, Jerry Lee will still be on a stage somewhere, singing it. (For the reasons why, see Nick Tosches's *Hellfire: The Jerry Lee Lewis Story*, New York: Delacorte/Dell, 1982. Robert Palmer's *Jerry Lee Lewis Rocks!*, New York: Delilah, 1981, combines excellent photos with a strong, personal essay; ignore Robert Cain's worthless *Whole Lotta Shakin' Goin' On*.)

Those were the titans of rockabilly. Other singers, deified by misty-eyed European collectors, are far less impressive, save for the occasional glorious one-shot: certainly there are gems to ferret out, and some take the rockabilly style to places Sun never got to. There is Sonny Fisher's smoky sexual menace, authentically tough stuff from 1955 (see *Texas Rockabilly*, Ace/Chiswick 10/14, UK); the Lonesome Drifter, whose authentically strange stuff can be found on *10 Years—Collector Records* (White Label 8816, Holland); thrillingly "pure" country rock (i.e., no drums) from Junior Thompson and Wayne McGinnis (see *Meteor: Hillbilly Bop, Memphis Style*, Meteor 5000, a good anthology that also includes Charlie Feathers's interesting "Tongue-Tied Jill"); and the stunning, Willie Johnson-influenced guitar playing of Paul Burleson (fronted by the far less convincing vocals of Johnny Burnette) with the very early Memphis rockabilly band the Rock 'n' Roll Trio (see *Tear It Up*, Solid Smoke 8001). But Warren Smith and Malcolm Yelvington had no real affinity for the black rhythms rockabilly took off from (though Smith, in truth a modern Appalachian balladeer, can be heard for the quirky delight he was on *The Legendary Sun Performers—Warren Smith*, Charly 30132, UK). Charlie Feathers, despite his unforgettable "One Hand Loose," cut for King in 1956, (see *King–Federal Rockabillys*, King/Gusto 5016), and his latter-day claim that he, *he* taught Elvis everything he knew, was just a rather odd country singer. (Feathers still performs in and around Memphis. After deification by rockabilly followers, he released numerous awful true-believer LPs in the '70s—and then, rather shockingly, redeemed himself with "Gone and Left Me Blues" and "Rockin' with Red," spooky, sensuous late '70s performances that have no parallels in rockabilly, but point to directions the music might have taken. See

Johnny Burnette's Rock and Roll Trio and their Rockin' Friends from Memphis, Rock-a-billy 1001). Carl Mann and Carl McVoy were not much more than fakes; Sonny Burgess, though wild-eyed enough, huffed and puffed more than he rocked (see *The Legendary Sun Performers—Sonny Burgess*, Charly 30136, UK). Outside of originals like Buddy Holly, (probably) Gene Vincent, and (perhaps) Eddie Cochran, most rockabilly singers weren't even imitating blacks, let alone listening to that inner voice: they were imitating Elvis Presley. Fanatics call the like of Alvis Wayne geniuses, but their aggression was full of self-doubt and the flash was always forced.

Rockabilly was a very special music. For all of its unchained energy and outrage, it demanded a fine balance between white impulses and black, between fantasies of freedom and the realities that produced those fantasies. The sound Sam Phillips got proves how well he understood this—but sometimes, working for that next hit, Phillips ran into mysteries in the music not even he could have expected.

In 1957, Phillips, Billy Lee Riley, and Jerry Lee Lewis were setting up to make "Great Balls of Fire," the follow-up to "Whole Lot of Shakin' Going On," Sun's biggest record. Suddenly, Jerry Lee objected. In 1949 as a kid in Ferriday, Louisiana, he had talked his way onto a bandstand for a chance to bang out "Drinkin' Wine Spo-Dee-O-Dee," but on the road to Sun he had also put in time at the Southwest Bible College in Waxahachie, Texas; like all rockabilly ravers, he was raised on the gospel. Sitting in Phillips's studio, reading over the lead sheet for "Great Balls of Fire," the meaning of the image must have hit him. "Great balls of fire": that was a Pentecostal image, that meant Judgment Day—and now Sam Phillips wanted Jerry Lee to turn that image into a smutty joke, to *defile* the image. Jerry Lee rebelled.

JERRY LEE LEWIS: H—E—L—L!
SAM PHILLIPS: I don't believe it.
JLL: Great Godamighty, great balls of fire!
BILLY LEE RILEY: That's right!
SP: I don't believe it.
JLL: It says, WAKE, MAN! To the Joy of God! But when it comes to worldly music—that's rock 'n' roll—

BLR: Rock it out!

JLL: —or anything like that, you have done brought yourself into the world, and you're in the world, and you hadn't come on out of the world, *and you're still a sinner.*
You're a sinner—and when you be saved—*and borned again*—and *be made as a little child*—
And walk before God—
And be holy—
And brother, I mean that you got to be so pure! No sin shall enter there: *No sin!*
For it says, *No sin!* It doesn't say just a little bit, it says, NO SIN SHALL ENTER THERE—brother, not one little bit! You've got to walk and *talk* with God to go to Heaven. You've got to be *so* good.

BLR: Hallelujah.

SP: Alright. Now, look, Jerry. Religious conviction—doesn't mean anything—resembling extremism. [Phillips suddenly goes on the offensive.] *Do you mean to tell me* that you're gonna take the Bible, you're gonna take God's word, and you're gonna revolu*tionize* the whole universe? Now, listen! Jesus Christ was sent here by God Almighty. Did He convince, did He *save,* all the people in the world?

JLL: Naw, but He tried to!

SP: *He sure did.* NOW WAIT JUST A MINUTE. Jesus Christ—came into this world. He *tolerated* man. He didn't preach from one pulpit. He went around, and He *did good.*

JLL: That's right! He preached *everywhere!*

SP: Everywhere!

JLL: He preached on land!

SP: Everywhere! That's right! That's right!

JLL: He preached on the water!

SP: That's right, that's exactly right! Now—

JLL: And then He done everything! He *healed!*

SP: Now, now—here's, *here's the difference*—

JLL [speaking as if horns have sprouted on Phillips's head]: *Are you followin' those that heal?* Like Jesus Christ?

SP [confused]: Whatta you mean, I, I, what—

JLL [triumphant]: Well, it's happening every day!
The *blind* had eyes opened.

        The *lame* were made to walk.

SP: *Jerry*—

JLL: The *crippled* were made to walk.

SP: Alright now. Jesus Christ, in my opinion, is just as *real today*, as He was when He came into this world.

JLL: Right, right, you're so right you don't know what you're sayin'.

SP [back on the offensive]: Now then! I will say, *more so*—

BLR: Aw, let's *cut* it.

SP: Wait, wait, wait just a minute, we can't, we got to—Now, look. Now, listen. I'm tellin' you outta my heart. I have studied the Bible, a little bit—

JLL: Well, I have too.

SP: I've studied it through and through and through and through and Jerry, Jerry, if you think, that you can't, can't do good, if you're a rock 'n' roll exponent—

JLL: *You can do good*, Mr. Phillips, don't get me wrong—

SP: Now, wait, wait—listen, when I say do good—

JLL: YOU CAN HAVE A KIND HEART!

SP [suddenly angry]: I don't *mean*, I don't *mean* just—

JLL: You can help people!

SP: YOU CAN SAVE SOULS!

JLL [appalled]: No. NO! No, no!

SP: Yes!

JLL: How can the *Devil* save souls? *What are you talkin' about?*

SP: Lissen, lissen—

JLL: I have the Devil in me! If I didn't I'd be a Christian!

SP: Well, you may *have* him—

JLL [fighting for his life]: JESUS! Heal this man! He cast the Devil out, the Devil says, Where can I go? He says, Can I go into this *swine?* He says, Yeah, go into him.
        Didn't he go into him?

SP: Jerry. The point I'm tryin to make is—if you believe in what you're singin'—you got no alternative whatsoever—out of— LISTEN!—out of—

JLL: Mr. Phillips! I don't care, it ain't what you believe, it's [as if explaining to a child], *it's what's written in the Bible!*

SP: Well, wait a minute.

JLL: It's what is *there*, Mr. Phillips.

sp: No, no.

jll: It's just what's there.

sp: No, by gosh, if it's not what you believe [and Phillips hits the clincher], *then how do you interpret the Bible!*

blr: Man alive . . .

sp: Huh? How do you interpret the Bible if it's not what you believe!

jll [confused]: Well, it's just *not* what you believe, you just *can't*—

blr: Let's cut it, man . . .

And so they did; *Good Rocking Tonight*, the bootleg that contains this conversation, follows it with a furious take of "Great Balls of Fire"—a take that, one might say, outsins the version Sam Phillips ultimately released to the public.

"Sam's crazy," Jerry Lee told John Grissim, many years later. "Nutty as a fox squirrel. He's just like me, he ain't got no sense. Birds of a feather flock together. It took all of us to screw up the world. We've done it."

INDEX